Poverty & the Public Utility

Poverty & the Public Utility

Building Shareholder Value through Low-Income Initiatives

Kevin Monte de Ramos

PennWell®

This book represents a summary of the author's experience with low-income programs, communications with industry professionals, and a review of publicly available documents. While efforts have been made to ensure the veracity of all claims and facts expressed within, this publication is not a formal assessment of existing products, programs, and/or services. As such, the text represents the perceptions and beliefs of the author and may not necessarily reflect the opinions, positions, or claims made by the organizations, individuals, or government agencies herein mentioned. Readers are advised to independently corroborate all facts, opinions, findings, or claims before citing in formal proceedings, such as rate hearings, legislative testimony, and program assessments.

Copyright ©2005
PennWell Corporation
1421 South Sheridan Road
Tulsa, Oklahoma 74112

1-800-752-9764
sales@pennwell.com
www.pennwell.com
www.pennwell-store.com

Managing Editor: Stephen Hill
Production Manager: Julie Shank
Cover Designer: Shanon Moore
Book Designer: Robin Remaley

Library of Congress Cataloging-in-Publication Data

Monte de Ramos, Kevin.
 Poverty and the public utility : building shareholder value through low-income
initiatives / by Kevin Monte de Ramos.
   p. cm.
 ISBN 0-87814-883-3 (3)
 1. Economic assistance, Domestic--United States. 2. Poor--Energy assistance--
United States. 3. Public utilities--Rates--United States. 4. Public utilities--Valuation--
United States. I. Title.
 HC110.P63M57 2004
 362.5'83--dc22

                                                                2004020380

Printed in the United States of America
1 2 3 4 5   09 08 07 06 05

This book is dedicated to the professionals and volunteers who make up the low-income provider network. The daily effort and loving commitment to humanity demonstrated by these individuals represent a humbling and powerful call to action.

CONTENTS

FOREWORD

T he timing of this book is pivotal to the influence it will have in the United States. The political process continues to determine the budget and resources that are available to address worsening economic conditions for those in or near poverty. As this book goes to press, the bad news keeps coming:

- The Census Bureau reports that 1.3 million more Americans were living in poverty during 2003, and this is the third successive increase in as many years. This means that 35.9 million Americans live below the federal poverty level – that is 12.5% of the population. In the South, which historically has had the highest poverty rate in the nation and the lowest median household income of the four regions, things are even more dire, with some states' poverty rates exceeding 20%.

- The price of natural gas has more than doubled since 2002, leading Federal Reserve Chairman Alan Greenspan to express concern over the increase and its drag on the economy.

- The price of oil has risen dramatically in the past year, hovering around its all-time high of more than $45 a barrel, driving gasoline prices ever higher, and placing a heavy burden on low-income and working poor families who drive older, inefficient cars.

- The price of eastern low-sulfur coal over the past 20 months is up 40–100 percent, raising the production cost of domestic electricity.

- By appropriating gapingly inadequate amounts for LIHEAP (Low-Income Home Energy Assistance Program), in the face of this growing need, Congress has allowed the federal utility bill-payment assistance program—the lifeline for many states—to languish for years. Since its inception in 1982, LIHEAP's inflation-adjusted buying power has shrunk more than 44 percent.

Given this deteriorating situation and growing need for assistance, only unconscionable indifference can explain the continued failure to dramatically increase LIHEAP funding, or even worse, the prospect of cutting its funding during these times.

So where can one turn to find an optimistic scenario for addressing the worsening plight of the poor? The answer given by Kevin Monte de Ramos in this thought-provoking, refreshing, and creative book will perhaps be counterintuitive to many readers: look to innovative, efficient, and bold public utilities that provide electricity and natural gas. Utilities are willing to form partnerships with similarly progressive public and charitable organizations providing energy assistance. And, he says, note that these companies are doing what they do for bottom-line business reasons. There are profits to be made in being an agent for change that really helps the poor and the near-poor in this country, while reducing utility collections costs and write-offs, and increasing the rate of return on utility investments in customer service.

Citing numerous examples of aggressive utility and non-profit initiatives, like utility and charitable fuel funds that provide emergency bill payment assistance to households facing financial or medical crises, Monte de Ramos shows how properly structured and incentivized programs designed and implemented by utilities and community agencies can help customers use less energy in their homes, reduce their bills and render them more affordable, and improve their payment behaviors. He also points out the major strides that can be taken when a state and its utilities harness the power of the ratemaking process to create public benefit funds supported by very small monthly surcharges on utility bills.

The book reveals how keeping low-income and working poor customers connected, safe, healthy, and able to afford their utility bills can reduce the costs a utility incurs when it has to engage in credit and collection activity. Once while I was practicing law two decades ago, I counseled a client about the senselessness of suing a person without any money, "You can't get blood out of a turnip," I said. "Well," he replied, "You may be right, but you sure can squeeze the greens!" My 25 years of observing utility companies leads me to believe that many of them, and many other companies providing services essential to life, have begun to see the futility of chasing dollars from people who have utterly no means of ever paying. So long as there is near consensus that electricity and gas service are necessities of life, there is a premium at hand for utilities that look for better ways to serve those in need. This book is a spotlight to find those ways.

The company for which I have worked since 1990, Entergy, has made determinations that both its customers and its shareholders are better off if those in need can pay their bills and the utility can avoid incurring costs of disconnection, reconnection, extensive call center activity, and write-offs of uncollectibles. The vast majority of our low-income customers are excellent credit risks. They pay their bills on time and rarely cause the company to incur credit and collections services.

Drawing on his knowledge of the internal workings of the utility business and stitching into it his understanding of how public and charitable organizations operate to help low-income households, Mr. Monte de Ramos creates a tapestry of strategies, business decisions, actions, and programs that can produce a victory banner for all the players. This confluence of winning results is broad and expansive: There can be direct help through bill payment assistance and weatherization for families and individuals in need; success for agencies and state programs that are seeking to move people to self-sustainability; benefits for utility customers in general, whose rates can be tempered by reduced uncollectibles and write-offs; and positive outcomes for utility companies and their shareholders, who can experience both a healthy return on their investment in low-income initiatives and satisfaction with their commitment to philanthropy and compliance with their public utility franchise obligation to serve and meet their corporate social responsibilities.

The essence of this book's contribution to progress on behalf of the poor, working poor, and utility customers in general is this: While the benefits to low-income program participants are clear, utility ratepayers also benefit. The rehabilitation and weatherization of low-income housing stock improves service reliability, and improves safety. Despite reduced billings caused by installing energy savings measures, the provision of affordable service allows occupants to pay down past arrears in addition to meeting current obligations. As a consequence, ratepayers no longer need subsidize the same level of bad debt. Even more important is the shareholder impact. Not only are cash flows improved by these actions, but also reduced credit and collection activities necessarily lead to accounting profits that accumulate exponentially over time. Monte de Ramos' message should be powerful and alluring to utility corporate executives seeking to strengthen their bottom lines in a way that allows them to demonstrate the bona fides of their corporate citizenship.

Wally Nixon
Director, Low-Income Programs
Entergy Services, Inc.
September 3, 2004

ACKNOWLEDGMENTS

T he commitment and effort required to publish a document of this import requires effort beyond any single individual or organization. Without the support and encouragement of Lucia Lelii, this book would not have been possible. For her page-by-page review and honest feedback, I am thankful beyond expression. As a business partner, she demonstrated both patience and wisdom in authorizing this project. As my fiancée, she continues to demand the best of me. Only by borrowing upon her strength did I gain the resolve to complete this work.

To those at Columbia Gas, I thank them for a decade of experience provided under the WarmChoice, CAP, and CARES programs. From them, I learned of the commitment needed to run the nation's best programs. The confidence they demonstrated in me so early in my career will always be appreciated.

To the utility executives, agency officials, and industry profes-sionals who contributed valuable insight and perspective, I express my gratitude. Only through your time and expertise was I able to compile the requisite knowledge base to formulate the opportunities that lie within the low-income population.

And, of course, I extend my sincere regards to PennWell for publishing this work.

INTRODUCTION

H istory has shown that corporate behavior must be monitored and regulated to prevent systemic abuse. Public utilities generally no longer charge unwarranted fees for service. Instead, more subtle and profitable endeavors have been used. Cannibalistic management schemes used to cheat investors and other public utilities are curbed by the shepherding of consumer advocacies and by the moral fiber of many top executives. Still, recent abuses are indicative of an infectious disease threatening the fiscal health of corporate responsibility. The proliferation of stock options and the rising expectations of Wall Street traders have resulted in myopia that impairs long-term strategic vision. As such, more and more Fortune 500 companies are acting like small entrepreneurial businesses, thereby raising the inherent risks assumed by shareholders.

While industry abuses are few in number, the public utilities were not immune. Arguably among the worst corporate offenders were public utilities: Enron, WorldCom, and Montana Power. This book asks industry participants to acknowledge their important role in utility governance and recommends actions needed to raise long-term shareholder value.

Rising fuel costs, utility deregulation, and the recent recessionary economy contribute to these ills. Utilities are struggling to balance shareholder expectations with the need to provide affordable and reliable utility service. Increasingly, utilities are opting for innovative cost recovery mechanisms instead of altering business practices to serve the emergent needs of their service territory. By doing so, the cost of utility service is raised even higher.

For the 17% of the U.S. population in financial distress, the continuing escalation of utility expense exacerbates financial distress and challenges the quality of utility revenues. Even the face of those living in poverty has changed. Administrators at the Salvation Army tell of middle class families who have lost their jobs and struggle to meet their financial obligations. Unwilling to sell their homes and claim the accumulated equity, these families allow foreclosure proceedings and watch their homes sold below market to pay off existing mortgages. Even with limited cash reserves and no short-term job prospects, these newly poor are better situated than those living in abject poverty. With the requisite skills, work experience, education, and mobility, the eight million displaced workers can return to the workforce during the next economic upturn.

For the 35 million households living near poverty, a number of barriers remain that limit job opportunity. Without reliable transportation, the only jobs accessible are those within the neighborhood. Without cash reserves, relocation is often impossible. Without access to consumer credit, unexpected expenses throw families into crisis. Without an advanced degree, job opportunities are rare, especially when industries have systematically outsourced labor and entry level positions to foreign lands. And without regional investment, prosperity seems an illusion created by the White House and Hollywood.

Entergy found that the poor, in spite of having energy burdens four times that of the average residential household, exhibit no worse credit behavior than any other customer class. People with low incomes often sacrifice food, medicine, and health just to maintain utility service. Working multiple low-paying jobs or living on a fixed retirement income, these individuals are still found helping others in the community. The deadbeat personas assigned to these customers are unfounded. In fact, the low-income represent a valuable market segment within utility service territory.

Forty-seven million individuals live near poverty, occupying 35 million households. Together, these households represent 28% of the $159 billion U.S. home energy market. In addition, four out of five low-income households rise from poverty within 12 months. While these homes may repeatedly transition into and out of poverty, their ability to raise household income is encouraging.

After researching this book, I am now convinced that an energy company specifically designed to serve the low-income population could do so effectively and profitably as the provider-of-last-resort. Towards this end, I have formed a think tank, KMDR Research, Inc., around Poverty and the Public Utility. Our goals are threefold:

- Facilitate an understanding of poverty-related issues

- Foster innovation to relieve the impact of poverty on the public utility

- Lower utility operating expenses through community-based outsourcing as an application of our knowledge and innovations.

However, to be successful in our efforts, we must establish a dialog with utilities, regulators, government agencies, and community-based organizations. If you deal with poverty-related issues, please contact me directly using e-mail at KMONTE@kmdr.net or contact our organization via our toll-free number: 1-800-563-7638.

For the reader, many of our strategies are highlighted in this book for your consideration. I hope to open the communication between the low-income provider network, the many public utilities, and those involved in utility governance. As such, the book is comprised of three sections. Section I highlights key statistics relating to utilities and poverty. Section II reviews the differing approaches used within the industry to improve access to and affordability of utility service. Section III describes the process necessary for community action agencies and low-income program managers to address shareholder concern.

After reading this book, you will have the requisite knowledge to effectively raise shareholder value through low-income initiatives. Still, every situation is unique; therefore, no singular strategy will properly address the emergent needs of your community. As such, we encourage collaborative strategic planning to identify available resources and leverage the efforts of existing community-based organizations. We espouse integrated service delivery through infrastructure enhancements. And foremost throughout, we repeat the need for an open mind.

Lifting ideas from one state to the next will not yield satisfactory results. Instead, new approaches must be developed that challenge our inherent biases. *Poverty and the Public Utility* is meant to facilitate this process and serve as a valuable resource when exploring opportunities within the low-income community.

SECTION I

AN INDUSTRY OVERVIEW

1

REALITIES OF
THE UTILITY MARKETPLACE

Many utilities struggle to profitably serve the low-income population. If given an option, many utilities would avoid this customer segment. For this reason, regulators have opted for universal service provisions modeled after those in the telecommunications industry. Yet, when it comes to marketing utility services, the gap between the two industries is substantial.

The telephone industry has utilized time-of-use rates within the residential sector for a long time. In comparison, electric and gas utilities have relied on a single uniform residential rate. With decreases in metering costs, time-of-use rates have been extended to the residential segment. However, there does not seem to be any significant adoption of these tariffs by homeowners to date.

The telephone industry has many options and packages available to their residential customers. Our industry offers residential customers a single choice: us or the other guys. Richard Wight, President of Energy Market Solutions, "Customers want choices within the utility, not a choice between utilities." Where regulators have authorized innovative rate designs, customers have demonstrated a willingness to try alternative pricing schemes.

Next, consider the number of viable market participants. Within any significant market, a dozen cellular and a handful of long-distance providers will compete for your business. Today, the typical city block and rural town will have at least one prominent reseller offering cellular service, prepaid long distance, and even options for local landlines. To obtain or change energy providers, most consumers would have to open the Yellow Pages. Even then, many would have difficulty finding even two or three energy providers.

Of course, comparing energy distribution to telephony is comparing apples to oranges. The underlying delivery infrastructure of gas and electric utilities limits many billing and marketing options. For example, time-of-use (TOU) rates require the installation of whole premises load recorders and special TOU bins to match appropriate tariffs. It also requires billing system modifications to accommodate the various plan options. For an incumbent utility, the necessary enhancements and procedural changes can easily cost hundreds of millions to implement. Absent competitive influence, most executives are reluctant to invest in these changes.

New market participants do not face such barriers. An energy provider wishing to offer TOU rates and other innovative rate designs could do so with ease. However, substantial risks are involved when taking on incumbent utilities, especially when their services are required for energy distribution.

Despite regulatory mandate, the local distribution companies are often uncooperative. This does not imply the local distribution companies are intentionally anticompetitive. Rather, most utilities are simply unable to assist emergent energy providers with innovative billing solutions and specialized service centers. As such, new market participants must build the capability to reliably install new meters, acquire meter data, generate customer invoices, process bill payments, and support customer initiatives.

Capital and operational requirements for market entry are substantial and tend to be underestimated. The failure of new market participants in emerging markets is evidence of this fact. Even with regulatory action to ensure competitiveness, many energy providers have lacked the necessary business delivery infrastructure to maintain their customers.

Because of the underlying risk and substantial investments required to support bold marketing initiatives, the industry remains in a familiar mindset where premises are served as opposed to the occupants who bear fiscal responsibility for energy use. Even within this re-regulated environment, a little unregulated thinking may reveal opportunities lingering within the utility market.

MARKET DIRECTION

Public utilities operate in an environment where market forces and regulatory constraint weave a complex web of special interest. Even the elementary interactions between buyer and seller are complicated. In a phenomenon I refer to as the *middle-class escalation of expectation,* competitive influences can have inflationary effects on the cost of utility service.

Instead of competitive pressures slimming profit margins, regulated industries selling basic necessities often raise retail prices. These increases fund infrastructure enhancements, value-added services, and marketing options. Within the public utility industry, increased revenue requirements are needed to cover operational enhancements and raise shareholder value.

While regulatory action protects ratepayers from unwarranted rate increases, public utility commissions are susceptible to the same inflationary expectations. As a result, nearly every regulated industry has been able to raise prices because of seemingly necessary service enhancements.

Grade-school educators must have advanced degrees to teach our children basic arithmetic functions. Hospitals must invest in the latest diagnostic equipment and maintain the best surgical staff available. Cable TV companies must offer 200 or more channels. Phone companies must offer DSL, even in the most remote communities. Electric utilities must offer online payment options and must provide uninterrupted service.

"The various mindsets acting on industry participants form a balance of power that mimics our political structure."

Of course, none of this actually must be done. Kids can learn basic math skills from almost anyone. Most illnesses can be diagnosed properly in a physician's office using only a thermometer, basic blood tests, and standard X-rays. Some families would be happy with the four broadcast network channels. Many families are satisfied with dial-up Internet accounts. Most householders continue to mail their utility bills despite dozens of payment options. Even temporary interruptions in utility service have little long-term consequence on most individuals.

Yet, because of our escalating expectations, we will jockey from one neighborhood to the next just to find the right balance between available service options, affordability, and convenience. In response, corporations will continue to design solutions for the middle class, leaving individuals at the lower economic extreme of our population without affordable service options.

Expectations are formed, in large part, by what we have now and can reasonably obtain in the near future. For this reason, low-income families will have very different expectations than others regarding power quality, service reliability, customer service, and affordability. The question remains, will energy providers recognize the low-income consumer as a viable market segment that can be profitably served?

UTILITY GOVERNANCE

Utility governance has grown increasingly difficult to understand and to implement. Regulators, advocates, and utility executives will often hold varied opinions on how to best meet the demands of the market. Similarly, utility employees will have varied opinions on how to best serve their customers or meet stated corporate objectives.

The various mindsets acting on industry participants form a balance of power that mimics our political structure. The varied opinions and values of industry participants generate incongruencies that prevent the formation of a cohesive approach to serving the weakest market participant: the low-income individual.

In this book, utility governance is simplified to encourage industry participants to move from well-entrenched positions. This will allow them to seek a collaborative strategic plan that identifies the low-income population as a valuable market segment with unique service expectations.

Industry participants will continue to acclimate to emerging market opportunities. In the process, service to low-income house-holds will be recognized as compatible with the natural corporate desire to expand long-term shareholder value.

Strategically simple, but tactically difficult, this book illustrates a framework through which a utility can profit from the implementation of low-income programs. The book is presented in three sections.

Section I introduces the fundamental concepts necessary to demonstrate the value of low-income programs, presented in chapters 1 through 3:

- Realities of the Utility Marketplace
- Evolution of Low-Income Programs
- Building a Business Case for Low-Income Utility Programs

Section II is a survey of existing low-income programs relevant to the public utility. Although our primary focus is on energy providers, government initiatives and programs from other regulated industries will be examined. These programs are divided into four categories and are presented in chapters 4 through 7:

- Household Subsidies
- Service Affordability Programs
- Market Transformation Programs
- Community Development Initiatives

Section III utilizes information from the first two sections to develop a pragmatic approach for the implementation of low-income programs within your public utility. Chapters 8 through 11 complete this book, putting all the factors together:

- Assessing Your Situation
- From Concept to Reality
- Designing Your Program
- Putting it All Together

A NEED FOR REGULATION

Railroads became the first postindustrial monopolies in the United States. During the mid-1800s, approximately 200,000 miles of track connected the Eastern Seaboard to the West Coast via the Great Lakes. The expansion of the rail system led to broad economic opportunities in many related industries. Among the benefactors was agriculture.

Following the Civil War, a migration began from the East to the West, forming cities around each railway station. Storage facilities were needed to house supplies and agricultural products. Private citizens utilized personal resources to construct and operate these facilities. Before long, grain elevators marked prosperity across the North American landscape.

With rising demand for grain processing and storage, private owners sought increasingly higher prices for their services. Northwestern farmers, known as grangers, banded together to fight the exorbitant rate increases. Despite their increased market power, the grangers were unable to regulate storage and processing fees through competition, because emerging towns could support only a single grain elevator.

As these makeshift railroad towns grew into cities, competition emerged through the construction of storage and processing facilities owned by a cooperative of local grangers. While this provided some relief, private owners could still charge higher prices when seasonal demands outpaced the capacity of cooperatively run grain elevators.

The grangers sought and were elected to government offices. Soon the granger movement gained momentum, allowing them to pass protective legislation on behalf of the communities from which they were elected. Collectively this legislation became known as the Granger Laws. These laws sought state control of private railroad and grain elevators.

Surviving a challenge in the U.S. Supreme Court, *Munn v. Illinois (1876)* established the principle of public regulation of private industries serving the public interest (see Fig. 1–1).

Speaking on behalf of the court, Chief Justice Waite wrote the majority opinion stating common law has supported from "time immemorial" the legislative right to regulate fair trade practices.

More laws would be passed over the proceeding century to discourage the abuse of market power. A chronology of relevant federal legislation is summarized below to introduce evolutionary aspects of public utility regulation.

MUNN V. ILLINOIS

In countries where the common law prevails, it has been customary from time immemorial for the legislature to declare what shall be a reasonable compensation under such circumstances, or, perhaps more properly speaking, to fix a maximum beyond which any charge would be unreasonable. [94 U.S. 113, 134] Undoubtedly, in mere private contracts, relating to matters in which the public has no interest, what is reasonable must be ascertained judicially. But this is because the legislature has no control over such a contract. So, too, in matters which do affect the public interest, and as to which legislative control may be exercised, if there are no statutory regulations upon the subject, the courts must determine what is reasonable. The controlling fact is the power to regulate at all. If that exists, the right to establish the maximum of charge, as one of the means of regulation, is implied. In fact, the common-law rule, which requires the charge to be reasonable, is itself a regulation as to price. Without it the owner could make his rates at will, and compel the public to yield to his terms, or forego the use.

But a mere common-law regulation of trade or business may be changed by statute. A person has no property, no vested interest, in any rule of the common law. That is only one of the forms of municipal law, and is no more sacred than any other. Rights of property which have been created by the common law cannot be taken away without due process; but the law itself, as a rule of conduct, may be changed at the will, or even at the whim, of the legislature, unless prevented by constitutional limitations. Indeed, the great office of statutes is to remedy defects in the common law as they are developed, and to adapt it to the changes of time and circumstances. To limit the rate of charge for services rendered in a public employment, or for the use of property in which the public has an interest, is only changing a regulation which existed before. It establishes no new principle in the law, but only gives a new effect to an old one.

– CHIEF JUSTICE WAITE
94 U.S. 113 (1876)

Fig. 1–1 *Munn v. Illinois*

The Sherman Act (1890)

The Sherman Act opposed the concentration of economic power in large corporations, trusts, or other entities that conspired to restrain interstate commerce or foreign trade. Both civil and criminal penalties were specified for the substantive violations of the act. In 1904, President Roosevelt successfully employed this act to dissolve the Northern Securities Company. This company was formed by James Hill, J. P. Morgan, and Edward Harriman to thwart competition within the railway industry. In 1911, President Taft used the Sherman Act to break up Standard Oil and the American Tobacco Company.

The Clayton Act (1914)

The Clayton Act assigned civil penalties for damages resulting from exclusive sales agreements and price fixing. The act prohibited joint directorship of corporations in the same line of business, legalized labor strikes, and regulated mergers and acquisitions.

The Robinson-Patman Act (1936)

The Robinson-Patman Act supplemented the Clayton Act and is sometimes referred to as the Anti-Chain-Store Act. This legislation forbade price discrimination when used to limit competition or effectively create a monopolistic position within a given market. The law originated to protect small independent retailers and wholesalers from domination by large chain stores.

Rural Electrification Act (1936)

This act empowered the United States Department of Agriculture (USDA) to facilitate rural electrification. USDA-backed loans are used to improve electric and telephone service in rural areas. Electric borrowers can use funds to implement demand-side management and energy conservation programs, as well as renewable energy systems.

The Emergency Price Control Act (1942)

The Emergency Price Control Act enabled the government to set prices for a number of industries during adverse national conditions. The legislation was adopted to ease the transition back to prewar economic conditions. Although this act was not part of the antitrust legislation, the law sought to limit profiteering through price controls.

The Celler-Kefauver Antimerger Act (1950)

This antimerger act closed a loophole found in the Clayton Act. Although the acquisition of equity positions to restrain competition was prohibited, businesses were allowed to purchase the assets of their competitors. The acquisition of strategic assets from competitors could yield market power and eliminate competitive influences. To close this loophole, the acquisition of strategic assets to limit or remove competition in the marketplace is forbidden.

Regulatory Agencies

A number of state and federal agencies emerged with broad investigative, judicial, and legislative powers. Those agencies with obvious roles relating to the public utility are highlighted in the following text. However, given the complexity of the industry and the interaction of government agencies, the reader should understand the following list is not meant to be comprehensive, either in depth or in breadth.

The Department of the Interior (DOI) (1849)

This department was established to oversee patents, government lands, and to conduct the nation's census counts. As the manager of U.S. lands and waters, the DOI plays an important role for the public utilities generation and transmission systems. Energy projects on federally managed lands and offshore areas supply about 28% of the nation's energy production.

The Department of Agriculture (USDA) (1862)

This department maintains the U.S. forests as well as other federal lands. The USDA oversees Rural Utilities Service (RUS), ensuring even remote areas of the United States have access to electric, tele-communications, and water service. The USDA also administers a number of business/community development initiatives, rural housing programs, and other technical assistance.

The Interstate Commerce Commission (ICC) (1887)

This commission became the first regulatory commission in the United States. The ICC sought to resolve the malpractice and abuse within the railroad industry. It was charged with the regulation of interstate commerce and was supported by President Roosevelt. As such, the role of the ICC included investigative, quasi-legislative, and enforcement powers across a diverse range of trade industries. While no longer in existence, the ICC laid the foundation for modern regulatory practice.

The National Association of Regulatory Utility Commissioners (NARUC) (1889)

NARUC promotes quality and effectiveness of public utility regulation. It also provides continuing education programs for its members, facilitates primary research via the National Regulatory Research Institute (NRRI), and interprets public policy. NARUC helps member organizations establish and maintain rates and conditions that are just, reasonable, and nondiscriminatory for all consumers.

State Public Utility Commissions (PUCs) (1907–1916)

These commissions were formed to regulate the public utilities. Following an era of corporate abuse, these regulatory bodies helped build trust between utility companies and their consumers. The first state PUCs were formed in 1907. With the support of investor-owned utilities (IOUs), the practice of state regulation spread quickly. Today, PUCs are present in every state and territory throughout the United States. Like the ICC before them, the state PUC acts without separa-tion of powers. This allows them to investigate, legislate, enforce, and rule on virtually any aspect of utility service provisioning.

The Federal Trade Commission (FTC) (1915)

The FTC monitors American businesses to ensure that open, fair, and efficient trade exists. The FTC enforces federal consumer protection law and antitrust legislation. It also conducts research in support of its actions and regularly participates in policy deliberations. Most notably, the FTC developed the National Do-Not-Call Registry to limit telemarketing and has been working on antispamming initiatives.

The Securities and Exchange Commission (SEC) (1933)

The SEC monitors the issuance and trading of public securities, requiring full disclosure of relevant financial data to potential investors. The SEC also enforces the Public Utility Holding Company Act of 1935 (PUHCA). PUHCA forbade the acquisition of multiple gas or electric utilities with the intent to stifle competition. As a result, the SEC must approve utility mergers where operations span noncontiguous service territories or cross state boundaries.

The Occupational Safety and Health Administration (OSHA) (1970)

OSHA ensures businesses maintain safe and healthy work environments for employees. As such, OSHA defines the safety guidelines for the employees of our country's IOUs who work with hazardous materials, mechanical equipment, and electric distribution equipment.

The Nuclear Regulatory Commission (NRC) (1974)

The NRC was formed out of the Energy Reorganization Act, which sought to limit civilian use of nuclear material. The NRC assumed the role of the Atomic Energy Commission (1946) whose responsibility was to ensure public health and safety as the nuclear power industry developed. Today the NRC governs reactor safety, license renewal, and waste management.

The Department of Energy (DOE) (1977)

The DOE advises the executive branch on all energy issues. As such, the DOE has substantial influence over the interpretation and application of rules governing public utilities. The DOE's Energy

Information Administration provides a wealth of timely and relevant research for anyone seeking to better understand the utility marketplace. In May 2003, Secretary Spencer Abraham spoke to the National Petroleum Council. He urged the incoming chairman to convene an emergency summit to address the anticipated rise in natural gas prices.[1] In doing so, he demonstrated the willingness of DOE to facilitate actions that address pressing energy issues.

The Federal Energy Regulatory Commission (FERC) (1977)

This commission originated in the Federal Power Act of 1935, granting government the right to set fair and reasonable wholesale electricity prices. With a board appointed by the president, FERC regulates the interstate transmission of natural gas, oil, and electricity, overseeing natural gas and hydroelectric power projects.

A number of other agencies have important roles related to the provision of utility service to low-income customers. These include the Housing and Urban Development Agency (HUD), the Administration for Children and Families (ACF), a division of the Department of Health and Human Services (DHHS), and the Federal Emergency Management Administration (FEMA). Although these agencies are not listed in this chapter, relevant programs are highlighted at more appropriate sections in this book.

THE STATUS OF UTILITY REGULATION

A number of federal laws are in place to regulate interstate and foreign utility holdings, while state PUC rules and regulations govern the practices of utility distribution companies. At this time, the energy industry is poised for significant changes at all levels of government.

At the federal level, an energy bill passed the Senate and a similar bill was passed by the House. This legislation seeks to significantly alter the landscape for utility holding companies and a number of energy service companies. Enactment of this legislation will have a significant impact on energy industry.

The Energy Policy Act of 2003 (EPAct 2003)

This bill is a comprehensive legislation affecting all energy sources including natural gas, electric, fossil fuels, and renewables energy sources. The bill also establishes energy efficiency standards, funds research activity, repeals existing legislation, and redefines current market interactions. Hence, the bill itself and the legislative attitudes behind the bill define the status of regulation at the federal level.

The following text highlights major components of the bill, without consideration of the specified guidelines, standards, or consequences.

Title I: oil and gas. Title I funds a comprehensive review of oil and natural gas reserves by the DOI. The review will help to set both onshore and offshore production incentives, clear regulatory production and transmission barriers, and subsidize abandoned or otherwise marginally viable reserves. It also establishes a new office within the executive branch called the Office of the Federal Coordinator for Alaska Natural Gas Transportation Projects. It empowers FERC regulatory oversight of the continued operation and immediate expansion of the Alaskan natural gas pipeline.

Title II: coal. Title II empowers the Secretary of Energy to fund research relating to the coal-based gasification technology. It also empowers the Secretary to provide university grants to establish Centers of Excellence for Energy Systems of the Future. The bill sets an agenda to ease federal coal lease restrictions and resolve shared mineral estates.

Title III: Indian lands energy. Title III encourages the use of Indian lands to increase resource development. Tribal grants, loan guarantees, and technical assistance are provided.

Title IV: nuclear. Title IV indemnifies all NRC licensees and DOE contractors indefinitely. It also provides federal subsidies and loan guarantees for the construction of nuclear and hydrogen cogeneration plants and sets standards for the sale and transfer of uranium.

Title V: renewable energy. Title V funds research and development of renewable energy on public lands, including all U.S. territories. Special consideration is also given to hydroelectric licensing, the use of federal lands for geothermal projects, and subsidies for biomass facilities.

Title VI: energy efficiency. Title VI specifies energy efficiency performance and measurement standards for all government buildings. Grants will be available to state and local offices to fund energy conservation, energy efficiency, and appliance rebate programs. Under the Energy Star program, energy-efficient consumer products will be developed and actively promoted. Additionally, HUD must reduce energy consumption in public housing. FHA mortgage insurance will encourage the purchase of energy-efficient housing.

Title VII: transportation fuels. Title VII encourages the use of dual-fuel fleet vehicles and idling reduction technologies for heavy-duty vehicles. Funds are also available to increase energy efficiency in locomotives and to produce dual-fuel automobiles. The bill also grants the Secretary of Transportation broad latitude in setting the maximum average fuel efficiency standard for motor vehicles.

Title VIII: hydrogen. Broad funding options are made available to promote, investigate, develop, and demonstrate the viability of hydrogen fuel cell technology.

Title IX: research and development. Title IX appropriates funding for the various components of this bill. The proposed eight-year budget for these programs includes $3.8 billion for energy efficiency, $1.25 billion for distributive energy and electrical energy systems, $3 billion for renewable energy, and $2.4 billion for nuclear energy. It also includes $2.8 billion for fossil fuels, $22.9 billion for science, $147 million for energy and the environment, and another $250 million for management. The total allocations approved by the enactment of EPAct 2003 will be $36.7 billion during the next eight years.

Title X: personnel and training. Title X provides for the monitoring of workforce trends and necessary training to ensure the energy industry has a skilled labor force to support our energy infrastructure.

Title XI: electricity. Title XI sets service reliability standards, defines regional markets, provides access to transmission grids by unregulated utilities, and obligates continuous service. The bill proposes significant changes to the Public Utility Regulatory Policies Act (PURPA) of 1978. Changes include implementing net metering, requiring smart metering, and ensuring the costs of electricity and capacity purchases are recoverable by the utility. The enactment of this bill would also repeal the Public Utility Holding Company Act (PUHCA) of 1935, with requirements for market and consumer protections.

While EPAct 2003 increases competition in the generation, transmission, and wholesale energy trade, state regulation of local distribution will remain in place. Consequently, each PUC holds the state agenda regulating the interactions between energy provider and energy consumer.

STATE ENERGY RESTRUCTURING

With a federal directive towards increased competition, a push for deregulation of the public utility emerged at the state level. The most common manifestation of this initiative was *customer choice* and the application of *universal service riders* to fund consumer protection.

Customer choice allows individual account holders to buy their fuel from the energy provider of their choice and have it delivered via the existing utility company. In theory, this process would unbundle energy supply from local distribution costs, providing consumers with added market power. In practice, the individual consumer has no access to the wholesale energy provider. Rather, retail energy marketers emerged, adding a new tier in the delivery of energy. As a result, the individual consumer often has decreased market power and more complicated buying decisions.

As a result, many states reasserted regulatory powers to protect individual account holders. Customer billing standards were established, along with universal service provisions. Even with these measures, retail customers no longer rely on average cost pricing and must cope with seasonal fuel price volatility. Many individuals and small businesses lack the tools to effectively manage this volatility. Because of this, deregulation has lost much of its momentum.

Today, the gas and electric industries are taking a more cautious approach to deregulation. This more cautious approach has resulted from rising fuel costs, energy shortages, and delivery constraints that exacerbate an already difficult market transition.

Today, the telecommunications industry has completed deregulation, while the gas and electric utilities are in the midst of the deregulation process. At the end of 2002, just five states and Washington, D.C. had completely unbundled gas service. These states were New Jersey, New Mexico, New York, Pennsylvania, and West Virginia. In addition, eight states were in the process of unbundling gas service, with another eight pilot programs. The remaining 29 states were not actively pursuing gas deregulation. Since then, Delaware and Wisconsin have discontinued efforts to unbundle gas service following initial pilots.

Electric utilities have moved forward with the deregulation process. As of February 2003, 24 states and Washington, D.C. allowed consumers to choose their electric providers. However, rising energy prices and anticipated shortages resulted in the delay of retail access in five states: Arkansas, Montana, Nevada, New Mexico, and Oklahoma.

California has suspended restructuring activities altogether and had to use state funds to guarantee electricity purchases. Because of suspected abuse by industry participants, a grassroots campaign for public power has begun. The movement would not only reverse deregulation, it would seek state ownership of all public utilities.

A precedent for public power exists in the state of New York. The Long Island Power Authority (LIPA) purchased Long Island Lighting Company's (LILCo) retail business, resulting in a 20% reduction in electric rates. The LILCo acquisition by LIPA has saved ratepayers an estimated $2 billion and has improved discretionary household income by 2%.

A report by the city of Davis compared the average rates between Sacramento's Municipal Utility District (SMUD) and Pacific Gas & Electric Company (PG&E). This report highlighted the fact that the average residential rates of SMUD have historically been 22% lower than those of PG&E. The rate gap grew to 49% in 2002.[2] If SMUD could offer the same rates outside its current territory, Californians would realize substantial reductions in energy costs.

This finding has fueled a campaign effort, Public Power Now. Although the acquisition of PG&E by SMUD is unlikely, Public Power Now has raised important considerations. Because municipalities are often exempt from property taxes and are usually backed by the state and federal guarantees, government-owned utilities enjoy a lower cost of capital. In addition, government-owned utilities operate without a profit motive. While government-owned utilities are positioned to offer lower rates, the incentives may exist solely because private industry found no viable means to enter and serve customers in the region. This does not mean all markets are better served by government-owned utilities.

The transportation industry clearly demonstrated that rapid advances in technology could leave many assets stranded. As rail transport shifted to flight, governments were unable to raise capital to effectively address shifting priorities. By allowing individuals to own public utilities, private markets could easily raise capital needed to adopt new technologies, explore market opportunities, and address consumer demand.

In fact, a number of government-owned European utilities have been privatized and the markets restructured. It appears that market forces offer some competitive advantages over long-term government control.

TENETS OF A PUBLIC UTILITY

Businesses vested with a public interest are often termed a public utility, and there are a number of industries considered public utilities. However, in the context of this book, a public utility is limited to either gas, electric, water, or telecommunication companies.

Public utilities have a number of shared characteristics that isolate them from other companies that may also serve the public but lack a vested public interest. Unlike a restaurant that serves the general populace, the public utility is vested with a public interest because the service provided is considered vital for public health and welfare. Without utility service, customers are placed at physical and economic risk.

Public utilities are often granted special rights by the government to ensure the availability of service to all. Among these are rights-of-way, eminent domain, and franchise territories free from competition. Because of this, public utilities operate as natural monopolies and are consequently heavily regulated to ensure public safety.

Common law

As affirmed by Chief Justice Waite, the right of a government to regulate prices predates written law. These rules, known as *common law,* apply to all businesses unless expressly overturned via local legislation. One such obligation, the duty to serve, represents the first tenet of a public utility.

The duty to serve. The duty to serve obligates the public utility to serve all entities that accept reasonable restrictions on the use of utility services and are willing to pay a fair price. This obligation requires the public utility to serve all customers and regions within the whole of its franchise territory. Consequently, a public utility may not exclude unprofitable segments of its market from service. As seen from the previous section, even within a deregulated environment, the public utility must provide universal access to service.

Continuity of service. Beyond the obligation to serve all customers, public utilities must do so in a safe and reliable manner. Services provided by the public utility are vital to public health and economic well-being. Rules and regulations exist to ensure a continuity of service, which represents our second tenet of the public utility.

To ensure a continuity of service, utilities must maintain excess capacity to ensure spikes in demand do not drain existing supplies. For natural gas and water utilities, storage facilities hold excess commodities in reserve to meet seasonal peaks in demand. Consequently, storage facilities will be underutilized, and commodities will remain in inventory. Counter this with the unregulated approach of *just-in-time* inventories, and the inherent inefficiencies will become clear.

"In short, the public utility holds a special place in society. This is because utility services are necessary for the general health and economic well-being of those communities served."

Similar inefficiencies necessarily exist within other public utilities as well. Because electricity cannot be efficiently stored, the electric utility must have the capacity to meet instantaneous consumer demand. To ensure energy availability when you turn on the lights or a business starts its production line, an electric generation facility always out-produces current demand.

When an electric generation system nears its capacity to deliver energy, another generator is started. However, like a pot of water, time is needed to bring it to a boil. Consequently, plants are turned on weeks in advance of forecasted demand. The generation system will become operational before the electricity is needed. The turbines are allowed to spin, but the gears are not yet engaged to produce electricity. Electric generation plants at this stage are considered spinning reserves.

Clearly, spinning reserves represent an inherent inefficiency of the electric system. Without the requirement for continuity of service, electric generation would lag demand to minimize these inefficiencies, raise market prices, and maximize profits. In an unregulated market, these inefficiencies could be used to exploit market participants.

Regulated average cost-based pricing. The third tenet of the public utility is regulated average cost-based pricing. In unregulated markets, pricing can take many forms to meet varied corporate objectives. For example, an antique dealer in one neighborhood may charge higher prices than a dealer with the same item in another neighborhood. Based on factors such as consumer demand and economics, each dealer can set his or her price without regard to actual costs.

Such an approach is termed market-based pricing. Market-based pricing seeks to maximize the sale price without regard to the actual cost of the object being sold. For a public utility, such an approach would inflate rates without theoretical limits. After all, the very nature of public utility says the commodity is necessary for public health. Because individuals cannot choose to forgo energy use without dire consequences, the demand for energy is considered nondiscretionary.

To compensate, public utilities must use cost-based pricing. Cost-based pricing uses a margin above the actual costs necessary to provide reliable service to all. In the public utility, this is called the revenue requirement. Regulators use this figure along with demand forecasts to set fair and reasonable charges for utility service.

The basic rate structure for public utilities consists of a fixed monthly customer charge plus a variable charge for energy use. With market forces driving utility fuel and operational expenses, the margins achieved by the public utility will vary from one quarter to the next. Yet, the consumer pays a regulated average cost-based price versus a fluctuating price that reflects the real cost of utility service. Under customer choice, fuel prices may vary between billings, but the delivery of utility service to the home remains cost-based.

Also included in regulated average cost-based pricing are the variable costs to serve each member of the community. The cost of providing equivalent utility service to one entity may differ from that of a different entity. Instead of charging each entity a different price, regulated average cost-based pricing provides a fair return on the overall cost to serve equivalent classes of entities.

Inelasticity of consumer demand. The final tenet of the public utility is the inelasticity of consumer demand. Given the vital nature of utility service, consumers will require some minimum quantity of service before suffering personal or economic harm. The resulting inelasticity of consumer demand allows for price gouging outside the regulated environment of the public utility. Although consumers may forgo utility service during extreme conditions, such elasticity is always to the detriment of other obligations or health considerations.

In short, the public utility holds a special place in society. This is because utility services are necessary for the general health and economic well-being of those communities served.

Because of these four tenets, public utilities remain regulated at the local distribution level. Whether by common or statutory law, consumers of public utility service will have historical precedence upon which to build the need for continued protections. Given recent allegations of abuse by Enron and WorldCom, politicians need not look deep into American history to justify the need for continued regulatory oversight.

A SIMPLIFIED BUSINESS MODEL

The public utilities have embedded economies of scale. Samuel Insull, president of the Chicago Edison Company, was the first to realize that fixed costs were disproportionately higher than the variable costs of providing utility service. He concluded that as more customers were added to the utility system, increased revenues would dilute the impact of substantial fixed costs. His conclusions have been borne out over time. Both ratepayers and shareholders benefit as the number of utility customers increases.

The same is not necessarily true of increased energy use. When projected demand outpaces supply, utilities must supplement existing generation, exploration, and delivery facilities. Building this infrastructure requires significant investments that quickly degrade utility cash flows.

Without appropriate protections, ratepayers would be burdened with increased rates long before these facilities are activated. Likewise, existing shareholders would be asked to assume risks beyond their original investment horizon.

While the utility indusry is complex, the business model can be reduced to basics. These include the number of customers on the system, their anticipated energy use, and the infrastructure needed to deliver reliable utility service.

NOTES

[1] Abraham, S. 2003. Speech to the National Petroleum Council.
Washington, D.C. (May 16). *http://www.energy.gov/engine/*
content.do?PUBLIC_ID=12801&BT_CODE=PR_SPEECHES&
TT_CODE=PRESSSPEECH.

[2] Knox, W. J., et al. 2003. Citizens Task Force on Energy Issues
Final Report. City of Davis. p. 26. *http://www.ci.davis.ca.us/story/*
pdfs/CTFEI-FinalReport.PDF.

2

EVOLUTION OF
LOW-INCOME PROGRAMS

Many Roman philosophers, politicians, and poets considered helping the poor a necessity of any responsible government. Juvenal (55–127 AD) recognized that "it is not easy for men to rise whose qualities are thwarted by poverty." This quote perhaps more than any other demonstrates the intent of this book. The poor are often stranded victims of economic downturns, restraining their ability to meet the demands of modern living.

Individuals living in poverty often lack the necessary cash reserves, equity holdings, personal income, and credit to migrate from areas of concentrated poverty to regions of greater prosperity. Hence, the poor must accept the economic realities of their community. As such, it is unfair for one to adopt the attitude reflected by James Dale Davidson, "When you subsidize poverty and failure, you get more of both."[1]

Davidson implies that once low-income support is removed, the poor will simply choose to become productive members of society. This deadbeat persona persists despite evidence to the contrary. The reality for the general low-income population, excluding the elderly and disabled, is that one or more members of the household are employed. These working poor are often stuck in low-wage jobs with limited opportunities for advancement. This is typically a function of local economic conditions rather than a rational choice made by the individual.

Talking with the underemployed, it quickly becomes apparent that they enjoy the comfort of a familiar community but would leave without hesitation for a viable employment opportunity. However, finding viable employment opportunities outside their communities can be difficult. Transportation costs and uncertain housing options make relocation a very real gamble, requiring nearly all the financial resources at their disposal.

"The reality for the general low-income population, excluding the elderly and disabled, is that one or more members of the household are employed. These working poor are often stuck in low-wage jobs with limited opportunities for advancement. This is typically a function of local economic conditions rather than a rational choice made by the individual."

As a result, many seek the few jobs available in their area. A chronic lack of communal prosperity can easily discourage even the strongest will. Removing low-income subsidies from the poor would simply further discourage them from pursuing legitimate opportunities and instead turn to acts of desperation. The result is a predictable degradation of housing stock, site abandonment, and ultimately, an increase in crime.

In realization of this consequence, governments throughout the ages have taken on the social responsibility of helping the poor. Over time, various organizations have evolved to provide specialized forms of assistance. In our time, private organizations recognize the value of community development and voluntarily fund economic development initiatives.

We shall trace low-income assistance from government programs, through public-private partnerships, to modern private-sector revitalization projects. We will lay the necessary foundation by chronicling the transition from public to private sector support. We will then demonstrate the value low-income programs hold for both the utility ratepayer and shareholder.

GOVERNMENT CONCERN FOR THE POOR

Ancient philosophers and all major religions have espoused the virtue of helping the poor. However, the state's obligation to the needy was not formalized until the Elizabethan Poor Relief Act of 1601. Taxes were levied and administered by the local parish. Individuals unable to work received necessary care at residences known as poorhouses, where food, shelter, and clothing were available. The young and able-bodied were required to participate in apprenticeships or to earn their keep living in workhouses.

Because of growing unemployment, home relief was developed to reduce pressures on poorhouses and workhouses. By 1834, the belief that poverty resulted from an unwillingness to work led to reforms in the Poor Law. Assistance levels were minimized to levels well below even the lowest wage jobs. The premise for this change was that individuals in need would return to work because earnings would outpace available assistance. When this approach failed, the Local Government Act of 1929 would establish more comprehensive and humane assistance to the poor of England.

Throughout the 1600s, the English would colonize what was to become the United States. These settlers viewed those living in poverty as part of a rigid hierarchy. Charity was an important aspect of religious practice, but no expectation existed for the underclass to rise from poverty and to prosper within the workforce.

From 1650 to 1800, the population of the United States grew from 50,000 to four million, marking a westward territorial expansion. Following the Civil War, the railroad industry spawned economic opportunity from untilled land. Formally erected in 1886, the Mother of Exiles utters a silent message heard by all, "Give me your tired, your poor, your huddled masses yearning to breathe free, the wretched refuse of your teeming shore. Send these, the homeless, tempest-tost to me, I lift my lamp beside the golden door!"[2] By 1900, the United States population grew to 75 million, due to a large immigrant workforce employed by the railroads.

The economic prosperity of America would soon come to an abrupt end. Production of goods outpaced the ability of the American public to consume. With repressed foreign markets and an overbought stock market, the Great Depression soon took hold. Nearly one out of three workers lost their jobs and found themselves unemployed. With 16 million Americans out of work, it was time for a New Deal.

Franklin Delano Roosevelt ran on a platform of business regulation, inflation, price stabilization, and public works projects. Through public spending, the New Deal laid the foundation for American economic and social policy. To revitalize the nation's economic status, the Works Projects Administration (WPA) sponsored construction projects. The WPA sponsored the construction of nearly 116,000 buildings, 78,000 bridges, 65,000 miles of road, and a number of other public spending projects. By investing in the American infrastructure, the nation's economic conditions improved. The WPA employed more than eight million individuals just before World War II. However, with jobs transferring to the private sector, the WPA closed its doors in 1943.

Still, a number of Roosevelt's initiatives remain in force today: increased consumer protections, improved working conditions, and social security. Like all industrialized nations, protections were established to provide basic economic security for workers and their dependents. The government expanded the social security to protect the aged, sick, and disabled. Over time, the expansion of social security led to federal and state unemployment insurance, retirement benefits, and health care provisions.

Today, a number of agencies and government initiatives form a network of social programs designed to move the able-bodied back into the workforce. Figure 2–1 presents a timeline of American social programs.

FEDERAL WELFARE LEGISLATION

1932—Reconstruction Finance Corporation (RFC). Initially an institutional lender, the RFC provided federal loans and loan guarantees as part of President Hoover's economic stimulus package.

1932—Emergency Relief and Construction Act. Federal funds petitioned by state governors to supplement local work and direct relief efforts; the cornerstone of President Roosevelt's New Deal with America.

1933—Federal Emergency Relief Administration (FERA). Provided more than $3 billion in direct relief to the poor via Home Relief Bureaus and Departments of Welfare for Poor Relief. Ultimately, the program directed aid to one-sixth of the population.

1933—Civil Works Administration (CWA). Provided block grants to individual states for the construction of schools, athletic fields, and roads.

1933—Civilian Conservation Corps (CCC). Administered by the U.S. Army, young men were relocated and offered jobs on a number of conservation, reclamation, and construction projects.

1935—Works Progress Administration (WPA). A massive federal work relief initiative to build America's infrastructure. WPA construction projects included highways, government buildings, urban revitalization efforts, and rural rehabilitation. During its 8-year history, the WPA employed more than 8.5 million persons for more than 1.4 million separate projects, with a total commitment exceeding $11 billion.

1935—Social Securities Act (SSA). Replaced FERA, providing direct assistance to the unemployed, aged, dependent, and handicapped. The program was financed by payroll taxes.

1940—Aid to Families with Dependent Children (AFDC). Established what we know today as welfare.

1964—Economic Opportunity Act (EOA). The centerpiece of President Johnson's Great Society, providing job training, adult education, and small business loans to improve unemployment and reduce poverty.

1988—Job Opportunities and Basic Skills Act (JOBS). A welfare-to-work program promoting self-sufficiency through job training, adult education, transportation, and child care.

1996—The Personal Responsibility and Work Opportunity Reconciliation Act (PRWORA). Welfare reform legislation that encapsulated AFDC and JOBS into a program known as Temporary Assistance for Needy Families (TANF). TANF provides assistance and work opportunities to needy families by granting states federal funds to customize welfare programs.

Fig. 2–1 Federal Welfare Legislation

PUBLIC–PRIVATE INITIATIVES

Federal, state, and local governments may struggle to meet growing infrastructure requirements, especially in times of economic extremes. Because of this, public entities often turn to the private sector for help. By combining resources and sharing the risk, public-private partnerships can accomplish what neither sector can accomplish alone.

During economic downturns, declines in tax revenue make it difficult for the government to maintain and operate existing properties. Coupled with increasing social demands, government spending is scrutinized and must be examined carefully. Keeping pace with infrastructure requirements becomes increasingly difficult for the public sector. Although tough economic times may limit private sector investment, the prospect of increasing the corporate revenue base can be alluring.

During economic booms, the cost of capital increases for the government. With funds transferring from bonds to equities, private organizations can efficiently raise capital. With available cash, private entities seek large government contracts to provide safe long-term returns on investment capital.

Economic extremes may well trigger interest in public-private initiatives. However, the interplay between public sector requirements and private sector ambition remains without regard to economic climate. These partnerships take many forms, but all involve private companies in long-term service contracts with the government. The following list highlights the typical arrangements that define public-private partnerships (see Fig. 2–2).

An example of one of the most successful public-private partnerships is the United States Postal Service (USPS). Although the USPS structure does not fit cleanly within the definitions provided above, the spirit of a truly public-private partnership is clear.

Via the Postal Reorganization Act of 1969, the Postal Service became an independent corporation owned by the government, but managed by a board of governors chaired by the Postmaster General. With the ability to raise capital, expand services, and set postal rates, the USPS effectively operates as a private entity. As such, the USPS strives to improve operational efficiencies. At the same time it tries to maintain the government directive of reliable, affordable, and courteous service, an unspoken mandate of any public utility.

PUBLIC–PRIVATE PARTNERSHIPS

Traditional Design and Construction (TDC). Private sector responds to a government request-for-proposal. In general, the government establishes the requirements, and the bidder designs and implements the solution for a specified fee.

Operation and Maintenance Contract (O&M). Public facilities are operated by private entities under contract with the government.

Lease-Develop-Operate (LDO). A private entity is offered a long-term lease to operate and expand existing facilities. By investing in the facility, the private entity can recover the investment plus a reasonable return over the term of the lease.

Build-Own-Maintain (BOM). A private entity builds, owns, and maintains a facility occupied by a government agency and staffed with government employees.

Build-Own-Operate-Transfer (BOOT). Private sector financing, construction, ownership, and operation of a facility over a specified period before returning the assets and operation to the government.

Build-Own-Operate (BOO). Similar to the BOOT project, except the private entity retains ownership of the facility and operates under the regulatory supervision of the government.

Fig. 2–2 Public–Private Partnerships

Public-private initiatives within the utility industry, such as many energy efficiency and home weatherization programs, have demonstrated success. By leveraging state community-based providers, utilities are able to lower implementation costs. Yet, they still maintain administrative control over program objectives and quality standards. Through this collaborative approach, utilities are able to create and brand notable initiatives. EnergyStar is well branded within a number of state, federal, and private energy efficiency initiatives.

President George W. Bush's Future Gen Initiative provides a good working example of how government objectives can be pursued through private sector participation. FutureGen "seeks the creation of a near zero-emission power plant and hydrogen production facility with integrated carbon dioxide management."[3]

Ten companies have formed an alliance to test the feasibility of FutureGen. Battelle, a nonprofit R&D institute, will coordinate the activities of several electric utilities and six mining companies. The goal is to make available low-cost electricity, limit U.S. dependence on foreign oil, and address public concern over climate change. The FutureGen initiative represents a 10-year federal commitment to generate electric power with limited environmental impacts through hydrogen fuel cell technology. If FutureGen proves viable, another public-private initiative will result. The U.S. DOE will facilitate the design, construction, and operation of an advanced coal-based power and hydrogen plant.

"Overcoming market barriers is the true value of the public-private partnership. No single entity, acting alone, could amass the necessary resources to realize such a bold vision. The success of this public–private partnership will be the combined expertise, financial strength, and risk sharing of its industrial allies."

Overcoming market barriers is the true value of the public-private partnership. No single entity, acting alone, could amass the necessary resources to realize such a bold vision. The success of this public-private partnership will be the combined expertise, financial strength, and risk sharing of its industrial allies.

A MORE NATURAL ALLIANCE

These public-private partnerships need not be as large as the USPS or FutureGen to be successful. Collaborations between the public and private entities, even on a small scale, have proven beneficial. Take for example, Columbia Gas of Ohio's WarmChoice Program.

Working together with the state of Ohio, Columbia Gas of Ohio has successfully operated one of the North America's most successful low-income home weatherization programs. Initiated in 1988, WarmChoice has served more than 45,000 low-income households with achieved energy reductions averaging 25% of preprogram levels. The reduction equates to 350 ccf per home per year. For occupants of these WarmChoice homes, monthly billings are reduced an average of 21% from pretreatment levels. The net result is that low-income energy burdens are reduced significantly. With energy savings proven to persist for as long as 11 years, WarmChoice has the potential to transform the low-income housing stock.

While the benefits to program participants are clear, utility ratepayers have also benefited. The rehabilitation of low-income housing stock has improved service affordability. Despite reduced billings, the provision of affordable service allows occupants to pay down past arrears in addition to meeting current obligations. As such, ratepayers are no longer subsidizing the same level of bad debt. Even more important is the shareholder impact. Not only are cash flows improved, but also reduced credit and collection activities necessarily lead to accounting profits that accumulate exponentially over time.

Sharing program costs with the state weatherization agency, the WarmChoice program from Columbia Gas has proven cost-effective over the long-term. No studies have estimated the cost-effectiveness of WarmChoice without this cost sharing and leveraging of resources. However, other utility weatherization programs have succeeded as public-private initiatives.

GOING IT ALONE

Whether coerced by regulatory pressures or self-initiated, the utility need not rely on government monies to implement demand-side initiatives. In fact, the private sector excels at marketing programs to create product demand. Millions of dollars are committed without any guarantee of success. Yet, when it comes to regulating or retarding demand, the private sector often fails to yield to this unnatural, but sometimes necessary, activity. Despite a strong theoretical benefit to the utility, shareholders and ratepayers may be reluctant to fund private efficiency programs. However, conditions do exist whereby these programs are economically feasible.

Take for example a utility with supply constraints. To meet the demands of their customers, utilities will negotiate interruptible rates with their largest customers to drop the necessary load. However, the more a utility relies on this tactic, the less reliable service becomes for the largest and most valuable customers. As such, there are significant risks associated with interruptible commercial and industrial programs.

Losing a large commercial account impacts the utility in more than just one way. Not only are the revenues from the account lost, the economic gains provided by a large entity are also lost. The socioeconomic impact of a departing manufacturer can have lasting effects. Plant closings will drive middle-class individuals to areas of greater economic opportunity. Left in the wake of the passing opportunities, areas of concentrated poverty evolve over decades.

With a change in attitude, utilities need not accept this risk. What if the utility could reverse the scenario? Instead of asking the largest customers to drop load to serve many customers, perhaps the utility could ask the many smaller customers to reduce demand to serve the largest customers. By focusing on the 32% of residential accounts representing those who struggle with service affordability, the public utility may be able to improve conditions on the entire system.

Entergy Corporation has employed such an approach. Studies of the low-income areas across Entergy's service territory have identified a number of opportunities. These opportunities have been embraced by senior management and supported by a wide range of stakeholders including regulators, interveners, and shareholders. In a speech at the Southern Governor's Conference, Wayne Leonard, CEO of Entergy Corporation, gets right to the point. He stated, "The housing stock in many areas is so poor, it is creating a dead weight economic loss to society."[4] To spur economic growth, Mr. Leonard calls on the nation's leaders to show compassion and weigh justice above all else. His enthusiasm was not limited to mere words for others. Rather, his words sponsored actions that permeated throughout his company.

> *"People living in poverty struggle to pay their bills and live from paycheck to paycheck. The IDA program gives them the ability to save money and accrue assets which are vital components to a complete program that helps people break the cycle of poverty."*
>
> **Curt Hebert,**
> *Entergy executive vice president of external affairs*

In June 2003, Entergy shareholders committed $1.2 million to establish independent development accounts (IDAs) for the low-income. This program matches contributions to personal savings accounts maintained by their low-income customers. Using a one-time tax-deductible donation, Entergy will encourage behavioral patterns that will have long-term benefits for utility shareholders and ratepayers. This is in addition to the empowering benefits gained by program participants.

"People living in poverty struggle to pay their bills and live from paycheck to paycheck. The IDA program gives them the ability to save money and accrue assets which are vital components to a complete program that helps people break the cycle of poverty," said Curt Hebert.[5] Hebert is Entergy's executive vice president of external affairs.

Not only will Entergy benefit from the participants' improved economic well-being, the company serves as a model for increased corporate involvement. In the future, greater corporate involvement will lead to exponential growth in the support available to the disadvantaged. In an effort to inform the public, Entergy has made much of its low-income research available online at *http://www.entergy.com/corp/lowincome/advocate.asp*. This is a good starting point for anyone hoping to understand the value of private-sector support for low-income initiatives.

Helping the poor step beyond their current socioeconomic conditions is more than just another corporate good deed. It is also good business. Horace Webb is president and CEO of the Entergy Charitable Foundation. He stated, "We are committed to making a positive and lasting impact on the communities served by the Entergy Corporation."[6]

Having carefully examined the low-income population, Entergy embraced the basic tenets of the public utility and aspires to provide affordable service to all. Through a suite of targeted programs, Entergy Corporation has sought to revitalize those areas stricken by poverty. With the support of the national consumer advocates and local regulators, Entergy will enjoy long-term economic benefits that are certain to result from their initiatives.

Although the benefits are straightforward, subsidizing the poor can be seen as a tax on the middle class. Consequently, we will arm you with the knowledge necessary to ward off this stigma and find support for your low-income initiatives.

Summarized by Wayne Leonard in an article written for *Electric Perspectives,* you have only to remember the following about the low-income population:

> Too many of them scrimp on food, drugs, and healthcare in order to keep the lights and gas on.
>
> They have jobs—often two of them that both pay minimum wage.
>
> They often are elderly, living on fixed incomes in homes that are old, leaky, and substandard, with inefficient appliances and heating systems.

They don't have paid lobbyists to champion their cause or seek changes in laws to improve their lot.

They have big hearts. They try to help their neighbors. Despite poverty, they contribute to others.

They are loyal customers, rarely complain, and almost never call our phone centers or seek special service or attention.

They give us high customer satisfaction scores.[7]

Avoiding the myths and misconceptions associated with the low-income population is the first step in realizing a lasting solution.

A COOPERATIVE APPROACH IN A COMPETITIVE MARKET

In a June 2003 ruling that forbade bankrupt Enron from trading natural gas and electricity, FERC Commissioner William Massey sent a clear message. He said, "Profit maximization is not an excuse for market manipulation." Given pending legislation that could repeal the Public Utility Holding Company Act (PUHCA) and rewrite U.S. energy policy, one can be certain that federal and state oversight will remain. This will be true even in the most competitive segments of the public utility industry.

For the local distribution company (LDC), a cooperative relationship with state regulators may increase shareholder value. Ronald S. Tanner, a utility industry analyst for Legg Mason Capital Markets, identified regulatory environment as a key component when valuating a public utility. Among the other factors considered are fundamentals, strength of the service territory, customer growth, and asset mix.

Factors such as service territory and customer growth relate to the economic health of the community. This is an area in which politicians and regulators have a vested interest. As such, the general well-being of a public utility's service territory can serve as a focal point for a cooperative approach within a competitive market.

Although socioeconomic factors can be difficult to quantify, their impact on the public utility can be predicted. Revenue growth, a primary concern of all businesses, is impacted directly by the economic condition and growth experienced by a utility's customer base.

Utility shareholder interests are vested in the general health of the pubic utility's service territory. In fact, the general socioeconomic condition of the community is the one factor whereby all public utility stakeholders benefit or suffer in unison.

Under strong economic conditions, jobs are readily available, allowing individuals to boost earnings. As earnings increase, consumers are better able to pay down existing obligations and increase discretionary spending. Within an economic resurgence, regional populations will grow as others immigrate to access new jobs. As long at the local infrastructure can effectively serve those entering the community, the growth will continue.

Part of that infrastructure is the public utility. As a result, utility shareholders and ratepayers can often benefit by encouraging regional growth. But what role should the utility play in the market? Should the public utility actively stimulate economic growth or simply remain a passive benefactor of broad economic cycles? If the utility remains passive, then opportunities may fall short of shareholder expectations. On the other hand, utility participation requires resource commitments. These commitments add to operational costs and to shareholder risk. At what point does utility participation in the market exceed ratepayer and shareholder tolerance?

Public utilities have been willing to actively participate in economic development by lowering rates to attract large commercial and industrial customers to their service territories. In some cases, the proposed rate would be well below the standard rate, and energy is sold near cost. To justify these preferential rates, utilities often argue two points.

First, where organizations can substantiate a lower cost-of-service, preferential rates may be offered. While this negates the concept of average cost-based pricing, regulators may approve custom rates to avoid cross-subsidization. To understand this, let us explore it in a little more detail.

Since rates are cost-based, accounts wishing to secure lower utility rates must establish that a lower cost-of-service justifies the discounted utility rate. To overcome the averaging aspect of utility pricing, the account must establish that peers either do not exist or that they benefit from similar discounts. These arguments have held in the past. Utilities have offered lower rates to commercial and industrial accounts with preferred load factors. Since load factors are improved as annual use increases, large energy consumers often benefit from preferred rates. Aggregators of residential accounts may be able to use similar arguments to reduce per-unit energy charges.

Second, new organizations add to the customer base and therefore contribute to fixed costs. Because large employers can stimulate residential growth, the contribution to fixed costs carries considerable weight.

This rationale is supported by the fact that fixed costs exist whether or not energy is delivered across the meter in question. Hence, this argument is typically used by existing companies considering relocation, rather than to justify rates for additions to the public utility system. Because large consumers of energy provide other socioeconomic stimuli, little opposition exists for this preferential treatment.

Similar arguments can be used for the low-income sector. By contributing to fixed costs, individual customers can argue continued service despite payment problems. Where billings exceed the variable cost-to-serve, then other ratepayers benefit from a contribution to fixed costs even where 100% of the costs are not covered.

Like the specialized commercial and industrial load-retention programs, low-income assistance programs are investments to secure long-term shareholder value. In November 2001, Jerrold Oppenheim and Theo Macgregor made a good case for this in *The Economics of Low-Income Electricity Efficiency Investment.* They concluded that "low-income energy efficiency is one of the most cost-effective investments a utility can make from the standpoint of program participants, non-participant customers, and society as a whole."[9]

LONG-TERM STAKEHOLDER VALUE

When a social program is implemented, the impact on a variety of industry participants is often measured and reported to sponsoring agencies. For programs within the public utility, impacts on program participants, program nonparticipants, ratepayers, the utility, and society as a whole are evaluated.

"Like the specialized commercial and industrial load-retention programs, low-income assistance programs are investments to secure long-term shareholder value."

At first glance, this appears to cover all industry participants in one form or another. While true in the strictest form, the broadly defined utility and society stakeholders are subject to interpretation. To identify the subjective nature of these stakeholders, consider how you would define society.

Is society limited to the service territory, the state, the country, or the entire world? In addition, you must also consider the timeframe. For example, society may benefit from the introduction of a manufacturing plant over the next 50 years. However, 1,000 years from today that same plant could be an environmental liability.

Like other accounting practices, a conservative estimate is used to evaluate net benefits. A predictable stream of net present benefits to a given stakeholder is tallied over the foreseeable future. If the benefit stream is positive, then the investment is considered wise for the given stakeholder. If negative, then the investment is considered a long-term liability from the given stakeholder's perspective. A similar analysis must be completed for each stakeholder to understand the potential benefits for the public utility.

Programs have obvious costs to implement in the form of salaries, expenses, and other resource allocations. When costs are compared to benefits over the same period of time, long-term benefits may be ignored or undervalued. Because benefits can lag expenditures, benefit streams may be out of sync with program costs.

A home weatherized in one year will improve energy efficiency in the following year. Comparing the one-time investment to the immediate one-year return would omit the long-term stream of benefits from being recorded. Consequently, great care must be taken to ensure an appropriate timeframe is used to assess long-term stakeholder value.

Another example of this mismatch in benefits and costs can be seen in the accounting practices of Enron and WorldCom to accelerate revenue recognition. In the short-term, utility earnings were improved along with growth expectations. Consequently, investor shareholder value skyrocketed. Very few found cause for alarm and touted both companies as leaders in the public utility field. Unfortunately, the mismatch in earnings to expenses would result in the destruction of long-term shareholder value. Today we find both companies under bankruptcy protection with negligible shareholder value.

These examples help to illustrate the subjective nature and trappings associated with the quantification of stakeholder value. Because of this, we need to specify the criteria by which stakeholder value will be assigned to programs evaluated in this text. The one constant of our analysis will be the focus on long-term stakeholder value, even when the long-term impacts are difficult to quantify.

BREADTH AND DEPTH

Every decision you make relies on a subjective analysis of the potential outcomes. Whether the reward is emotional, financial, or otherwise, our choices define our actions and set in motion a stream of consequences. If our actions are beneficial to those around us, we will realize widespread support and recognition for our contribution.

Businesses take action in a similar manner. Marketing programs have impacts on a broad range of industry participants, with each impacted to a lesser or greater extent than the other. When choosing between two different actions, the public utility will consider the breadth and depth of impacts resulting from these actions. In fact, regulators often demand this type of analysis before making a ruling.

Since no two stakeholders will realize the same depth of benefit from a given action, the public utility seeks to maximize the breadth of positive stakeholder impacts. This forms the foundation for any win-win outcome. The objective is to find a strategy that minimizes harm to any one stakeholder and maximizes the number of benefactors.

Because of this, the public utility can find support for its decisions by focusing on long-term utility shareholder value and ratepayer impacts. At first glance, this ignores the practice of maximizing the number of benefactors. However, these two stakeholders constitute the largest range of individuals. Because these two parties are juxtaposed, a balance of power is formed. A decision providing long-term value to both parties will not find significant opposition.

To illustrate this point, we need to understand the key factors relating to each stakeholder perspective. At first, the ratepayer perspective appears to have only a single factor: price. Economists would have you believe that price takes into account a breadth of social values and can be taken as a single measure. However, this does not hold true in a regulated environment in which the consumer has no viable alternative other than to pay the approved rate.

Consequently, ratepayer value has imbedded other socio-economic considerations. According to Oppenheim and Macgregor,

"The societal benefit stemming from the reduction of this gap [electric energy burdens of the poor versus that of the average American, 7.7% to 23% and 2.4% of annual household incomes respectively] is reflected not only by increased fairness, but also by the reduced requirement of low-income households to forego other necessities. The public, in recognition of the benefit associated with reduction of the energy burden gap, has shown strong support for taking care of the energy needs of low-income households."[10]

"In many cases, low-income populations exist in areas of repressed economic growth, serving as a guidepost to needed stimuli. Low-income customers and the working poor can account for as much as 32% of the residential market. "

In fact, a number of independent studies have found and reiterated ratepayer support for public welfare. A public opinion survey conducted in 1999 found that 84% of respondents supported the federal low-income energy assistance. In addition, 68% supported higher funding levels for the Low-Income Home Energy Assistance Program (LIHEAP).[11] Customers of El Paso Electric Company rated the basic tenet of meeting everyone's basic energy requirements as very important (8.9/10).[12] John M. Kennedy verified the public belief that access to public utility service was a right in our society.[13]

Societal and regulatory perspectives are represented by the ratepayers, which include program participants and nonparticipants. As such, ratepayers are the most important consideration for the public utility, especially when considering shareholder value.

In many cases, low-income populations exist in areas of repressed economic growth, serving as a guidepost to needed stimuli. Low-income customers and the working poor can account for as much as 32% of the residential market. Given that fact, ignoring their needs can have serious impacts on ratepayer and shareholder interests.

The ratepayer is the customer of the public utility and the source of most revenues. For this reason, shareholder value is tied to ratepayer numbers and satisfaction. Clearly as ratepayers grow in number, utility operations become increasingly efficient. This is especially true in a mature market where market saturation has peaked. To prevent revenue erosion and efficiency reductions, public utilities must retain existing customers and implement long-term strategies to improve economic conditions at the local level.

Low-income programs can accomplish both of these goals. In many cases, low-income populations exist in areas of repressed economic growth, serving as a guidepost to needed stimuli. Low-income customers and the working poor can account for as much as 32% of the residential market. Given that fact, ignoring their needs can have serious impacts on ratepayer and shareholder interests.

Consequently, public utilities will leverage federal and state resources to spur economic development, encourage energy assistance programs, and negotiate affordable payment options with those financially distressed. By doing so, public utilities can maintain their customer bases. In addition, they can reap other benefits. These can include improving cash flow, generating corporate goodwill, enhancing regulatory relations, and stimulating socioeconomic conditions within their service territory. What better way to ensure long-term strategic growth and shareholder value!

Notes

[1] Davidson, J. D. 1994. *The Great Reckoning: Protecting Yourself in the Coming Depression.* Fireside, p. 433.

[2] Lazarus, E. 1883. The New Colossus. Inscription on the Statue of Liberty.

[3] Southern Company. 2003. Industrial Alliance Formed to Support Near Zero-Emission Power and Hydrogen Production Facility. Press Release: Atlanta (Apr. 22).

[4] Leonard, J. W. 2002. Southern Governor's Conference Speech. Entergy (Aug. 25) *http://www.entergy.com/corp/speeches/leonard_08_25_02.asp.*

[5] Entergy Corporation. 2002. Entergy Donates $1.2 Million to Create Savings Programs for Low-Income Families—Partners with Foundation for the Mid South to create Mid South IDA Initiative. Press Release: Beaumont (Nov. 6).

[6] Entergy Corporation. 2003. Entergy Charitable Foundation Focuses on Grants to Low-Income Areas. Press Release: New Orleans (July 11).

[7] Leonard, J. W. The Most Important Customer. *Electric Perspectives. http://www.entergy.com/corp/community/ most_important.asp.*

[8] Tanner, R. 2001. Analyst Showcase: Ronald S. Tanner Legg Mason Capital Markets. *Buyside Magazine* (Mar.) *http://www.buyside.com/mag/0301/as_legg_tannr.asp.*

[9] Oppenheim, J., and T. Macgregor. 2001. The Economics of Low-Income Electricity Efficiency Investment (Nov.), p. 11.

[10] Ibid.

[11] Behavior Research Center. 1999. Public Opinion National Survey on Low-Income Home Energy Assistance Program, p. 2.

[12] Guild, et al. 1997. Southwest Town Meeting on Electricity Issues. El Paso Electric Company.

[13] Kennedy, J. M. 1987. Public Support for Residential Energy Assistance. *Sociology and Social Research.* Vol. 71, p. 308.

3

BUILDING A BUSINESS CASE FOR LOW-INCOME UTILITY PROGRAMS

Over the past decade, many companies invested millions to better identify and track their customers. Yet, even today, most public utilities cannot identify a growing customer segment that purchases $43 billion of home energy annually.[1] What other industry would require regulatory coercion to develop special programs to address a market segment of this size?

The public utility should not be an exception. Just look at the following statistics. The customer segment to which we refer comprises the 35 million low-income households across the United States.[2] To put this number into proper perspective, one home in every three shelters a low-income family. These households translate to 47 million individuals living within 125% of the federally established poverty guidelines.[3]

With nearly 17% of the U.S. population living in financial distress, the low-income problem can seem daunting and appear hopeless.[4] This is especially true for those who consider the poor to be a persistent group of deadbeats without any realistic prospect of self-sufficiency. Yet, a deeper look at poverty statistics will reveal that this perception is a myth.

> *"According to the September 2003* **Current Population Report** *on Consumer Income,* *80% of individuals rise from poverty in just 12 months."*

According to the 2002 statistical abstract, 11 million individuals were recently unemployed and two million were disenfranchised.[5] Although it may take an individual several months to reenter the workforce, we rarely hold any contempt for these individuals. We simply understand that it takes time for an individual to rise from such a setback.

The same is true for those living in poverty. Often time is all that is needed to overcome poverty. According to the September 2003 *Current Population Report on Consumer Income,* 80% of individuals rise from poverty in just 12 months![6] While individuals may transition into and out of poverty, the fact that households can achieve self-sufficiency, if only temporarily, should encourage even the greatest skeptic.

The public utility struggling to serve the low-income sector should look closely at the population as a viable market segment. According to the 2001 IRS tax filings, 7,794 utility companies had business receipts in excess of $1 trillion, with $159 billion in residential sales.[7,8] Using these estimates, low-income energy consumption accounts for 6% of gross annual sales and 28% of residential energy sales.

To better understand the low-income energy market, consider the energy consumption of LIHEAP-eligible households. In total, households eligible for energy assistance consume 2.7 quadrillion BTU (quads) annually; again, 28% of the residential total.[9] On average, low-income households consume 80 million MMBtu and spend $1,264 on home energy annually.[10,11] In terms of typical fuel use, the average low-income household consumes the equivalent of 8,832 kilowatt-hours (kWh) of electricity, 640 CCF of natural gas, or 553 gallons (gal) of fuel oil annually.[12] When compared to the energy use of the average American household (10,596 kWh, 700 CCF, or 589 gal, respectively), another myth is dispelled.[13] Low-income consumers are no more wasteful of our energy resources than the general population.

A LATENT ENERGY RESERVE

In August 2003, parts of the United States and Canada experienced a severe disruption in electric service. Although the cause of the blackout resulted primarily from faults in FirstEnergy's distribution system, the event reminded us that energy resources are limited.[14] When utilities are confronted with unexpected energy demand, both voluntary and involuntary service interruptions can significantly impact utility revenues. Investments in new power plants and storage facilities can also affect revenues. For this reason, utilities invest in energy efficiency and appliance cycling programs.

Where load demand can be shifted from residential accounts in adequate amounts, service interruptions to commercial and industrial segments can be avoided. Where transmission constraints are an issue, targeted usage reduction programs can forestall costly power outages.

"... energy inefficient homes represent a significant energy reserve, while weatherized homes represent an energy source."

Participants in existing home weatherization programs can easily achieve a 20% reduction in home energy use.[15] If the 35 million low-income households were weatherized, a reduction in energy demand would total 540,000,000 MMBTU annually, or 10.8 quads of energy over the 20-year expected life of measures.[16] Using the standard point-of-use heat rate, the savings potential for low-income weatherization is the equivalent of an 18-GW power plant. As such, energy inefficient homes represent a significant energy reserve, while weatherized homes represent an energy source.

FUNDING FOR LOW-INCOME PROGRAMS

Historically, low-income programs were expensed by the utility. Program expenditures were simply rolled into the operational budget. To recover program costs, utilities were simply reimbursed for program expenses by other residential ratepayers. This approach proved problematic.

Utilities considering low-income assistance programs needed to initiate rate filings to cover program costs. Because rate filings involve a downside risk and many hours of effort, the development of a single program would not justify such an action.

Another problem was that program expenditures were not disclosed to the general consumer. Buried by other operational costs, even mandated programs added to the basic residential rate. With asynchronous adoption of low-income initiatives, some utilities would have artificially higher rates. Even within a regulated environment, the added competitive pressure of higher utility rates was undesirable. As a result, valuable initiatives could be delayed for years.

With deregulation pending in many states, industry participants looked towards the telecommunications industry for guidance. Funding for universal service and emergency systems came from surcharges added to customer bills. Separated from the basic rates, surcharges avoided problems highlighted in the previous paragraphs. Because surcharges remove barriers for emerging initiatives, this funding mechanism has become the preferred funding mechanism for utility demand-side management programs.

While utility surcharges have been favored, they are not without issue. Line items on utility bills are distinct and quantifiable, aiding organized opposition. As such, they can be targeted for added scrutiny. In a time when new taxes are heavily scrutinized, proposed surcharges do not pass without notice.

The following excerpt exemplifies this fact. A legislative memo from the Business Council of New York State, Inc. was drafted to oppose a $1 monthly surcharge for continued operation of New York's emergency 911 service. "In an age where competition is being instituted in our energy and telecommunications industries with the intention of reducing high utility costs, we must be especially careful in approving new and added surcharges or taxes for costly programs. As vendors and businesses make choices about whether to locate or expand in New York, utility prices such as telecommunications services are given great consideration."[17]

Similar attitudes may arise even from those supportive of the underlying programs. The Oregon Public Utilities Commission approved a request by Avista Utilities to add a $\frac{1}{2}\%$ surcharge. The surcharge will raise $200,000 in energy assistance for 1,000 low-income families. While unanimously supported, the commission chair, Roy Hemmingway, characterized the surcharge as a *hidden tax*. He suggested that it "would not be needed if the Oregon Legislature had fully funded low-income programs from general tax revenues."[18]

In March 2003, the Association of Energy Services Professionals notified its membership of attempts by state governments to access monies collected through utility surcharges. "Several states [considered] using accumulated energy efficiency funds to pay-off state debt."[19]

Massachusetts outgoing Governor Jane Swift proposed the use of the $160 million trust fund established by the 1998 electricity deregulation law to offset the $2 billion budget deficit. Wisconsin defeated an attempt to access $38 million in public benefits funds. In Connecticut, annual collections for energy conservation and renewable resources are approximately $106 million. In the proposed 2003–2004 state budget, Governor Rowland has proposed that 100% of these funds be allocated to the general fund. Where legislators allow this to occur, ratepayers would indeed have cause for concern.

Initially, surcharges mimicked
early regulatory action that simply
reimbursed utilities for program
expenses. For mandated assistance
programs, the approach worked well.
However, surcharges spread to encom-
pass wider initiatives, including broad
energy efficiency initiatives and renewable energy sources. As a consequence,
programs were not tailored to specific
utility requirements.

"Through collaborative planning
and integrated monitoring,
broad stakeholder support
has resulted for California's
low-income initiatives.
Most importantly, utility shareholders
are rewarded with both
short- and long-term benefits."

Instead industry advocates shaped programs around societal
concerns, broad consumer protectionism, and environmental issues.
Without broad internal support from participating utilities, operational
efficiencies were not realized. In many cases, the programs existed
solely to appease regulatory mandate. Such gold plating raised utility
rates without generating adequate ratepayer benefits.

To overcome this, negotiated resolves gave consideration to
shareholder incentives, lost revenue, and stranded assets. While each of
these claims must be weighed individually, the use of shareholder
incentives for low-income initiatives has gained increasing acceptance.

California, as an example, offers shareholder incentives to
utilities with low-income energy efficiency programs that exceed
established performance standards. By offering shareholder returns,
low-income programs can be treated as investments. As a result,
utilities can develop initiatives to address specific needs. In addition,
utilities shareholders are vested in the programs. Ratepayers are
further protected through integrated monitoring and evaluation that
can detect and eliminate systemic inefficiencies.

Through collaborative planning and integrated monitoring, broad
stakeholder support has resulted for California's low-income
initiatives. Most importantly, utility shareholders are rewarded with
both short- and long-term benefits. This balance is an important
consideration for the utility company.

CONTINUED OPPOSITION

Program expenditures are considered direct expenses. This is problematic for the utility shareholder. Expenses appear on the income statement immediately. It is true that shareholders benefit from improved socioeconomic conditions, environmental compliance, and reduced capital expenditures. However, these benefits do not appear within the same accounting period as program expenses.

"Given the breadth of benefactors, you would expect low-income programs to be well supported within the industry. Unfortunately, this is not the case. Misconceptions regarding the low-income can blind utility employees and even regulators to otherwise profitable programs."

As a result, corporate earnings are reduced, and revenue growth is slowed. These factors negatively impact shareholder value. Until the Financial Accounting Standards Board addresses utility investments in energy efficiency, the appropriate accounting mechanisms to capitalize program expenditures remain absent. As a result, utilities are unable to treat low-income initiatives as an investment.

The authorization of shareholder incentives by the public service commission can provide a tangible short-term return for the utility. With both ratepayer and shareholder concerns addressed, utility opposition is eliminated. As such, broad stakeholder support has resulted for low-income initiatives. Supporters include program participants, low-income advocates, environmental lobbies, ratepayers, regulators, and the utility.

Given the breadth of benefactors, you would expect low-income programs to be universally supported within the industry. Unfortunately, this is not the case. Misconceptions regarding the low-income can blind utility employees and even regulators to otherwise profitable programs.

Because utility allotments within housing authorities and energy assistance grants do not provide adequate incentives toward energy conservation, a misconception exists that low-income families refuse to regulate household energy use. The stereotype is of a bare-chested male sitting comfortably in his trailer enjoying a beer in the dead of winter, with the front door left ajar by his children. This negative image often displaces a more placid example. Consider instead an elderly widow bundled in a long wool sweater living in just a fraction of available square footage to conserve energy.

While both examples represent extreme behaviors within the low-income community, such imagery is used to align industry participants with respect to low-income initiatives. These extreme images are more easily recalled because they represent extraordinary events.

> *"The public utility,*
> *as an essential service provider,*
> *can provide the necessary stimulus*
> *to raise financial resources*
> *and improve*
> *socioeconomic conditions."*

Yet a more appropriate representation of the typical low-income family is that of your neighbor. Demographically, the low-income mirror the general population in age, diversity, and geographic distribution. Lacking financial resources upon which to draw, low-income households make choices that seem counter-productive. For many, these choices result in contempt. This is represented by the following attitude: Why should I support those who refuse to help themselves?

Despite the great care and attention given to the issues at hand, anyone who has lived in poverty can attest to the ease with which situations degrade. For those of us who have not experienced poverty first-hand, simulations are available to illustrate the very real difficulties involved. Participants in these poverty simulations struggle to emerge from the grips of poverty, despite advanced degrees, specialized training, and informed options. The underlying truth is that within a bad situation, there are few good options.

Poverty simulations reveal that abhorrent social behavior does not necessarily result from a lack of education, general knowledge, or the presence of mental illness. Rather, it appears overwhelming social conditions, lack of available resources, and general human behavior perpetuate socioeconomic segregation.

Where socioeconomic conditions are improved and financial resources made available, many disadvantaged families can rise from poverty and become productive members of the community. The public utility, as an essential service provider, can provide the necessary stimulus to raise financial resources and improve socio-economic conditions.

UNDERSTANDING ENERGY AFFORDABILITY

For families living near poverty, the utility bill as a percent of household income will be much higher than that of the average home. In a study conducted by the National Low-Income Energy Consortium, the energy burden of the average U.S. household is just 5% of annual income, while those in poverty have energy burdens approaching 20% of household income. As such, $1 out of every $5 is spent on home energy.[20]

To understand how this is possible, we must look at what is meant by poverty. Poverty in the United States is defined as a function of income, household size, and age distribution. A single person making just $13,000/year or $6.50/hour would be at the upper bounds of our federal poverty guidelines. That means the average family living in poverty has less earning power than your teenage daughter.

As such, low-income families often have difficulty prioritizing household spending. Consider the following testimonial from America's Second Harvest. "Patsy had always been able to support herself and her three children with jobs in the hotel and food service industries, but when her mother died six years ago, that changed. Patsy developed a system to handle her bills. 'I would pretty much just pay half of each—the electric bill, the phone bill. That would keep them on, but some months were harder than others were. I was forced to make the choice between feeding my kids and being in the dark or having electricity. I chose to feed the kids.'"

Having applied for government assistance and successfully completed culinary school, Patsy was able improve her situation. She now has a new job with higher wages. Due to her initiative and patience, Patsy and her family now live comfortably.[21]

However, many low-income are not as fortunate. The National Consumer Law Center has published a number of studies demonstrating that families living in poverty have incomes below the level necessary to maintain a minimum standard of living. As such, poverty is more about subsistence rather than inequality.

One such study conducted in 1989 found half of households living below 50% of the federal poverty guideline did not earn enough money to pay essential household expenditures. Similarly, 85% of families living between 50% and 99% of poverty had less than $24 of monthly discretionary income before paying their utility bills.[22]

Consequently, one-time expenses such as car repair or medical expenses can cause the low-income family to fall behind in their payments. In fact, with little discretionary spending, even small events can upset the household budget. Despite utility bills having a high priority within the low-income household, continuity of service may be difficult to maintain. This is especially true during times of rising fuel prices.

Charles Givens, in his book, *Wealth without Risk,* recommends that individuals must pay themselves first. He highlights the value of this golden rule and argues convincingly against those who suggest that saving 10% of one's take-home pay is impossible. While his rhetoric is convincing and his words well known, few Americans are able to heed his advice.

For families in poverty, even a modest cash reserve would be a luxury. When bills cycle unpaid, many utilities begin a process that disconnects nonpaying customers from their system. The practice of mass disconnects during nonheating seasons is unfortunate, not only for the low-income family, but also for the utility.

Data concerning nonpayment disconnects has been reported to the Bureau of the Pennsylvania Public Utilities Commission. This data suggests a very high percentage, 42% in one filing, of low-income homes disconnected for nonpayment will remain vacant through the following heating season. The implication is that low-income families are forced from these properties once utility service is lost.

Low-income tenants wishing to reduce expenses may elect to forego utility service. Although reconnection fees may raise overall utility costs, seasonal utility service may assist families juggling payment priorities. However, leasing terms may require tenants to maintain utility service throughout the rental period. As such, low-income families risk eviction when employing voluntary service termination outside prepaid metering pilots.

This forced mobility of low-income families only exacerbates their struggles. The cost of moving into a new residence adds significantly to household expense. Deposit requirements and bulk payments to creditors severely limit access and affordability of utility service.

A 1995 study sponsored by the Energy Coordinating Agency of Philadelphia found that unaffordable utility service was linked with homelessness.[23] For the utility, these customers are lost from their system along with any hope of collecting outstanding balances.

Although utility debt is not solely a low-income problem, low-income programs that reduce the accumulation of accounts receivable can benefit the utility and its shareholders. In 1999, public utilities wrote off just 0.3% of gross revenues as bad debt. However, notes and accounts receivable represented 22% of gross receipts. With rising fuel prices, increased unemployment, and a soft economy, utility executives have grown increasingly anxious about the potential risk associated with the outstanding receivables.

While uncollectible accounts receive much of the attention, even delayed payments can raise operational expenses and diminish long-term shareholder value. Roger Colton suggests the following scenarios.

When utility bills are paid after the due date, two costs are incurred by the utility. The first is the cost of working capital. For a utility that must borrow cash to fund day-to-day operations, every dollar past due must be supplied via a debt instrument. With this debt, carrying costs are incurred. In a scenario where the utility has cash beyond its daily requirements, the unpaid bills have a second cost that limits investment opportunities.[24]

These costs can accumulate rather quickly. Colton provides an example using data from a Philadelphia utility to exemplify the cost of working capital. Although his estimates are not meant to quantify the precise amount, they do show the costs of working capital can be substantial. For a sample of 19,000 LIHEAP participants, the working capital cost for just one month exceeded $100,000.[25]

It would be unfair to extrapolate this number across the 35 million low-income households or across a lengthy planning horizon. Even so, simple deduction suggests that the cost of working capital coupled with lost opportunity can have substantial impacts on shareholder returns.

In the face of rising receivables, many utilities will increase collection activity, adding to their operating costs. The utility is better off only when more money has been collected than is spent on the process of debt collection. If the collection activity fails to yield a net positive result, the additional collection activity has simply compounded the problem by raising operating costs.

Collection costs are even further exacerbated by a common misconception that the threat of service disconnection is an effective method of collecting arrearages. Paul Komor addresses this fallacy in the following statement, "This heavy-handed method has been found to be surprisingly ineffective. Consumers will almost always pay whatever is demanded to ensure reconnection, but they will usually not improve their payment performance after that."[26]

"Luckily, low-income initiatives can mitigate the added expense of serving those near poverty. When well coordinated and effectively implemented, the utility will profit from low-income offerings. However, to appreciate these gains, a fresh prospective may be required."

His statement really gets at the point. Current methods, while effective in the short-term outlook, lack long-term resolve. As a result, utility credit and collection activities are often repeated, with additive effects.

Under ordinary circumstances, utilities invest cash to generate additional income for shareholders. Managing cash accounts to maximize reliable returns for the shareholder is a necessary competency for any finance manager. Untimely bill payment will substantially lower investment income.

Still, other shareholder concerns remain. The reliability and timeliness of accounts receivable are key factors in the assessment of credit worthiness. Corporations rely on credit ratings to access capital and support growth. A solid credit rating will yield less expensive capital and enhance growth expectations. For an investor-owned utility, credit worthiness translates directly to higher stock price and increased market valuation.

While operational practices must be implemented in a timely manner, a long-term outlook is needed to resolve corporate inefficiencies. Luckily, low-income initiatives can mitigate the added expense of serving those near poverty. When well coordinated and effectively implemented, the utility will profit from low-income offerings. However, to appreciate these gains, a fresh prospective may be required.

INVESTING IN LOW-INCOME PROGRAMS

The potential return from low-income programs is dependent on the specific needs and opportunities within the utility. Conventional thinking has theorized potential benefits as expense reductions and offsets. However, the potential benefits of low-income initiatives extend well beyond cost containment. Long-term shareholder value can be raised through low-income initiatives.

By thinking long-term, public utilities can improve their fundamentals. Utility cash flow, growth expectations, earnings, net assets,
as well as many valuable intangibles are often improved from the
implementation of low-income initiatives. To illustrate this point, let
us consider each component of shareholder value.

Utility cash flow

Utility cash flow has been the target of many low-income
initiatives. The results are immediate but often short-term. Energy
assistance is the most lucid example. National fuel funds and
government grants help the low-income maintain utility service.
These grants are one-time payments made directly to the public
utility on behalf of the customer.

Payment assistance programs and home weatherization improve
cash flow, but other programs also have proven effective. Negotiated
payment plans, payment counseling, and arrearage forgiveness
programs lead to long-term improvements in customer payment
behavior. While these programs may not have the immediate effect of
energy assistance, the achieved benefits may extend well past the
point of intervention.

Growth expectations

As cash accumulates within your organization, growth expectations are improved. The reality of this is rather simple to understand. While daydreaming at work, you may have contemplated
starting your own business. What stopped you? Most likely the
answer will be cash. As part of their day-to-day activities, utility
executives must develop strategies to grow shareholder value. In
many instances, that growth requires a cash investment.

Earnings and net assets

As cash flow improves, a cascade of benefits result. Credit
ratings improve, working capital expenses are reduced, and investor
confidence rises. Utility executives can leverage these events to raise
capital. The impact to the shareholder is immediately reflected in
higher price-to-earnings ratios and elevated stock expectations.

With increased market capitalization, corporations can realize even greater growth by using stock as a surrogate to cash. While the accumulation of cash can lead to growth, other factors are also important. These include the economic condition of the utility service territory, operational efficiency, customer growth, brand loyalty, and corporate leadership. Surprisingly, many low-income initiatives also help with these issues.

Conservation programs and energy efficiency initiatives delay investments in added generation capacity and fuel purchases. Therefore, substantial cash outlays and added debt are averted. As seen from an earlier example, the cost of capital can be significant. For large multi-billion dollar investments, such as a power plant, project costs can lower utility earnings for many years. While utilities eventually realize a return on the investment, it is only after the plant has been brought online. Consequently, 10 years may pass before a single dollar is returned to the shareholder.

"Without proper shareholder incentives, low-income programs funded through system benefit charges and designed outside the public utility will deteriorate in size and effectiveness."

With the recent deregulation, many utilities are no longer vertically integrated. Therefore, the building of new generation plants, fuel reserves, and transmission facilities may exist outside the local distribution company. Still, programs that delay these invest-ments remain beneficial to the utility.

The local distribution company has primary responsibility for delivering energy to the general population. As such, the local distribution company bears the risks associated with generation and transmission, even when those facilities are owned by other entities. Just as McDonald's must secure high-grade beef long before meat is turned into patties, local distribution companies employ long-term market instruments to meet future energy demand. Therefore, demand-side initiatives and integrated resource planning remain important internal controls.

A number of legislative actions and regulatory guidelines have emerged following deregulation. The public utility commission often drafts the emerging regulations on statewide concerns. As a result, these regulations do not effectively address the specific needs of the public utility. Without the proper checks and balances, broad regulatory guidelines must compete with the internal priorities of the utility.

Broadly defined affordability and energy efficiency programs lack the specificity to resolve pressing issues. Because of this, operational inefficiencies will exist. Although low-income initiatives have the ability to improve long-term earnings, short-term improvements are difficult to document. Consequently, low-income programs require a strong insightful utility executive who favors long-term shareholder value.

In a volatile market that rewards high-growth industries, stodgy old reliable utility stocks trade at low multiples. As such, a utility must be mindful of its financials. Without proper shareholder incentives, low-income programs funded through system benefit charges and designed outside the public utility will deteriorate in size and effectiveness.

To rectify this problem, low-income programs must be integrated within utility operations and viewed as an investment. Many advocates have recognized this problem and support utility-designed programs with guaranteed returns for the utility shareholders. While a step in the right direction, the industry must go further.

For example, current accounting practices hinder investments in energy efficiency. Currently, a disparity exists between the immediate recognition of program expenses and long-term benefits resulting from low-income initiatives. By booking expenses in the current year, utilities must absorb program costs well in advance of the expected benefit. This is problematic across a number of industries.

In recognition of this, the banking and insurance industries have recommended changes to Generally Accepted Accounting Principles (GAAP) for community development and affordable housing initiatives. Since many low-income programs are both, the utility industry should support GAAP treatments that would recognize the investment made in low-income programs. Similarly, an Emerging Issue, *90-8 Capitalization of Costs to Treat Environmental Contaminants,* is under consideration by the Financial Accounting Standards Board (FASB). The ruling on this issue may provide a base to change current accounting rules for low-income investments.

In fact, the FASB has allowed the capitalization of expenses where clear evidence of future revenue could be demonstrated. This is the case with fund-raising efforts. If the same treatment were allowed for low-income weatherization, program expenses could be capitalized over the 20-year expected treatment life. Such an accounting treatment would be a great improvement over current practices.

In addition, an argument can be made to treat energy efficiency investments as an asset. For example, energy efficiency programs have been used for decades as an alternative energy supply. Throughout the late 1980s and 1990s, many organizations accepted demand-side alternatives along with traditional supply options in their fulfillment strategy. As such, integrated resource planning justified usage reduction programs as an alternative fuel supply.

While this was the correct handling of these demand-side programs, utilities were unable to capture their investments on the balance sheet. With the support of industry participants, the public utility has available research needed to justify consideration of this issue by the appropriate accounting standards board. Changes in accounting practices would then give incentive for low-income program development.

Instead, utilities rely on the reduction of accounts receivable to justify low-income initiatives. As a result, program administrators must seek support from sympathetic executives and lobby ratepayer support to fund low-income initiatives. While contributions to corporate goodwill and participant benefits generate support, the true benefit and scope of program impacts are often understated within such a framework.

BENEFITS RESULTING FROM LOW-INCOME PROGRAMS

Low-income programs improve utility financials in a number of ways, as demonstrated in the previous text. However, understanding the impact of specific low-income programs on the utility as a business can be challenging. Perhaps this is why a stronger case for low-income programs has been ignored for so long. The primary impacts resulting from various classes of low-income programs are outlined for your consideration.

Household subsidies

The benefits of household subsidies to the utility are perhaps the most easily understood and are by far the easiest programs to implement. Many household subsidies exist outside the utility framework. Government programs, nonprofit agencies, and charitable foundations exist to assist struggling households with necessary living expenses. These include food, shelter, health, transportation, and child care.

The public utility can benefit indirectly from all these programs. Research of customer payment behavior has demonstrated that utility bills receive a very high priority. When customers prioritize their monthly expenditures, rent and utilities are among the first to be paid. As such, household subsidies are often directed to the public utility.

In fact, a number of household subsidies are specifically designed to pay utility bills. The federal LIHEAP allocates $1.7 billion annually to reduce the energy burden of low-income households. In most states, these payments are sent directly to the public utility on behalf of customers. Similarly, most major cities and many states have fuel funds that supplement the LIHEAP program.

While these payments do not raise revenues, utility cash flow and net earnings are improved. In recognition of this, many utilities actively lobby LIHEAP authorization. Still, more can be done.

A number of issues remain with the federal program: the level of funding, allocation of the funds, timing of allocation, and qualification of eligible households. Even with the nearly $2 billion in energy assistance available, only 10–15% of eligible households are served.

The public utility must sponsor research and lobby for increases in LIHEAP and the development of more fuel funds. In addition, utilities should establish shareholder-sponsored fuel funds to target payment-troubled populations in their area. By doing so, utilities benefit from short-term balance sheet improvements while building a network to raise additional cash grants.

Other sources of energy assistance are often overlooked. Many housing programs and general assistance programs have within them utility allotments. These allotments are designed to cover anticipated utility costs. Yet, many times these allotments are underestimated or redirected. By working closely with community-based organizations, utilities could recover revenue that has otherwise been lost in the process.

Similarly, public utilities can benefit as household incomes improve. Because of this, the public utility should highlight programs assisting low-income customers. These programs include the earned income tax credit, local empowerment programs, and economic stimulus packages. In fact, a number of programs exist whereby the utility could benefit indirectly. However, without a strategic directive to identify and promote these programs, available shareholder benefits are lost.

Payment stabilization programs

Almost every utility has some form of payment stabilization program. The most common of these programs are the budget plans, deferred payment plans, and referral services. While these programs are helpful, the low-income population may require even greater assistance.

Budget counseling services help those struggling with current financial obligations. Deciding how much to pay on which bills is a difficult task when resources are insufficient. An experienced and understanding advisor can guide a lost sailor to shore.

Utility customer service centers simply cannot provide this type of assistance. This is understandable, given the volume of calls, but unfortunate. Individuals and families in financial distress require access to these services. Customers having trouble with the gas or electric bill are likely going to have trouble maintaining phone service. The first call made by the consumer may be the only chance for the utility to serve that person's needs. A call center unprepared for this call exacerbates an already worsening situation.

Routing low-income customers to service representatives or community-based organizations with the appropriate tools can better address the issues of poverty. An even better option is to open centers in those communities most in need. Community-based outsourcing provides the best aspects of both.

Experienced social workers empowered by utilities to negotiate payment arrangements will more effectively resolve special needs than the average call center representative. For some households, the correct solution can be as simple as changing the billing cycle to match the customer's earnings cycle. For others, a prepaid meter may be viable. Others with greater needs may require arrearage forgiveness.

The payment counselor interacting with the low-income customer must understand the issues surrounding poverty. The counselor also must demand personal responsibility and maintain the interest of the public utility. To do so effectively, utilities must better target program services, train frontline employees, expand payment options, and invest in program delivery.

Many firms have experience with these programs. However, research firms that understand affordability issues and can identify the specific needs of your payment-troubled population are the best resource for the public utility. With proper assessment and program design, payment stabilization programs can enhance shareholder value.

Bill reduction programs

Today utilities have more options to reduce customer billings. Low-income rate reduction programs and aggregate fuel purchases have become popular. By lowering the energy costs passed to the customer, the public utility can improve the energy burden of those living near poverty. By doing so, utilities can experience reductions in top-line revenue without reducing net earnings.

While bill reduction programs existed prior to deregulation, utilities now have options that were once unavailable. These include prepaid services, customer choice, and even fuel-switching programs. With a push to allow market drivers to guide service options, fuel switching may resurface as a viable option to lower energy costs. The intent of low-income assistance is to improve affordability and lower energy burdens. Consequently, regulators and interveners should not object to the use of alternative fuels for heating and cooling.

In some states, utilities can even benefit from rate discount programs because funding mechanisms exist to offset the fuel subsidies. Similarly, fee waivers can be used to improve service affordability to the low-income and elderly."

With advances in metering technology, pricing options may demonstrate increased elasticity in consumer demand. Time-of-use rates, successfully implemented by the telephone companies, may be useful for certain consumers. Household occupancy patterns should be examined for opportunity. However, a relatively safe assumption is that low-income occupancy will differ from that of the general population. As such, price incentives could be used to modify consumption behavior, especially heating and cooling loads. With easily tailored pricing options and the proper technology, load shifting can be used to improve service affordability.

If utilities can lower current bills by just 20%, low-income customers are often able to pay the current usage charges and avoid the accumulation of arrears. Once affordability of utility service is achieved, the repayment of past debt becomes more probable. In fact, many customers will not lower their payment amounts simply because current bills are reduced. Evidence has shown consumers are willing to pay fixed affordable installments without regard to the current billings. Bill reduction programs improve credit and collection ratios, improve growth expectations, stabilize cash flows, and promote long-term earnings.

Usage reduction programs

Usage reduction programs and bill reduction programs are closely linked from the customer prospective. Both seek to improve low-income service affordability. However, significant differences exist when viewed from the perspectives of the various stakeholders.

Usage reduction programs require substantial initial investments. For example, replacing heating and cooling systems can cost thousands of dollars. Because returns on this investment trickle in over an extended period, short-term earning improvements can be difficult to demonstrate. Utility ratepayers subsidize these investments, but it is the shareholder who benefits most from market transformational changes in the low-income housing stock.

With low-income consumers cycling in and out of affordable housing, the utility can realize a continuous stream of benefits. These can result from one-time investments in heating/cooling efficiency, baseload reductions, and energy education. This recurring benefit separates the usage reduction programs from many payment programs.

For the program participant, property values are stimulated. While the promise of improved property value supports program participation, those living on fixed incomes have been targets of many restoration scams. Because of this, usage reduction programs often require the support of broad energy awareness programs and community support.

Once participation has been secured, utilities can reap long-term benefits that extend beyond a single household or low-income family. The result is a subsidized energy source that can lower future fuel costs and delay infrastructure investments. With proper management, utility shareholders may benefit from short-term improvements in growth expectations, corporate goodwill, and balance sheet improvements.

Health and safety programs

Health and safety programs often refer to appliance repair and other in-home services. However, utility access programs must be considered within this framework. Utility service is just as important to one's health as properly functioning home appliances. Following this approach, emergency assistance grants that ensure utility service can be viewed as a health and safety program.

Initiatives that lower deposit requirements also improve access to utility service. Crisis assistance that restores utility service following disconnection also provides access to utility service. Without these programs, low-income consumers must choose between food, medicine, heat, or air conditioning. This involuntary game of Russian roulette is certainly detrimental to people's health and well-being.

Equally dangerous to those living on limited means is the sudden malfunction of home appliances. Many people are aware of the danger of improperly vented gas appliances and aging electrical circuits. However, some families do not recognize the existence of these problems or simply cannot afford to remedy existing hazards. Such threats have very real societal implications. In addition, these threats also have consequences for the utility, its shareholders, and its ratepayers. Because of this, utilities provide safety education and referral services for their customers. In addition, utilities promote health and safety within existing marketing and assistance programs.

Ignoring the presence of health hazards by utility employees can lead to costly litigation and punitive damages. Every contact with those living on limited means can be used to identify and remedy family crisis.

Through positive community intervention, the utility can generate added loyalty, improve corporate goodwill, stabilize the residential customer base, and limit liability claims. Since the incremental costs of these programs are often trivial, utilities incorporate health and safety programs into their daily operations. In addition, utilities can leverage opportunities to raise service standards, improve regulatory relations, and enhance customer loyalty.

Community development programs

Programs such as affordable housing, empowerment zones, loan guarantees, and economic development initiatives generate lasting impacts for the local distribution company. Yet, within the context of a low-income framework, market transformation programs are often ignored. A close examination across the entire system will demonstrate that load building programs targeted at areas of concentrated poverty can outperform projects that extend service lines.

Take for example a large employer considering a move within your utility service territory. Typically, the employer would be subsidized through rate incentives and line extensions. Given a choice between new construction and renovating vacant properties within a repressed service territory, the utility should consider increasing subsidies for the latter.

Not only does the utility avoid the investment in new service lines, the economic stimuli provided by the employer has broad implications for any repressed service territory. Unlike areas targeted for new construction, depressed service territories are in decline. Upwardly mobile populations are migrating from the area, along with the larger employers. The remaining populace will have increasingly lower median incomes and fewer opportunities to improve their situations. As such, those living in these areas will begin to experience many of the problems associated with low incomes. Such problems include increasing energy burdens, growing payment troubles, declining housing stock, and limited job opportunities.

Without some economic stimuli, these areas will continue to decline. They will begin to demonstrate increased vacancy rates, payment negotiations, uncollectible accounts, and service discontinuity. For the utility, the decline often results in regionally higher operational costs, declining revenue, and negative customer growth. In extreme cases, areas of concentrated poverty arise, with added problems of employee safety and infrastructure decay. Because of this, economically repressed areas can negatively impact the fiscal health of the utility. Without intervention, repressed service areas will escalate both in number and financial consequence. As such, the utility must identify and promote revitalization of areas in economic decline.

Bringing a large employer into the utility service territory increases median incomes, stimulates customer growth, and results in added utility revenue. Large employers spur utility prospects and foster growth. Such stimulus in properly targeted regions can add significantly to long-term shareholder and ratepayer value.

The economic incentives offered by the utility should reflect the depth and breadth of achieved benefits. While line extensions build load, they do not help with the socioeconomic condition of the existing service territory. As highlighted earlier, poor payment behavior can lead to substantial costs. These costs must be considered when offering rate incentives to large employers who could stimulate an otherwise repressed service territory.

Too often, the number of jobs created by a new employer overshadows the persons filling those jobs. If the payment-troubled have access to these jobs, then additional incentives can be offered. The reversal of an economically repressed service area will generate sustainable returns for the utility shareholder. Sponsoring the entrance of a market driver into an area of concentrated poverty is by far the best opportunity for those struggling with high-energy burdens.

INDICATIONS OF NEED

With a number of low-income programs available to the public utility, identifying the right combination for your organization can be daunting. In fact, many employees within the public utility are simply unaware when and if low-income programs are needed.

Since low-income programs are justified by the financial health of the utility, an assessment of utility financial statements is required. However, do not expect your financial advisor or online broker to highlight the importance of these programs to the fiscal health of your organization. The special needs of the public utility cannot be found from accounting summaries alone.

Instead, the need for low-income programs requires an understanding of socioeconomic conditions within the service territory and the payment practices of individual customers. It also requires knowledge of the network of community service providers, the regulatory temperament, and a good handle on the fiscal fitness of the utility. It is no wonder that low-income program administrators have trouble qualifying the need and quantifying the impact of their programs.

At the time of writing, very few organizations have compiled the necessary information to properly assess the value of low-income programs to the utility. Instead, public utilities often rely on the external pressures to identify need and to recommend solutions. Advocacies may be necessary to call attention to systemic problems. However, the public utility must take more proactive steps to address the low-income market segment within a competitive context. After all, 28% of a utility's residential sales and 6% of gross receipts come from the low-income customers.

> *"Without sufficient documentation of program performance and demonstration of corporate returns, low-income programs will not receive proper consideration."*

Utilities have taken steps to better understand their payment-troubled customers. Yet, the best indications of need come from within the organization. We will highlight a few indicators in the following text. Sometimes several indications coexist within a given utility and across the service territory. When this is the case, you can be confident that the programs highlighted in this text can add long-term shareholder value and protect existing ratepayers.

Mergers and acquisitions

With the EPAct 2003 passing both the House and Senate, a repeal of PUHCA seems imminent. PUHCA dates back to the Great Depression restricting mergers and acquisitions within the utility industry. If the two bills can be reconciled, President Bush has acknowledged that he will sign EPAct into law. Should this occur, public utility holding companies are likely to build revenues and seek operational efficiencies through acquisitions.

While the local distribution company may remain an independent entity, changes in leadership, strategic direction, and financial circumstance will alter support for existing low-income initiatives. In most cases, expense reductions will be sought to offset acquisition costs. Given that the bottom line impacts of low-income programs are poorly understood, these programs are at great risk. Highly effective programs may be trimmed and marginal programs cut altogether.

Program administrators, regulators, and interveners should realize that leadership changes within an organization often trigger a multiyear review of existing operations. Without sufficient documentation of program performance and demonstration of corporate returns, low-income programs will not receive proper consideration.

If low-income initiatives are to continue, an understanding of the bottom-line impact is mandatory. Waiting until an internal review has been ordered down from the top is simply insufficient. The study of program impacts may take years from initial study design through data analysis. Corporate managers, even if sympathetic, cannot forestall decisions over this timeframe. Because of this, program administrators must have information available and be willing to stand by their programs despite an uncertain future.

Rate filings

Rate filings are costly and time-consuming. Consequently, the public utility will not enter the process without adequate cause. In general, the public utility will seek to amend its rate structure only when significant changes in operational efficiencies or market forces alter revenue requirements.

No better time exists to roll out and expand low-income initiatives than during a rate filing when program costs can be embedded in the base rates. The presence of customer-centric programs can be used to leverage support from a breadth of industry participants. For the utility shareholder and ratepayer, a rate filing is an opportunity to expand programs with a demonstrated business case. Efforts to prepare for this eventuality should not be delayed. The information gained through a rigorous analysis of operations will have many areas of applicability within the public utility.

External pressures

A number of external forces may require the implementation of low-income initiatives. Competitive pressures such as deregulation resulted in the establishment of systems benefit charges and regulatory pressure for universal service, energy efficiency, and utility service affordability options. When such pressures materialize at the regulatory level, the public utility must acquiesce and offer the programs demanded. Even within this framework, the utility should adopt a proactive response. Utilities can offer programs that fit the regulatory constraints but also address issues and customer segments relevant to the utility. Maximizing low-income initiatives in such a framework has rarely been seen.

Other, less obvious influences may exist. For example, in the summer of 2003 Philadelphia Gas Works announced the use of mass disconnects to address its growing number of uncollectible accounts. While the threat may or may not be carried out in full, the utility managed public scrutiny by promoting the many payment options available to those in need. By doing so, the utility demonstrated a concern for the poor while demanding personal responsibility for unpaid balances.

Like other marketing programs, utilities must integrate available programs with their strategic goals. Low-income programs are available in many utilities and can be used to leverage corporate goodwill. Community involvement has always been a hallmark of the public utility. Why not promote utility-sponsored assistance programs to demonstrate sensitivity and concern for the local issues?

Imagine the impact of a utility affordability program announced in response to a mass downsizing by a large employer in your service territory. The proper timing and promotion of available payment options can improve participation rates while at the same time establishing the public utility as a caring corporate citizen.

Internal pressures

Internal pressures may also serve as an indication of need for low-income initiatives. Revenue warnings, spending constraints, excessive uncollectible accounts, and load curtailments are all signs that affordability and energy efficiency programs are needed. Talking with strategic planners and revenue recovery personnel can help you understand strategic objectives. At times of rising internal controls, low-income programs can yield long-term benefits to utility shareholders and ratepayers.

PROFITING FROM LOW-INCOME PROGRAMS

In this chapter, a lot of ground has been covered. First, the low-income consumer was identified as a valuable and sizable customer segment. Second, a few myths regarding the low-income population were dispelled. Third, programs designed specifically for the low-income market segment were highlighted. Finally, markers indicating the need for low-income programs were revealed.

While these topics are necessary to build a business case for low-income initiatives, this chapter lacked specific program examples. In the following section, each class of low-income programs is considered. Existing programs serve as examples, but more importantly, they indicate the range of possible innovation.

As you move into the following section, you should challenge yourself to ask the following questions. These will ensure that long-term shareholder value and utility ratepayer protections have been properly considered.

- Does the program improve utility cash flow?
- Does the program result in balance sheet improvements?
- What impact does the program have on annual earnings?
- How will the program influence utility growth expectations?
- Can program intangibles be used to instill investor confidence?

By asking these questions, you arm yourself for the many challenges that lie ahead.

NOTES

[1] U.S. Department of Energy. Energy Information Administration. A Look at Residential Energy Consumption in 2001. Table CE1-3e.

[2] Number of U.S. households eligible for federal assistance as reported by the Energy Information Administration in their 2001 Residential Energy Consumption Survey, adjusted for 2003 using a 1.5% annualized growth rate.

[3] Proctor, B. D., and J. Dalaker. 2002. Poverty in the United States. U.S. Census Bureau, *Current Population Reports,* p. 12.

[4] Ibid.

[5] The term *recently unemployed* includes persons 16 years or older without work for six months or less with the disenfranchised represented by those unemployed for six months or more. *http://www.census.gov/prod/2003pubs/02statab/labor.pdf.*

[6] Proctor, B. D., and J. Dalaker, p. 14.

[7] *http://www.irs.gov/pub/irs-soi/01co14b.xls.*

[8] U.S. Department of Energy. Energy Information Administration. A Look at Residential Energy Consumption in 2001. Table CE1-3e.

[9] U.S. Department of Energy. Energy Information Administration. 2001 Residential Energy Consumption Survey. Table CE1-3c.

[10] Ibid.

[11] U.S. Department of Energy. Energy Information Administration. A Look at Residential Energy Consumption in 2001. Table CE1-3e.

[12] Ibid.

[13] Ibid.

[14] U.S.-Canada Power Outage Task Force. 2004. Final Report on the August 14, 2003 Blackout in the United States and Canada, Causes and Recommendations (Apr.), pp. 17–21.

[15] Berry, L. 1997. State-Level Evaluations of the Weatherization Assistance Programs in 1990–1996: A Metaevaluation that Estimates National Savings, p. 7. She found typical savings from state weatherization programs ranged from 18% to 24% of preprogram consumption levels.

[16] Calculated from statistics presented earlier. 2.7 quads x 0.20 = 0.54 quads or 540,000,000 MMBTU. Multiplying this by 20 results in 10.8 quads of energy savings.

[17] Evers, J. 2002. Legislative Memo: Bill S.7650 / A.11721 (June 12). *http://www.bcnys.org/inside/Legmemos/2002/s7650a11721.htm.*

[18] Weiss, S. 2002. Avista Moves to Help Struggling Oregonians. *NW Energy Coalition Report*, Vol. 21, No. 3.

[19] Alliance to Save Energy. 2003. State Energy Efficiency Funds at Risk. *AESP Member Newsletter* (Mar.).

[20] NLIEC. The Cold Facts: The First Annual Report on the Effect of Home Energy Costs on Low-Income Americans. http://www.nliec.org/cold.pdf.

[21] Utilities or Food. Issues Paper No. 1. Minnesota. *http://www.secondharvest.org/site_content.asp?s=147.*

[22] Colton, R. D. 1995. The Forced Mobility of Low-Income Households. National Consumer Law Center (NCLC) (Aug.).

[23] The Institute for Public Policy Studies at Temple University. 1991. An Examination of the Relationship Between Utility Terminations, Housing Abandonment and Homelessness. Energy Coordinating Agency (June).

[24] Colton, R. D. 1994. Low-Income Programs and Their Impact on Reducing Utility Working Capital Allowances. Fisher, Sheehan, and Colton (July).

[25] Ibid.

[26] Komor, P. 2000. The Low-Income Market: That Overlooked 25 Percent. RES Currents (Dec.).

SECTION II

EXISTING PROGRAMS
AND PRACTICES

4

HOUSEHOLD SUBSIDIES

STATEMENT OF OPPORTUNITY

The Low-Income Home Energy Assistance Program (LIHEAP) allocates approximately $2 billion annually to offset extreme energy burdens. Private fuel funds and utility allowances from HUD, TANF, and FEMA add to traditional energy assistance. Current estimates suggest $6 billion annually is linked directly to utility bill assistance.

These cash grants flow into the public utility as customer payments and account credits. While household subsidies already represent 14% of low-income home energy billings, the totals could be even higher. Budgetary constraints have placed downward pressures on governmental allowances for utility expense. As a result, many eligible households struggle needlessly against increasing energy burdens.

With available subsidies serving only a portion of the total need, households must file a complete and timely application to be eligible for energy assistance. Organizations that actively promote and ease the application process help those in need by effectively raising household income.

With utility bills given high priority over other monthly expenditures, additions to household income should result in added revenue and more timely utility payments. Yet, few utilities can identify the amount of assistance provided their low-income customers. With current household income subsidies nearing $90 billion annually, utilities seeking working capital improvements can no longer remain passive benefactors.

Increasingly, household subsidies are being cut at all levels of government. Moreover, state legislators have recently plundered universal service riders to offset budget deficits. As a result, utilities suffer both top-line and bottom-line consequences. Allowing such actions to take place without voicing opposition has lasting impacts on utility shareholders and ratepayers.

Energy consumption is correlated with household income. Consequently, utilities should leverage existing household subsidies and economic development incentives to improve the socioeconomic conditions within their service territories. By accessing payments that would otherwise be lost or directed to competing utilities, cash flow improvements will enhance utility fundamentals. To be effective, the public utility must better understand the low-income provider network and catalog available assistance. Through collaborative strategic planning, utilities can improve service affordability across the system while realizing lasting cash flow improvements.

Below is a survey of existing low-income assistance programs. You will find that household subsidies are distributed at all levels of government. While the majority of funds flow from federal programs, the reader should not underestimate the role of regional fuel funds. Fuel funds are now supported by private endowments and have just begun to develop. With increased corporate participation, private fuel funds will add significantly to available energy assistance.

KEY CONCEPTS

Households

Households, as defined by the LIHEAP statute, are persons living as a "single economic unit" within a given structure. These provisions were designed to protect renters within public housing projects. However, this provision has hindered states trying to serve households with the greatest energy burdens.

Several states have attempted to include the income of unrelated boarders when considering program eligibility and prioritizing. Consumer advocates successfully challenged the inclusion of this income. They cited strict guidelines defining the household and argued that the two tenants were not acting as a "single economic unit."

The presence of nontraditional family units and extended families living under the same roof may require additional clarification from Congress. The wording "single economic unit" portends the income from all working adults living within the same structure. However, judicial rulings have applied strict interpretations of the LIHEAP statute, thereby excluding income from tenants unrecognized by the state as a family. Because of these rulings, household assistance is given to homes that would otherwise exceed income eligibility guidelines.

By clarifying legislative intent, Congress could ensure families with the greatest need are protected. One way to accomplish this would be to ignore the utility service point and utility account-holder provisions. Each postal address identifies a unique and distinct housing unit. Adult earners at each postal address contribute to the household in one manner or another. Despite recognition of this fact, states have struggled to implement more inclusive definitions.

Energy burden

Energy burden is defined as the cost of home energy expressed as a percent of household income. While the average family has an energy burden of 7%, low-income families may have energy burdens exceeding 14% of household income.[1] When utility costs rise unexpectedly, the low-income are severely disadvantaged and often fall behind in their financial obligations. With fuel prices nearing record levels, energy burdens have grown disproportionately large within low-income households.

Growing need and declining assistance

Needs have grown and assistance has declined during the last two decades. The number of individuals living in poverty has remained at 1982 levels, while LIHEAP appropriations have declined 44% when adjusted for inflation.[2] In 2003, LIHEAP allocated nearly $2 billion to ease the energy burdens of those with the lowest incomes.

Despite federal support, LIHEAP serves just a fraction of eligible households. Approximately 4.1 million households are served each year. Clearly, this is just a small fraction of the 50 million individuals in need.

Following the example of Victorine Q. Adams, private fuel funds werc created to supplement federal energy assistance programs. Although private sector support represents a growing resource for low-income providers, private sector funding remains comparatively small. Yet with tightening state and federal budgets, privately funded energy assistance may represent the greatest potential for addressing increasing need.

Utility service allotments

Utility service allotments are embedded in many federal assistance programs. Without these grants, utility uncollectibles would certainly rise. Federal programs offering utility allotments include, but are not limited to, the following:

- Temporary Assistance for Needy Families (TANF)
- Emergency Shelter Grants (ESG)
- Emergency Food and Shelter Program (EFSP)
- Subsidized housing programs under HUD and the USDA

The impact of these programs on the utility has been largely ignored. Specialized studies will be required to fully understand the scope of utility service allotments. While funding trends have not been well studied, pressures on public housing authorities to reduce utility costs are troubling. Concern is rising as to whether reductions are the result of energy efficiency improvements or simply reductions in the availability of utility service allotments.

Charitable gifts

Charitable gifts made to fuel funds return to the utility via customer payments. Since most fuel funds are charitable organizations, corporations can claim deductions for contributions up to 10% of their net income. In addition, charitable contributions in excess of 10% can carry forward.

For the public utility, fuel funds can be a valuable tax shelter. First, charitable donations offset corporate income. Second, energy assistance funds return to utilities as customer payments. Third, energy assistance funds keep customers from being disconnected. As a result, fuel funds effectively transfer receivables from the balance sheet to the income statement without affecting cash. This transfer alone could yield significant cost savings and improve shareholder return.

Another benefit of charitable giving is the support of emerging fuel funds. Foundation grants offered to charitable organizations serve as seed money from which a viable and sustainable entity emerges. As a result, a single contribution provides continuous support to families in financial distress.

Utility service disconnects

Utility service disconnects have a negative impact on the public utility. Service terminations expose the utility to the risk of litigation, erode corporate goodwill, and reduce the existing customer base. Even worse, service terminations are a nonbillable expense that can exceed $100 per incident. As such, it is often difficult to justify these actions.

A better strategy is to use the *threat* of disconnection to access available financial resources. Many energy assistance programs focus on the preservation of utility service rather than the restoration of service. Consequently, the threat of service termination could be a stronger collection tool than the termination itself. This is an important concept for any collections manager.

SURVEY OF EXISTING PROGRAMS

The purpose of household subsidies is to help families through times of financial crisis. Short-term assistance programs allow those living near poverty to build resources and ultimately become self-sufficient. To meet the diverse circumstances of low-income families, assistance programs have evolved to serve a niche within the community.

We have chosen the following programs to highlight this diversity. We look first at the most prominent federal programs and then examine regional offerings. Special emphasis has been given to emerging fuel funds. Each has its own organizational structure, source of funding, eligibility criteria, and assistance levels.

While a number of programs are highlighted throughout this chapter, the reader must realize that new programs and program features appear each year. Our survey simply introduces the low-income provider network. The scope and availability of providers will vary between states, counties, and cities. Although it is a laborious process to identify and document low-income providers across your service territory, utilities undertaking such a project can expect significant returns. Early indications suggest utilities are not taking full advantage of available resources.

Low-Income Home Energy Assistance Program

The Oil Embargo of 1973 resulted in drastically higher oil prices. Energy burdens placed on low-income families prompted the formation of Project Fuel in 1974. The program began in Maine via a $478,000 grant by the Office of Economic Development. In 1975, the Emergency Energy Conservation Program was created with an appropriation of $16.5 million to provide home weatherization and crisis intervention services. By 1980, an outline for the modern Low-Income Home Energy Assistance Program (LIHEAP) emerged.[3] Public Law 96-126 provided $1.6 billion to fund three key programs.

The U.S. Community Service Administration received $400 million for the Emergency Crisis Assistance Program. Additionally, the U.S. Department of Health and Human Services received $1.2 billion to administer two separate initiatives. The first was a special one-time energy allowance of $400 million to supplemental security income. The second initiative was the Emergency Assistance Program. The Emergency Assistance Program received $800 million, which was distributed to individual states as block grants.

In 1981, the passage of Public Law 97-35 created LIHEAP. LIHEAP receives funding through the Department of Health and Human Services' Administration for Children and Families (DHHS ACF). Although the program exists largely unchanged in form, funding levels have varied over the years. A close look at historic funding levels may be surprising to many. Under Republican administrations, LIHEAP has reached historic levels (see Fig. 4–1).

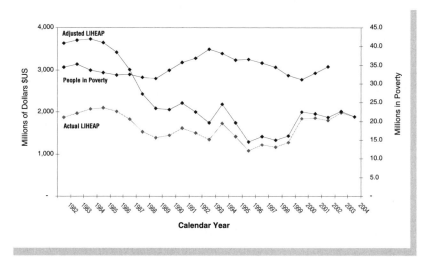

Fig. 4–1 Historical Appropriations for LIHEAP

LIHEAP funding peaked under the Reagan administration in 1985 at $2.1 billion. In 1996 under Clinton, LIHEAP funding bottomed at slightly more than $1 billion. Under the second Bush administration, LIHEAP allocations have returned to their highs. However, when funding is adjusted for inflation, funding levels are clearly inadequate. LIHEAP funding is down 44% from 1982, while the official poverty estimates have remained stable.

The discrepancy between increased need and decreased funding has consequences. Testifying before the Senate, David Bradley stated, "It [current LIHEAP funding] was not enough to meet the needs of even a quarter of those eligible for help." He went on to say that "[funding] fell so far short that many utilities…are reporting record debts…and record number of households are entering these cold months disconnected from their utility heat because they cannot pay."[5]

Households transitioning from welfare to work are part of an emerging demographic known as the *working poor.* Trading government assistance for low-wage hourly positions can be difficult. Faced with increasing responsibility and the continued challenge of poverty, our working poor struggle with increased rents and lowered household subsidies. During congressional testimony, Caroline Myers, chairperson of the National Fuel Funds Network, expressed this concern, "As welfare caseloads have generally gone down across the nation, energy assistance caseloads have gone up."[6] She concluded by saying, "Energy assistance is an important factor in the success of welfare reform."[7]

LIHEAP remains the primary resource for those struggling with home energy costs. To extend the impacts, LIHEAP has developed three notable program components. These are home weatherization, Assurance 16, and REACh. A brief description of each is provided for completeness.

Home weatherization. State home weatherization assistance programs (HWAP) may receive supplemental funding from LIHEAP. States supporting home weatherization through LIHEAP often allocate just 10% to 15% of the LIHEAP funds to home weatherization. However, the LIHEAP statute allows up to 25% of the state allocation to be used for home weatherization. By trading short-term energy assistance for long-term reductions in energy use, states can lower future need for short-term cash assistance.

Assurance 16 services. Assurance 16 allows 5% of state LIHEAP allocations to be used on "services that encourage and enable households to reduce…the need for energy assistance, including needs assessment, counseling, and assistance with energy vendors."[8] To date, 29 states have implemented Assurance 16 initiatives.[9] These initiatives include payment support services, energy education, family management, and referral services. Assurance 16 services represent a significant strategy to encourage individual self-sufficiency. However, a question remains as to whether or not the spending cap has prohibited implementations and evaluations necessary to promote viable alternatives to cash assistance.

Residential Energy Assistance Challenge. The 1994 LIHEAP reauthorization bill created Residential Energy Assistance Challenge (REACh) grants. REACh grants support a limited number of innovative pilot projects each year. Since REACh grants are highly competitive, it is important to understand their intent. The statute defines several desirable impacts used to evaluate REACh funding requests. The stated impacts are as follows:

1. Minimize health and safety risks resulting from high energy burdens placed on low-income Americans

2. Prevent homelessness as a result of inability to pay energy bills

3. Increase efficiency of energy usage by low-income families

4. Target energy assistance to individuals who are most in need[10]

Although only a handful of programs are funded each year, REACh grants can provide start-up capital for large programs. In a review of programs funded in 2002, four of the six programs received grants of $1 million or more. With start-up requirements covered, grantees can find necessary program sponsors for continued operations.

At the time of writing, LIHEAP is authorized through 2004. Federal funding levels, state allocations, advanced appropriations, and REACh grants were expected to be hotly debated issues during these hearings. However, such discourse was not realized. The House and Senate bills have suggested only modest changes to LIHEAP through 2010.

Temporary Assistance for Needy Families

The welfare reform law established the TANF program through the Personal Responsibility and Work Opportunity Reconciliation Act of 1996. TANF replaced the national welfare program known as Aid to Families with Dependent Children. It also replaced related programs such as the Job Opportunities and Basic Skills Training program and the Emergency Assistance program.[11]

TANF is a federal block grant program that helps state welfare programs to assist needy families through financial hardship and to create employment opportunities. In addition, states supplement federal grants with local funds to provide a number of supportive and employment-related services. Services are directed towards family preservation, health care, substance abuse, education, and job skill training.

In fiscal year 2000, TANF allocated $24 billion to state welfare programs. Nearly 48% of this expenditure, $11.5 billion, was distributed in cash grants to an average caseload of 2,272,282 households.[12] These cash grants assisted with living expenses, such as rent, mortgage, utility bills, medical expenses, and dependent care.

Although direct payment of the utility bill is not a universal feature of TANF, requirements for utility service are embedded in the calculation of cash grants. Historically, states have supplied emergency assistance via the welfare program, thus preventing utility service termination. During the winter of 1999, governors were urged to provide emergency heating assistance through TANF, making the program a valuable source of energy assistance.

Readers should realize that TANF recipients have little or no income outside these cash grants to pay their utility bills. Without TANF grants, recipients would either lack access to utility service or would suffer high energy burdens. Where consumers are unable to access utility service, utilities have a reduced customer base, resulting in lower revenues and reduced operating efficiency. Where consumers struggle against high energy burdens, payment behavior can lead to diminished cash flow and increasing arrears. As such, TANF has a significant role in regional low-income provider networks.

While TANF provides necessary assistance to the low-income population, the stigma associated with welfare may keep eligible consumers from participating in the program. Utilities contacted for payment negotiation should review TANF eligibility and make the appropriate referrals. Unlike LIHEAP, TANF assistance is provided throughout the year and over an extended period. As such, referrals to TANF can have compounding returns for the public utility.

Emergency Shelter Grants program

The Homeless Housing Act of 1986 established the Emergency Shelter Grants (ESG) program to address a growing homeless population. In 1987, the ESG program was incorporated into subtitle B of title IV of the McKinney-Vento Homeless Assistance Act (42 U.S.C. 11371–11378).[13]

The ESG program provides basic shelter and essential support services to the homeless. In addition, financial assistance is offered to persons at imminent risk of losing their housing due to eviction, foreclosure, or utility shutoff.[14] In order to qualify for these grants, recipients must have received notice of eviction, foreclosure, or utility termination. They must demonstrate a sudden loss of income as well as the ability to resume payments through a pending income stream. This could include a job offer, welfare eligibility, or social security income.[15]

The ESG program allows 30% of its allocation for prevention services. However, only 17% of ESG providers offered any prevention services.[16] With an annual budget exceeding $1 billion, the ESG program could add $300 million in short-term household subsidies.[17] Because utilities are essential services for any household, ESG prevention funds could be leveraged when service termination appears imminent.

In an area where mass disconnects have been threatened, ESG homeless prevention services may serve as a specialized fuel fund. However, with matching funds required for governmental support, many ESG providers were unable to initiate homeless prevention projects. Private funding of ESG providers could open avenues for improved utility cash flow.

Emergency Community Services Homeless Grant programs

DHHS allocates funding for the Emergency Community Services Homeless Grant (ECSHG) program. This program has many similarities to ESG and may be administered by the same community action agencies.

Through the ECSHG program, funds are available to assist with utility bill payment. Funding levels for the ECSHG program are difficult to ascertain because DHHS reporting requirements do not track allocations at this level. Consequently, local providers may be difficult to identify.

Since the DHHS offers block grants to individual states, local governments may have information regarding available ECSHG programs. If not, local ESG administrators may be able to offer guidance. While the ECSHG program remains a relatively small component of government low-income assistance, it provides services specifically designed to address local need.

Emergency Food and Shelter Program

EFSP was created through a $50 million grant from Congress in 1983. The EFSP is administered nationally through the Federal Emergency Management Agency (FEMA). It provides food and shelter to the homeless through a network of 11,000 community agencies in 2500 locations across the country.

Since its inception, the EFSP has disbursed more than $2 billion.[18] Annually, the EFSP receives funding from Congress. The current budget allocates $140 million through a continuing resolution but may be subject to change.[19] Limitations on the use of these funds help to ensure resources go directly to those in need. Administrative costs are capped at 2% of agency funding, with a national administrative expense not to exceed 1% of the total allocation. An additional 0.5% of local funds can be used to administer state set-aside programs.[20]

The remaining dollars are expended on behalf of those in need. The EFSP allows the money to be used on food, mass shelter, repairs, and equipment. The EFSP also helps recipients pay overdue rent, mortgages, and utilities. Although financial assistance is limited to one month, the amounts nationally are significant.

In 2001, the EFSP allocated 13% of its budget to utility bill payment, amounting to nearly $18 million. Approximately 200,000 bills were paid in 2001, averaging $94 each. Since 1986, the EFSP has provided $219 million in energy assistance. This represents nearly 12% of total EFSP funding.[21]

ESG, ECSHG, and the EFSP grants work independently to ensure families are able to maintain their homes. To reduce homelessness, low-income families must access programs before utility service termination or eviction. Unfortunately, community agencies serving the homeless may not identify customer need until after a family enters a shelter. While these programs may successfully restore households, a more timely interaction could have prevented the abandonment of suitable housing.

With emergency assistance triggered by termination notices, utilities may have both a stake and role to play in these programs. In many cases, simple referral services, lobbying efforts, or in-kind contributions toward these efforts could reduce the number of service terminations and improve utility uncollectibles.

Utility allotments for subsidized housing

Subsidized housing exists in many forms to ensure families are provided safe, sanitary, and affordable housing options. First, the Public Housing Authority (PHA) may own and operate subsidized housing. Second, the PHA may contract with private landlords for Section 8 housing. Third, the Federal Housing Administration (FHA) provides section 236, section 235, and section 202 projects. Fourth, the Department of Housing and Urban Development (HUD) administers the largest federally assisted housing service in the country. In total, Mary Ferrey estimates that public housing may represent as much as 20% of the low-income rental stock.[22]

"Where terminations are scheduled for tenants of subsidized housing, utilities may review the reasonableness of tenant energy use. By so doing, utilities could demonstrate that the energy use is not excessive and thereby support a claim for an increased utility allotment."

Individuals and families living in public housing generally must have incomes significantly below the median income for the area and are required to maintain utility service to their unit. To help provide for these families, the U.S. government has certain stipulations under the Brooke Amendment of the United States Housing Act. According to the amendment, tenants must not be charged more than 30% of the family's monthly-adjusted income or 10% of the family's monthly income for their shelter. The term shelter typically refers to rent and an estimate of reasonable utility expenses.

Whether tenants obtain utility service directly or obtain service through an agreement with the property owner, an allowance is provided for reasonable utility expenses. These utility allotments help to ensure the federal limits on shelter costs are maintained. Although in theory this task is simple, a report to Congress in March 1991 found that "about 45% of public housing households and approximately 70% of Section 8 households…had utility expenses that were higher than their allowances. This results in rent burdens exceeding 30% of adjusted income. Because the deviations were so great… paying utility bills can pose financial hardships."[23]

For the tenant, such hardship is often compounded when threatened with utility service termination. Tenants of subsidized housing are often required to maintain utility service as a condition of the lease. Consequently, when service terminations occur, tenants not only lose essential energy services, but also must face losing their homes.

Margot Freeman Saunders of the National Consumer Law Center states, "The greatest share of the blame for these problems lies with HUD, which has deliberately shifted the burden of utility costs from HUD's budget to subsidized housing tenants. HUD has done this by failing to guarantee to PHAs adequate allowances for each project… or to provide proper weatherization of the housing projects."[24]

HUD provides only a vague standard for the calculation of utility allowances. PHAs "approximate a reasonable consumption of utilities by an energy-conservative household of modest circumstances consistent with the requirements of a safe, sanitary, and healthful living environment."[25]

Where terminations are scheduled for tenants of subsidized housing, utilities may review the reasonableness of tenant energy use. By so doing, utilities could demonstrate that the energy use is not excessive and thereby support a claim for an increased utility allotment.

If the utility allotment can be raised to a point where service termination is avoided, all parties would benefit. HUD and the PHA will be better able to demonstrate the appropriateness of the utility allotments. The tenant will retain his or her home. The utility will avoid termination costs, improve future payment streams, and avoid revenue erosion from tenants who would have otherwise been evicted.

Earned Income Tax Credit (EITC)

The Earned Income Tax Credit (EITC) is a refundable federal income tax credit for low-income workers and their families. Established in 1975, the EITC sought to remedy burdensome social security taxes and provide work incentives.

The federal EITC returns $33 billion to nearly 20 million low-income households filing returns each year. EITCs offset tax liabilities resulting in larger tax refunds for qualifying individuals. Where the EITC exceeds federal withholding, the credit is fully refundable. As such, household income is improved.

Susan Boehmer, IRS National EITC Program Manager, told the American Bankers Association that "the federal Earned Income Tax Credit (EITC) boosts a family's gross annual income by as much as a third, and if complemented with a state EITC, gross annual income may increase by as much as 57%."[26] Clearly, these credits are an important financial resource for the low-income family.

With a prompt tax filing, federal refunds serve as a timely supplement to household income, especially at a time when state moratoriums on utility service disconnects are lifting. For the low-income worker with outstanding arrears, the availability of state and federal refunds presents a unique opportunity. These refunds can be used to reduce liabilities accumulated over the winter holidays or to ensure the availability of summer cooling. However, these refunds also represent a discretionary windfall that may be used to fulfill long-delayed desires.

The use of refunds will coincide with the information and pressures present at the time of receipt. A study presented in the *American Economic Review* found "increased spending on non-durables at the time of refund-receipt by those likely to be liquidity constrained."[27] Increasing savings may lead to improved fiscal responsibility. However, current economic theory suggests that spending increases with the amount of cash flowing into a household. In addition, households desire improved cash flow. This is true even at the cost of high-interest rapid refund or payday loans.

Remembering statistics from chapter 3, you will realize EITCs are provided to nearly one-half of the low-income households in the United States. These credits exceed one-half of the low-income household energy market. As such, the earned income tax credit represents a significant resource for both low-income families and their creditors.

To ensure the continuity of utility service, agencies and utilities must promote the use of refunds to pay outstanding arrears. Otherwise, the refund will be lost to other vendors. Developing programs to inform customers of the availability, size, timing, and use of EITC payments could improve collections and service affordability for many low-income households.

Advance child tax credit payments

The 1997 Taxpayer Relief Act created the child tax credit. Under the Jobs and Growth Tax Relief Reconciliation Act of 2003, the Child Tax Credit was accelerated. In 2003, a nonrefundable tax credit of $1,000 was available for each qualifying child. The child must be under 17 years of age, a citizen or resident of the United States, and claimed as a dependent of the taxpayer.

Included in this legislation are provisions for immediate tax relief. The Treasury Department sent out checks for $400 per qualifying child claimed on the 2002 return. This advance child credit represents the anticipated 2003 child tax credit. The program was designed to provide immediate relief to low- and middle-income earners. As such, advance payments could contribute to household cash income.

However, some low-income families will not benefit from the increased child tax credit or the advance payments. In fact, a number of families were unable to use even the $600 credit offered in 2002. Families unable to utilize the full credit that year did not receive that payment in later years, because the child tax credit is nonrefundable.

Additional child tax credits

While the child tax credit is nonrefundable, provisions have been made allowing some families to qualify for the additional child tax credit. Individuals who get less than the full amount of the child tax credit because their tax is too low may be eligible for the additional child tax credit.

To qualify, individuals must fill out Form 8812 and file income taxes using an IRS Form 1040 or 1040A. Individuals whose total taxable earned income exceeds $10,350 may claim the smaller of the following: the unused child tax credit or 10% of the excess earned income.

While the additional tax credit excludes the very low-income, some families living in poverty may claim the additional child tax credit and become eligible for a refund. However, to utilize this resource, the taxpayer must understand recent changes in tax law and tolerate a more complex filing process.

Unclaimed tax refunds

Every year, refunds are unclaimed or returned to the IRS as undeliverable. In 1999, $2.5 billion awaited 1.9 million individuals who failed to file a tax return. More than one-half of those who failed to file a claim would be eligible for a refund in excess of $500.

Many individuals were simply not required to file returns because their income resulted in no tax liability. However, many low-income individuals fail to realize the EITC can be claimed even if no taxes were withheld. Although eligible taxpayers qualify for a refund when their EITC is more than their tax, filers whose returns are more than three years late qualify only to offset their tax. As such, their refund is lost.

As April 15 approaches, low-income households should be encouraged to file promptly for the current tax year. In addition, previous tax years should be reviewed to ensure outstanding entitlements do not expire. Utilities seeking payment of outstanding liabilities should be aware that unclaimed tax refunds provide an untapped financial resource. Simply referring individuals to the IRS tax assistance line, 1-800-829-1040, or to local service centers could result in tax refunds that could offset accumulated liabilities or secure access to utility service.

United States Department of Agriculture (USDA)

The "people's department" was established under President Lincoln. With more than $63 billion in grants awarded each year, the USDA is an important resource for rural America. For the public utility wishing to extend services into remote areas of our nation, the USDA provides loans and grants. In a January 28, 2004 news release, Agriculture Secretary Ann Veneman clarified the objective. According to Veneman, "Expansion of rural infrastructure is a first step in opening the door for expanded rural economic development and improved quality of life for rural residents."[28]

Individual assistance provided by the USDA includes hardship loans, housing assistance, energy efficiency grants, and federal nutrition programs. Annual expenditures of nearly $32 billion are used to support federal nutrition programs. Such programs include the school breakfast program, national school lunch program, food stamps, and emergency food assistance.

Utility service riders (USRs)

With a review of federal programs complete, we now move to state-funded assistance mechanisms. With the recent deregulation of the energy industry, many states have mandated the adoption of USRs before authorizing retail competition. These USRs typically appear as required usage charges ranging from 0.5% to 3% of gross sales across various customer segments. The proceeds generated by these USRs are used to guarantee universal access to utility service and to enhance the efficiency of the utility system. As such, USRs are commonly referred to as *systems benefit charges, universal service charges,* or *public benefit funds.*

According to statistics compiled from the LIHEAP Clearinghouse, 27 states have specific legislative language to either create or maintain existing low-income programs.[29] Of those states, 20 require universal service charges to fund low-income initiatives. The following text exemplifies a few USRs.

In Georgia, large industrial accounts opting for interruptible service pay a surcharge set by the Public Service Commission. In Illinois, residential customers pay $0.40/month and commercial accounts pay $4/month, while the largest accounts are charged $300/month. The state of Oklahoma is considering an access fee to fund its universal service program. Perhaps the most original funding mechanism was chosen by the state of Michigan. Savings from *securitization,* financial instruments used to offset stranded assets, are allocated to existing low-income and energy efficiency funds. There are provisions to ensure service continuity for customers with special needs.

No matter what mechanism is used to collect USRs, the monies raised can be significant. Oklahoma USRs generate $60 million annually. In Georgia, the USR was capped at $25 million, while Maryland will raise $34 million through its USR. Other states have no limits on size and even have provisions for added funding mechanisms. In February 2002, Michigan announced that $27 million would be allocated for energy assistance to leverage existing community action agencies and the state LIHEAP program.

USRs support short-term and long-term energy assistance in the form of rate discounts, conservation initiatives, and direct bill assistance. As more states enter into retail competition, similar ratepayer-funded initiatives will be available for energy assistance.

The use of USRs has been widely adopted by the industry, mainly because usage surcharges create identifiable funds that can be legislatively restricted to specific uses. Perhaps the most successful and obvious examples of usage surcharges exist in the transportation industry. The costs to construct and maintain roads and bridges are collected from those using the assets in the form of tolls. Similarly, taxes on gasoline and diesel help build and maintain public transportation infrastructure and fund environmental programs.

Revenues generated through USRs are typically placed in special accounts and restricted to authorized programs. While the utility bills and collects these funds, the money is often controlled or even transferred to an external entity. While this protects against utility misuse of funds, the use of USRs is not without disadvantages.

First, programs funded through USRs often originate outside the utility. As such, these programs are based on assumed need and generally understood socioeconomic trends. These efforts lack a detailed analysis of need in the utility service territory. They also lack an assessment of the local low-income provider network and the study of existing utility customer service options. These externally developed programs lack the strategic vision necessary to address long-term shareholder value and the operating efficiency needed to control ratepayer expense.

Second, utilities are not offered a return on the expenses of USR-funded programs. Instead, regulators and program administrators rely on general operational/complaint ratios to guide program offerings. As such, utilities are tempted to reduce program expenses while maintaining the minimal level of customer satisfaction. Where these programs provide a return on actual program expense, utilities would seek to expand program offerings and maintain the highest level of customer satisfaction.

Third, some USR funds are allocated to external corporations. These corporations in turn operate programs designed to improve utility energy efficiency. While this ensures societal needs are met, utilities lose the goodwill and trust that low-income programs can cultivate. As such, utilities act as tax collectors for the state. Given many USRs require legislative support, ratepayers often vote down or negatively perceive USRs as hidden taxes. Because of this, USRs have become taboo in many states.

Lastly, USR funds, since they are controlled legislatively, also can be legislatively redirected. In some states, legislators have proposed tapping USR funds to serve unrelated programs in the state budget. The redirection of USR funds breaches a sacred trust that has long existed between states and industry. Historically, surcharges have been used to offset societal damages associated with the taxable asset. It is true that the legal question as to whether USRs represent an inappropriate delegation of power to tax has been answered. However, no protections exist to prohibit legislative actions from tapping special purpose funds.

For example, the state of Washington is currently considering a tax on espresso-based drinks to fund education initiatives. Since coffee consumption is correlated with price, revenue growth of coffee outlets in the state may be slowed. Because of this, legal challenges in opposition to the proposed tax may prove to be landmark cases. Within a deregulated market, utilities may face increasing price sensitivity. With the emergence of customer choice, utilities will seek to be the least-cost provider. Telecommunication companies have sought to maintain the lowest per-minute charge by adding USRs to fund expanded service offerings.

With USRs now being used to address competitive pressures and to fund unrelated causes, the future of USRs is uncertain. Consumers looking only at the per-minute charge are often surprised at the number and extent to which USRs can raise the cost of service. While most USRs are valid in scope, increasing ratepayer scrutiny is sure to challenge them in the future.

National Fuel Fund Network (NFFN)

Fuel funds were established to assist households troubled by increasing energy burdens resulting from rising oil prices. Private fuel funds that emerged had a unique blend of donors, varied organizational structures, and differing growth potentials. Over time, a niche developed for a national organization to promote low-income energy assistance through private fuel fund initiatives.

In 1987, the NFFN was established.[30] Since its inception, the NFFN has increased awareness of the low-income energy problem. It also has advanced energy policy, provided technical assistance to new and existing fuel funds, and promoted the development of regional fuel fund networks. Under the direction of George Coling, the NFFN will build capacity for fuel fund banks, continue member services, and advocate for expanded government funding.

With more than 200 agency members, the NFFN provides a national grassroots perspective on the difficulties facing low-income households struggling against insurmountable energy burdens. The NFFN promotes all types of energy assistance programs and advocates fair home energy policies. Today, the NFFN compiles, analyzes, and disseminates information regarding energy assistance. Utilities wishing to further develop energy assistance programs should consult the NFFN about emergent trends and funding opportunities.

Until the formation of the NFFN, identifying the size and number of fuel funds was difficult because of the number of agencies operating across North America. To compile information about fuel funds, the NFFN actively polls member organizations tracking funding and service levels as well as other important data. More recently, the NFFN has begun soliciting information about funds outside its membership. The results of this ambitious and valuable undertaking should be available in 2004.

Developing a comprehensive list of available funds is just the first step. To develop a working knowledge of fuel funds, a more detailed technical analysis will be required. To assess the long-term value of a given fuel fund, there are several things that must be considered. These include the maturity of the fuel fund, the stability of funding sources, and the condition of the low-income provider network.

The presence of the NFFN can simplify this task and provide timely data to interested parties. For example, the NFFN can combine data from a number of surveys to identify key success factors and define strategic initiatives for fuel funds across the nation.

Fuel funds operate in all states, serving urban, suburban, and rural neighborhoods. Their organizational structures vary and are often interrelated with other public and private organizations. Because of this, fuel funds can be customized to address regional legislative actions, economic conditions, and utility initiatives.

EXISTING FUEL FUNDS

The following pages will highlight a number of active fuel funds. These funds were selected to demonstrate various funding sources, notable achievements, or organizational structures. For more information on these programs, you may wish to contact the program administrators, visit their Web sites, or request information from the NFFN.

Victorine Q. Adams Fuel Fund

The Victorine Q. Adams Fuel Fund was formerly known as the Baltimore City Fuel Fund. It was the first fuel fund in the nation solely dedicated to serving poor families with their energy needs.[31] In the first 10 years of operation, the Victorine Q. Adams Fuel Fund served more than 47,000 households, distributing more than $14 million in energy assistance.[32] Today the fund remains one of the largest fuel funds in the nation.

The fuel fund bears the name of Baltimore City Councilwoman Victorine Q. Adams, whose leadership resulted in the creation of the Baltimore City Fuel Fund in 1979. However, this is just one of her many accomplishments. She was profiled in a PBS documentary, *The Colored Women's Democratic Campaign Committee.* This program highlighted her role as a civil rights leader, community activist, entrepreneur, and philanthropist. According to the Web site for the documentary series, "Victorine Q. Adams exemplifies a segment of American Society that is often overlooked: the African-American woman whose strength and compassion combine into a powerful force capable of changing the world around her."[33]

Today her name is associated with a philanthropic foundation, a youth scholarship fund, and a humanitarian award. Perhaps most relevant to our discussions, her name is also associated with the most prestigious award for excellence and innovation in fuel funds. Victorine Q. Adams, now in her 90s, serves as honorary chair for the Fuel Fund of Maryland.

NJ Statewide Heating and Referral for Energy Services (NJ SHARES)

NJ SHARES won the 2002 Victorine Q. Adams Award for fuel fund innovation. George Coling, Executive Director of the National Fuel Funds Network, described the accomplishment of NJ SHARES. He said, "Their innovation was developing a coalition of charitable organizations and utilities who demonstrated to the legislature the wisdom of using state funds to assist those, who through no fault of their own, fell behind in their utility bills. The NJ SHARES Program is an investment in family stability for New Jersey."[34]

NJ SHARES successfully advocated for new state laws that resulted in a nearly 10-fold increase in the number of homes served and 1300% increase in funding between fiscal years 2000 and 2001. In 2001, NJ SHARES served 32,071 homes with $8,931,049 in energy assistance. Compare this to fiscal year 2000, where NJ SHARES served just 3,496 homes with $684,693.[35] The increase in funding resulted from new laws. These laws made a retroactive allocation of unclaimed utility deposits and directed excess revenues from taxes on natural gas to the NJ SHARES program.

In addition to helping low-income customers, NJ SHARES made grants available to victims of the September 11, 2001 attack on the World Trade Center. "Eligibility is based on need, not income, so that a temporary financial hardship resulting from a lost job, lost income or injury related to this disaster could qualify an individual or family for a grant," said Larry Savitsky. Savitsky is the executive director of NJ SHARES.[36] The grants awarded up to $750 for natural gas service and $250 for electric service.

In 2002, NJ SHARES planned to return to its standard grant levels, $500 for each household, limiting eligibility to those individuals and families that do not receive assistance from other programs.[36] This was necessary as 2002 funding levels were expected to be significantly less than the 2001 funding levels. Of unclaimed utility deposits, 75%, or approximately $2.1 million, were to be allocated to NJ SHARES for energy assistance. However, the windfall revenues from 2001 natural gas sales would no longer exist.

Even without the windfall revenues, the lobbying efforts of NJ SHARES and other grassroots initiatives have successfully raised the annual funding levels by more than 400%. They will continue to serve an increased number of homes due to their efforts.

The National HeatShare program

HeatShare is a voluntary nongovernmental energy assistance program established in 1982 and administered by The Salvation Army. Financial support for the HeatShare program is derived from monthly bill contributions, individual donations, matching grants, and corporate gifts.

Monies contributed by individuals and matched by corporate grants are directed to those in need. Emergency energy assistance is provided year-round to utility customers without regard to fuel type.

In addition, HeatShare provides furnace system repairs, energy education, budget counseling, and social service referrals.

Administrative costs for the HeatShare program are covered by corporate gifts and through the general operational budget of The Salvation Army. The resulting oversight ensures administrative expenses are kept to a minimum. For example, a 1997 audit of the Minnesota HeatShare program showed that expenditures for administrative and fund-raising activities were just 7% of total revenues.[37]

Although national statistics regarding this program were unavailable, the success of HeatShare can be demonstrated at the state level. In Minnesota, HeatShare annual revenues between 1994 and 1997 averaged $1,105,162, which served a total of 43,801 individuals.[38] These individuals had to meet eligibility criteria for emergency assistance. In order to participate, the client

1. Must be a customer of a participating utility
2. Must have received a termination notice
3. Must be at or below 155% of poverty
4. Must exhaust options for governmental assistance
5. Must have a crisis situation that was directly responsible for the nonpayment, with the exception of elderly and disabled individuals, who are given special consideration.

These eligibility requirements help exemplify the ability of non-governmental fuel funds to serve a selected niche within the community. While LIHEAP seeks to reduce the energy burden felt by the low-income population, HeatShare serves individuals who have few options to maintain utility service.

Alabama's Project SHARE and Business Charitable Trust Fund

The Alabama Business Charitable Trust Fund was established in 1992 by the shareholders of Alabama Power Company. The fund provides emergency cooling assistance to households experiencing severe financial difficulty or health risks. In addition, the trust funds energy efficiency improvements and counseling services.

Notably, Project SHARE resulted from the early involvement of two large utilities. With a relatively small contribution of $50,000 from Alabama Power Company and $25,000 from Alabama Gas Corporation, Project SHARE was established in the early 1980s. From its modest beginnings, Project SHARE and the Alabama Business Charitable Trust Fund now distribute an average of $2.3 million annually.[40] With these funds ultimately returning to the utilities in the form of customer payments, utility cash flow improvements justify the shareholder investment.

Over time many of the state's municipalities and electric cooperatives now contribute to Project SHARE. Energy suppliers ask customers to contribute $1/month to help qualified low-income elderly and disabled individuals facing financial or medical emergencies. Larger donations are accepted at the Birmingham Area Chapter of the American Red Cross.

Project SHARE has provided more than $14 million to pay the energy bills of more than 165,000 qualified households. "Project SHARE and the Birmingham Area Chapter of the American Red Cross help nearly 6,500 people per year across six counties."[41] Project SHARE and the Alabama Business Charitable Trust Fund demonstrate that a single donation can generate a persistent stream of support for low-income consumers struggling with utility service affordability.

Utility Repair, Replacement, and Deposit Program (URRD)

With limited resources in reserve, low-income families are often unable to meet utility deposit requirements and unexpected repairs. In response, the state of Arizona utilized unclaimed utility deposits to create the URRD Program. The revised statutes of 1989, title 46, sections 731–732, created an assistance fund to provide utility deposits and system repairs for customers living near poverty.[42]

Utility deposits are paid by various community-based organizations to secure utility service for program participants. These deposits are governed by the same tariffs, rules, and procedures used by the utility for those who are not program participants. Refunds and accumulated interest are returned to the assistance fund at the end of the deposit period. This allows one-time contributions to provide ongoing aid to those in need.

Utility system repairs and replacements are paid by administrative agencies directly to selected vendors. The general intent of the program is to restore functionality of the delivery system via repairs. Where repairs are impractical, faulty systems are replaced. To ensure service standards, administrative agencies withhold vendor payment until jobs are completed to the satisfaction of program participants.

Notably, water and sewer system repairs are included and may account for as much as 10% of the total URRD fund. Funding levels for the URRD have varied since program inception. In 1991, the allocation to the URRD was $346,000. In 1992, the allocation peaked at $641,000. In 1996, the allocation was just $282,181. Yet by 2001, program funding had once again grown to near-record levels.[43] Although these allocations remain well below the legislative cap of $1,000,000, the URRD remains an expanding resource for low-income families.

In the case of the URRD, the state of Arizona created an assistance program from unclaimed resources. These resources would have otherwise been allocated to the general operational budget of the state. The URRD demonstrates the ability of lawmakers to remove barriers for innovative utility programs.

Low-Income Fund for Emergencies (LIFE)

In 1996, Tucson Electric Power Company shareholders contributed $4.5 million to create LIFE. The interest generated from the fund, about $250,000 annually, has been used to offset cuts in LIHEAP.[44]

Using a one-time charitable contribution to generate energy assistance funds can yield a three-fold financial impact for the utility. First, charitable donations can leverage tax incentives to offset corporate income. Second, energy assistance funds return to utilities as customer payments, resulting in balance sheet improvements. Third, energy assistance helps customers with utility service affordability, which maintains utility revenues and avoids additional operational expense.

The LIFE program demonstrates a win-win-win scenario serving program participants, ratepayers, and shareholders. As such, the LIFE fund serves as an investment model for utilities seeking to resolve the financial impacts from poor payment behaviors.

Colorado's Property Tax, Rent, and Heat Rebate

The state of Colorado created a tax rebate program to assist low-income elderly and disabled customers. Assistance with property taxes is coupled with rebates for home heating expense. Formed in 1971, the Colorado Property Tax, Rent, and Heat Rebate program refunded nearly $3.2 million annually for many years. In 1998, legislation passed that more than doubled the level of assistance to $7 million annually.[45] The maximum level of assistance rose from $160 to $192, while expanded income guidelines allowed greater participation.

To participate, applicants must be either 65 years of age, a surviving spouse of at least 58 years of age, or disabled without viable employment options. Annual income for singles may not exceed $11,000, or if married, combined income from all sources may not exceed $14,700. Participants must maintain a Colorado residence and may not be a dependent of another individual. Lastly, the program acts as a refund. Therefore, actual payment of property tax, rent, and/or heat expenses must precede any rebate claim.[46]

The current guidelines were supported by the Property Tax Credit Coalition (PRCC) of Colorado, formed in 1995 to ensure rebates remained at meaningful levels. The coalition stated, "We fear that without an update, the rebate will become useless and pass out of existence altogether."[47]

In fact, without the lobbying efforts of the PRCC, it is entirely likely that no reform would have been enacted. The PRCC effectively demonstrated that even very small contributions to their efforts resulted in effective legislative reform. As such, Colorado's Property Tax, Rent, and Heat Rebate program demonstrates the ability of an organized grassroots campaign to generate short-term energy assistance from growing public sentiment.

The Colorado Energy Assistance Foundation (CEAF)

In 1989, the Colorado Commission on Low-Income Energy Assistance (CCLEA) was formed to bridge the gap between decreasing federal funding for energy assistance and the persistent home energy needs of Colorado's low-income families. The CCLEA created the CEAF as the vehicle to achieve that goal.[48]

The CEAF helps low-income households meet their home energy needs by supporting existing energy assistance and energy conservation programs. The CEAF supplements the Low-Income Energy Assistance Program (LEAP) and distributes funds through the Catholic Charities Emergency Assistance Centers. Using community-based organizations, the CEAF kept administrative costs below 5% of annual donations, while assisting more than 80,000 households in 2001.

Since its formation, the CEAF has distributed more than $28 million to supplement LEAP. Interestingly, only one-half of those served in the prior year returned for energy assistance in 2001. Of the households served five years prior, only 8% continued to request energy assistance through 2001, suggesting the LEAP provides a hand up, not a handout.[49]

The CEAF also created a Utility Grant Program to provide assistance during periods when LEAP was unavailable. In 2000, the program distributed $970,000 to 4,100 households throughout the state. In 2001, the program distributed more than $2.1 million due to extraordinary need.[50]

The CEAF provides a number of financial vehicles through which contributions can be made. Contributors may donate assets as well as cash. The CEAF will accept securities, bequests, beneficiary designations on financial instruments, and directed annuities. It will also accept retirement plan assets and matching grants, in addition to one-time cash contributions.

Although many not-for-profits accept delivery of similar assets, the proactive effort of the CEAF to clarify these options has helped them accumulate noncash investments and receivables exceeding $20 million. In addition, the CEAF received cash contributions of $4,774,382 from individuals, $2,544,655 from utilities, and another $1 million from other sources.[51]

The CEAF distinguishes itself from other assistance funds by its ability to raise both cash and noncash contributions. A quick look at its Web site, *www.ceaf.org,* helps to explain this success. The site supports prospective donors with planned giving. By doing so, CEAF was able to articulate the many options for charitable giving.

Relying on the benevolence of individuals within the community, the CEAF has established a foundation to expand energy assistance programs. Providing individuals with a feel-good option makes giving easy.

Private foundations in other regions may find the efforts of the CEAF instructive and encouraging. The demographic served by energy assistance programs coupled with past program performance can be leveraged to spur charitable giving. This is true especially in regions where growing need is exacerbated by cuts in governmental assistance programs.

Michigan's Low-Income and Energy Efficiency Fund

Savings generated from securitization bonds, financial instruments used to offset stranded assets, provide for low-income energy assistance programs in Michigan. The Customer Choice and Electricity Reliability Act of 2000 (CCERA) resulted in seven organizations receiving a total of $27.4 million for energy assistance.[52]

The Family Independence Agency received $19 million to supplement home heating credits, expand Michigan's state emergency funds, and address emerging priorities.[53] The Michigan Community Action Agency Association received $3,110,000 to match funds raised through the annual Walk for Warmth.[54,55] The Salvation Army received $3 million to serve households ineligible or unable to receive assistance from the Family Independence Agency.[56]

The Heat and Warmth Fund (THAW) received $2 million for their safety net program.[57] Newaygo County Community Services, Wayne Metropolitan Community Action Agency, and Leslie Outreach received proportional levels of funding to serve their residents.[58,59]

Following utility restructuring, the Michigan Public Service Commission ensured support for statewide low-income and energy efficiency programs. As shown previously, a wide range of energy assistance programs can be supported to ensure broad economic assistance is provided to families and individuals in need. Similar restructuring will continue throughout the United States as well as internationally. The CCERA illustrates an effective resolve to the complex interactions rising from utility deregulation by recognizing stranded utility assets to improve utility service affordability.

The Crisis Assistance Ministry

Outside of state and local government agencies, religious organizations can provide an established infrastructure in which to deliver community services. Overwhelming demand on missionary budgets resulted from the economic recession of the early 1970s. In 1974, the clergy of Mecklenburg County examined options to address local demand. Shortly thereafter, the Crisis Assistance Ministry (CAM) was formed, and CAM and Leslie Outreach received proportional levels of funding to serve their residents.[60]

Today CAM provides financial assistance, mentoring services, clothing, and furniture to families in crisis. In 2001, CAM expended more than $6 million to serve its community. Of this expenditure, CAM provided nearly $3.5 million for energy assistance. Coupled with other household subsidies, financial aid provided CAM clients represented 71% of community service expenditures.[61]

The North Carolina Crisis Assistance Ministry demonstrates the ability of religious organizations to contribute significantly to housing affordability. Religious organizations have established congregations from which to draw volunteers. They also have facilities to deliver program services and access to community leaders. Consequently, religious organizations possess the necessary infrastructure to offer household subsidies.

Under the current administration, faith-based initiatives are gaining momentum. Churches, temples, and synagogues are more viable than ever as low-income providers. As such, faith-based organizations are certain to become a funding source for emergent household subsidies and utility assistance programs.

Oregon HEAT

Oregon HEAT was established in 1987 using $1.5 million from the Exxon Petroleum Violation Escrow.[62] Bolstered by individual donations and corporate matching grants, Oregon HEAT remains a vital resource for low-income families. To encourage local donor participation, Oregon HEAT distributes cash assistance in proportion to regional contributions.

Balancing environmental concern with social welfare, Oregon HEAT recovers unused heating oil that would otherwise be left to contaminate the environment. Individuals switching to other fuels may be left with excess heating oil. Oregon HEAT collects the oil and redistributes it to low-income families with demonstrated need.

Oregon HEAT demonstrates that judgments resulting from legal action can be leveraged to fund home energy assistance programs. This is especially true when the awards are targeted for environmental remedies. However, to access these funds, political support may be needed from established environmental lobbies and community providers.

Pennsylvania's Dollar Energy Fund (DEF)

Since its inception in 1983, the DEF of Pittsburgh has distributed more than $33 million in energy assistance grants to more than 132,000 homes. Today the DEF remains one of the largest private fuel funds in the United States. Contributors who participate in fund-raising activities will see their donations matched by corporate sponsors and delivered directly to eligible customers via energy assistance grants.

In 2002, the DEF distributed $3 million in grants and provided $2 million in services.[63] Under the leadership of Cindy Datig, the DEF focuses on self-sufficiency, not only for its clients, but also for the organization as a whole. The DEF serves as an example of social entrepreneurship, whereby existing roles are leveraged to expand services that generate revenues.

The DEF works with 14 utilities and 150 community-based organizations. Several of these relationships have been in place for more than 15 years, and many others more than 10 years. The longevity of these relationships results from the commitment DEF has to service quality and the ideals by which it operates. In recognition of this fact, several philanthropic foundations have awarded grants to support a number of entrepreneurial initiatives. The resulting impact is that DEF earns 36% of its revenue from service contracts.[64]

Growing organizations like the DEF should be commended for their efforts and supported by corporations. Established and well-respected organizations can often generate greater contribution levels than can a number of smaller entities. DEF demonstrates that emergent nonprofit organizations can attract and prosper under strong leadership. More importantly, DEF serves as a single coordinating agency for low-income energy assistance.

Emergency relief funds

When extreme climatic events occur, individuals are exposed to dramatically higher energy burdens. Low-income populations are particularly sensitive to pricing spikes. With extreme energy burdens, any increase in utility expense can result in a very real fiscal crisis. In 1998, Texas Governor Bush provided a one-time allocation of state funds in response to a summer heat wave.[65] During the same period, Tarrant County made similar allocations. As a result, additions of $1,302,000 were made to existing fuel funds.[66]

To access discretionary funds, extraordinary need must first be demonstrated. Utilities are uniquely positioned to identify the presence of extreme circumstance. First, climatic events place additional demands on the utility infrastructure that are noted by system operators. Second, accounting and metering systems easily identify significant changes in revenue billings. Third, utilities will see arrearage increases because abnormal weather patterns are not included in budget payments. Fourth, individual accounts will begin to cycle unpaid, increasing collection activity and payment negotiations.

> *"A certain percentage of households facing service terminations are willing to make prompt payment, even as other necessities (food, medicine, etc.) remain unmet. However, to do so, households must have the necessary financial resources available."*

When these conditions are noted, utilities should alert federal, state, and local governments of the pending crisis. In many instances, state leadership must be notified before initiating actions to mitigate family crisis. These one-time allocations can be substantial. Consequently, emergency relief should be sought as early as possible to ensure bureaucratic delays do not exacerbate already strenuous conditions.

Toronto's Share the Warmth Program (TSWP)

Fuel funds are not unique to the United States; TSWP is one such example. TSWP currently works within more than 400 municipalities serving more than 4,000,000 households. TSWP purchases heat and energy on behalf of families, seniors, the terminally ill, and disabled persons living near poverty. TSWP converts 100% of all public donations to heat and energy for low-income households.[67]

GENERAL CONSIDERATIONS

Our review of existing programs has identified a number of issues that require special attention to address long-term shareholder value and fundamental ratepayer concerns. These issues are identified in the following text to raise industry awareness and promote industry discussion.

Service terminations as a collection method

During Senate testimony, the National Consumer Law Center highlighted its concerns over "increasing use of disconnection by utilities as a collection mechanism."[68] Such a policy has both positive and negative consequences that must be weighed carefully by the utility.

A certain percentage of households facing service terminations are willing to make prompt payment, even as other necessities (food, medicine, etc.) remain unmet. However, to do so, households must have the necessary financial resources available. Many low-income households lack cash reserves or access to credit, thereby making immediate payment unrealistic.

To prevent termination, customers must contact the utility to make payment arrangements or find community support. Fuel funds often remain the last line of defense. Yet, awareness of regional funds and eligibility criteria must be improved.

Utilities can assist in this effort by identifying, documenting, and publicizing the low-income provider network. Financial assistance to prevent utility service terminations is often available. This can be through government programs, pending tax refunds, and specialized charitable organizations. One strategy for utilities would be to include provider information along with service termination notices. By directing consumers to funded providers, utilities offer meaningful guidance in times of crisis.

Still, some customers will not follow up out of fear, embarrassment, lack of telephone service, or other domestic concern. As a result, service termination may be unavoidable. Once service has been terminated, the utility books an expense related to the physical termination followed by an immediate loss of revenue.

To restore service, customers can contact the utility to establish a new payment arrangement. However, a perpetual cycle of disconnection and reconnection can escalate the cost of utility service. Where customers reconnect without significantly improved economic circumstance, service fees inflate outstanding balances. This exacerbates an already unfavorable circumstance.

Without utility service, subsidized leases can be terminated, leaving low-income families without independent housing options. Families forced into temporary housing, public shelters, or even homelessness by service termination could even result in high-profile litigation. As a result, physically disconnecting customers for nonpayment may erode utility revenue. It can also increase operational expenses or even lead to unfavorable media exposure and regulatory scrutiny.

While mass utility disconnects have largely negative impacts on the utility, the *threat* of utility disconnection can be a valuable tool. A strategic axiom from chess may apply well. Jose Raul Capablanca, a Cuban World Chess Champion, summarized the principle. He said, "It is always an advantage to threaten something, but such threats must be carried into effect only if something is to be gained immediately. For, holding the threat in hand, forces the opponent to provide against its execution and to keep material in readiness to meet it."[69]

Concerning utility service termination, the threat of disconnection engages most customers and establishes a mutually beneficial goal of avoiding service termination. While many fuel funds provide for customers with severe payment problems, few funds provide assistance to reestablish utility service once a disconnection has occurred.

Were it legally plausible, the utility could benefit most by serving disconnection notices without the intent of actually disconnecting utility service. Since this is not possible, utilities should maintain the threat of service termination for as long as possible. Service terminations should come only after all available resources have been exhausted.

Tax credits and unclaimed refunds

Pending credits and unclaimed refunds serve as financial resources for those households ineligible for other household subsidies. A number of refundable tax credits are available to workers with low incomes. The earned income tax credit provides the greatest potential for the working poor. Each year, the federal government issues more than $33 billion in refundable tax credits to nearly 20 million households.

In 1999, $2.5 billion went unclaimed because 1.9 million individuals did not file a federal tax return. Educating the population about available tax credits and unclaimed refunds has become a priority for the banking industry.

Recently, public utilities have become aware of this resource and have initiated public awareness campaigns. By directing low-income persons to tax advisors, tax credits and refunds may be leveraged to eliminate arrears accumulated over winter heating or summer cooling seasons. At the state level, similar initiatives may be available for low-income wage earners. Although an investment is necessary to document available incentives, the potential return will justify most efforts.

Federal LIHEAP Reauthorization

LIHEAP will seek reauthorization in 2004. Interested parties have a rare opportunity to lobby for increased funding, state allocations, advanced appropriations, and REACh leveraging grants. With many outstanding issues facing LIHEAP, utilities are best served through direct participation, rather than simply relying on industry trade organizations.

Through direct participation, utilities can influence formulations that reflect their service territory. For example, a southern electric utility with a large low-income population may wish to raise federal appropriations to trigger favorable state allocations. By doing so, the utility can access federal assistance without diminishing existing state allocations. Once appropriations are directed to the state, the utility can lobby state administrators for allocations and specific eligibility guidelines that match utility demographics.

When adjusted for inflation, LIHEAP allocations are down 44% from historic levels. Only a fraction of those eligible for LIHEAP receive assistance. Although state participation levels vary, on a national level, just one in four eligible customers receive LIHEAP grants.

Increased funding and higher participation rates should be sought amidst rising oil prices. Historically, increased fuel costs result in increased arrears. Since bad debt reserves are not typically adjusted for rising fuel prices, increased arrears directly impact net earnings. A formula that ties LIHEAP appropriations to oil and natural gas prices should be evaluated. Linking energy assistance to inevitable price variability hedges against increased uncollectibles.

Agency administrative costs

Advanced appropriation of LIHEAP funds is just one topic of contention sure to arise during LIHEAP reauthorization hearings. Public law emphasizes the need for advanced appropriations concerning state LIHEAP grants. However, little action has been taken to ensure state funding is in place before critical needs arise. In fact, 2002 LIHEAP appropriations were not made until October, when the Office of Management and Budget allocated $812 million under a continuing resolution.[70]

Advanced appropriations at the state and federal levels may have little consequence. However, for the community action agencies, LIHEAP allocations must be received before the onset of extreme weather. Without timely receipt of federal funds, resources are unnecessarily delayed and administrative costs are met with great difficulty.

State and utility support is often required by community action agencies to cover administrative expenses. However, smaller community-based organizations and emergent fuel funds may be forced to close their doors during the off-season. To ensure the provider network, grants and financing options are needed to cover the year-round administrative expenses. Even simple low-interest loans can stimulate regional fuel funds and support the existing low-income provider network.

Definition of household

This seemingly trivial detail has been the point of contention within low-income programs. Total household income defines program eligibility, while household size determines assistance levels. Federal LIHEAP statute defines a household as "any individual or group of individuals who are living together as one economic unit for whom residential energy is customarily purchased in common or who make undesignated payments for energy in the form of rent."[71] The statute continues recommending that homes with the greatest energy burdens should be given priority and offered the highest levels of assistance.

Although Congress has deferred to other low-income programs for their definition, the current definition has prevented states from implementing policies that would better realize congressional intent to prioritize households with the greatest need. As such, congressional action is needed to clarify the definition of a household.

Advocates have supported individuals and opposed state initiatives to address the problem of unrelated boarders. Under the Food Stamp Program, individuals living together constitute a single economic unit only if they routinely purchase food together. This means that all individuals could claim food stamps individually by simply purchasing their food and preparing meals separately. To avoid this problem, unrelated boarders at a given physical address are denied food stamps unless they are designated as the head of household.

> *"Utilities could also become more active in promoting available funding sources and tax credits.*
> *With utility bills entering nearly every residential household, utilities have the ability to disseminate information in a cost-effective manner."*

Since this problem was not relevant to energy assistance, such language was omitted from the LIHEAP statute. Utility accounts are established under a single name, so premises with more than one tenant must designate a responsible party for home energy. By selecting an individual with a low income, financial resources can be accessed, even when the other residents effectively contribute to household income. So long as the boarders do not routinely act as a single economic unit, little can be done to exclude shared households from energy assistance. As a result, a very real potential for abuse exists.

The current definition of household poses a significant threat for needy families who cannot access assistance because of limited funding. Despite recent efforts to streamline program enrollment, families remain frustrated by the bureaucracy. If the intended socio-economic impacts are to be realized, state agencies and public utilities must collaborate to increase and improve access to household subsidies. It would be more effective to define *household* as "all occupants living at a unique postal address." In this manner, a number of troublesome issues for state and local agencies could be avoided.

TAKING ACTION

The utility and energy industry lobby

Utility distribution companies represent a significant industry group. Total market capitalization for distribution companies alone exceeds $688 billion, while energy companies add $1.3 trillion in market capital. Together, utilities and energy companies represent a significant governmental lobby. As a secondary beneficiary of household subsidies, the utility and energy industry lobby must support LIHEAP funding increases. It must also develop regional fuel funds and target governmental programs with embedded utility allotments.

Utilities could also become more active in promoting available funding sources and tax credits. With utility bills entering nearly every residential household, utilities have the ability to disseminate information in a cost-effective manner. Where effective messages are developed, utilities can raise awareness. By promoting action and supporting community redevelopment, utilities can assist low-income communities and increase funding for energy assistance.

Strategic use of fuel funds

Private fuel funds present a unique opportunity for utilities. Private fuel funds are registered 501-3(c) charities to which corporations can give up to 10% of their earnings. For even a modest utility, charitable giving could exceed $10 million annually. Unlike other charitable gifts, contributions to fuel funds return to the utility as customer payments. This can offset otherwise burdensome bad debt and prevent costly service terminations. Coupled with tax incentives that offset corporate income, utilities can effectively expense low-income receivables.

Although the support of fuel funds could be viewed with some suspicion, the fact remains that energy assistance provides very real support to a financially troubled segment of our population. With less than 25% of eligible low-income customers receiving energy assistance, many families must do without winter heating and summer cooling. Without utility service, families can become homeless and properties left abandoned.

With the support of utilities, household subsidies and energy assistance can generate measurable societal benefits. Continued support for energy assistance programs remains across a diverse group of stakeholders. As such, utilities should support subsidization programs at all levels of government and actively develop regional fuel funds.

By developing an understanding of, and interactions with, the low-income provider network, utilities can improve the socio-economic condition of their service territory. By doing so, investor confidence will rise along with growth expectations, fueling long-term shareholder value.

Utilizing refundable tax credits

Approximately one-half of all low-income customers qualify for the EITC. Yet many working poor fail to file a tax return necessary to access this credit. In April 2003, 1.9 million low-wage workers lost their right to obtain their share of $2.5 billion in unclaimed tax refunds.

In 2003, 20 million working poor were expected to receive $33 billion in refundable EITCs. This is more than one-half the cost of home energy utilized by the entire low-income population. As such, tax credits and pending refunds cannot be ignored by the industry.

Programs must be developed to help consumers access and wisely use the windfall revenues flowing from government tax initiatives. The IRS must better publicize available low-income credits and simplify the filing process for low-income individuals. Use of tax professionals by the low-income simply erodes the intended benefit of many low-income tax credits. This problem is further exacerbated by the use of rapid refund loans.

By sponsoring informational seminars for the low-income, utilities can build positive relationships within the low-income community while boosting household financial resources. Given the importance placed on utility service by energy consumers, utility payments improve with the socioeconomic conditions of the service territory. As such, programs designed to assist consumers struggling with increasing energy burdens generate a sustainable benefit for utility ratepayers and shareholders.

Just the beginning

While nearly all utilities recognize the existence of a low-income segment, few utilities fully appreciate the value of this market segment. They also fail to realize the complex issues that exist within this market segment. Utility executives looking to make a significant impact must not underestimate the long-term strategic value of serving those currently in poverty. Strategic consideration of the low-income customer class and related service providers is wise. It will uncover latent operational efficiencies, growth opportunities, and a common ground with state and federal regulators. Funding research to identify the low-income provider network and to design strategic initiatives can yield unexpected growth within a stagnant, maturing marketplace.

NOTES

[1] Thomson, K., Bracy Tucker Brown, Inc. 2004. *The LIHEAP Data-book: A State-by-State Analysis of Home Energy Assistance.* Campaign for Home Energy Assistance (Jan.).

2 Calculated by looking at U.S. Census poverty estimates from 1982 and comparing to 2002 estimates. LIHEAP appropriations remain near $2 billion. However, when adjusted using the CPI, LIHEAP levels are considerably lower than in 1982.

3 *http://www.acf.dhhs.gov/programs/liheap/history.htm.*

4 *http://www.ncaf.org/lihpncaf.pdf.*

5 Ibid.

6 *http://www.nationalfuelfunds.org/testimonyapril2000.html.*

7 *http://www.nationalfuelfunds.org/testimonyapril2000.html.*

8 Public Law 103-252 Section 2605 (b) (16).

1 *http://www.ncat.org/liheap/tables/FY2003/a16fy03.htm.*

10 *http://www.acf.dhhs.gov/programs/liheap/statute.htm#Sec2607B.*

11 *http://www.acf.hhs.gov/programs/ofa/exsumcl.htm.*

12 *http://www.acf.dhhs.gov/programs/opre/ar2001/indexar.htm.*

13 *http://www.hud.gov/offices/cpd/homeless/library/esg/ esgdeskguide/introduction.cfm.*

14 *http://www.hud.gov/offices/cpd/homeless/programs/esg/index.cfm.*

15 *http://www.hud.gov/offices/cpd/homeless/library/esg/ esgprevention2.PDF. p. 7.*

16 *http://www.hud.gov/offices/cpd/homeless/library/esg/ esgprevention2.PDF. p. 4.*

17 *http://www.hud.gov/about/budget/fy03/appenb.pdf. p.* 1.

18 *http://efsp.unitedway.org/efspnew/Pages/about.cfm.*

19 *http://efsp.unitedway.org/index.cfm.*

20 *http://efsp.unitedway.org/efspnew/Pages/about.cfm.*

21 *http://efsp.unitedway.org/efspnew/Pages/spendingnatl.cfm.*

22 Ferrey. 1986. Cold Power: Energy and Public Housing. *Harvard Journal on Legislation* 23 (33).

23 General Accounting Office. 1991. *Report to Congress on Committees, Assisted Housing, Utility Allowances Often Fall Short of Actual Utility Expenses. Vol. I* (Mar.).

24 Saunders, M. F., National Consumer Law Center. 2001. *Access to Utility Service.* 2d ed.

25 24 C.F.R. §965.505.

26 EITC 2003 and Beyond. Internal Revenue Service. *http://www.irs.gov/individuals/article/0,,id=107549,00.html*

27 Souleles, N. S. 1999. The Response of Household Consumption to Income Tax Refunds. *American Economic Review* 89(4) (Sept.), pp. 947–58.

28 USDA Newsroom. 2004. USDA Announces $32.8 Million in Rural Electric Loan Guarantees. News Release 0046.04, (Jan. 28).

29 *http://www.ncat.org/liheap/tables/resleg.htm.*

30 *http://www.nationalfuelfunds.org/who.html.*

31 *http://www.fuelfundmaryland.org/FactSheet.html.*

32 *http://www.nationalfuelfunds.org/faq_ans2.html.*

[33] *http://www.visionaries.org/index.php?contentmenu=series&page=season8#812.*

[34] *http://www.ppag.com/trenton/8-2002.pdf.*

[35] *http://www.ppag.com/trenton/8-2002.pdf.*

[36] *http://www.njshares.org/pr060402.shtml.*

[37] http://www.lswebdesign.net/heatshare-mn/stats.html.

[38] Ibid.

[39] *http://www.lswebdesign.net/heatshare-mn/criteria.html.*

[40] *http://www.ncat.org/liheap/leverage/alff.htm.*

[41] *http://chapters.redcross.org/al/bham/Progsvcs.htm #Project%20SHARE.*

[42] *http://www.ncat.org/liheap/legislation/azua.htm.*

[43] *http://www.ncat.org/liheap/leverage/azstfd.htm.*

[44] *http://www.ncat.org/neaap/programs/lowincome/az-li.htm.*

[45] *http://www.ncat.org/liheap/newslett/30net.htm.*

[46] *http://www.revenue.state.co.us/PDF/00104ptc.pdf.*

[47] *http://bcn.boulder.co.us/community/easycall.html.*

[48] *http://www.ceaf.org/about.htm.*

[49] *http://www.ceaf.org/AR2001.pdf.* CEAF 2001 Annual Report, p. 7.

[50] Ibid.

[51] *http://www.ceaf.org/AR2001.pdf.* CEAF 2001 Annual Report. p. 11.

[52] *http://www.cis.state.mi.us/mpsc/orders/electric/2002/u-13129c.pdf.*

[53] *http://www.michigan.gov/fia/0,1607,7-124-5453---,00.html.*

[54] *http://www.mcaaa.org/New_Info_2002/CAA_Mission.htm.*

[55] *http://www.acset.org/CAA/CAAHTM/W4W.htm.*

[56] *http://www.usc.salvationarmy.org/www_usc_arc.nsf.*

[57] *http://www.thawfund.org.*

[58] *http://www.michigan.gov/mcsc/0,1607,7-137-6116_8159_8162-24965--,00.html.*

[59] *http://www.freep.com/news/childrenfirst/sd2002/action2_20020502.htm.*

[60] *http://www.crisisassistance.org/history.html.*

[61] *http://www.crisisassistance.org/AR.pdf.*

[62] *http://www.ncat.org/liheap/leverage/orfuelfd.htm.*

[63] *http://www.dollarenergy.org/DE2002AR.pdf.*

[64] The 1$ Fund 2002 Annual Report, p. 6. *www.dollarenergy.org/DE2002AR.pdf.*

[65] National Consumer Law Center. 2001. Access to Utility Service. 2d. ed., p. 586.

[66] *http://www.ncat.org/liheap/pubs/98stlvsm.htm.*

[67] *http://www.sharethewarmth.org/.*

[68] *http://www.consumerlaw.org/initiatives/energy_and_utility/ senatets.shtml.*

[69] Capablanca, J. R. 1949. Chess Fundamentals. 18th ed., p. 82.

[70] *http://www.aga.org/Template.cfm?Section=News&template= /ContentManagement/ ContentDisplay.cfm&ContentID=9304.*

[71] *http://www.acf.hhs.gov/programs/liheap/statute.htm#Sec2603.*

5

SERVICE AFFORDABILITY PROGRAMS

STATEMENT OF OPPORTUNITY

Watching news reports and business updates, you may be under the impression that spending has risen to unmanageable levels and that consumer debt is a modern phenomenon. While dramatic increases in spending may be based in fact, the overwhelming concern for consumer debt is far from modern.

In early America, colonists bought goods on credit issued by local merchants. By the late 1800s and early 1900s, newspapers, politicians, and even President Warren Harding expressed great concern over frivolous spending. He espoused, instead, a greater virtue: thrift. Yet, our Victorian notion of ancestral thrift is little more than a romantic ideal. More realistic is the fact that America has always been a society of consumerism.

The Pilgrims in 1641 used debt to cultivate the new land. To fund the Revolutionary War, Continental currency totaling $135 million was printed, backed by *bills of credit.* In the 1800s, consumer credit allowed individuals to *buy up,* raising social stature. Soon installment loans became necessary tools for many retailers. Store credit enabled Americans to purchase automobiles, clothing, pianos, sewing machines, furniture, phonographs, as well as other household appliances.

"Individuals in financial distress often falter and engage in a cycle of destructive behavior. Even solid and otherwise satisfying employment can become an unbearable burden. How long could you remain productive if every dollar earned was spent on basic necessities, and your family still remained in need?"

Credit has evolved into a necessity rather than a luxury. In the early 1900s, nearly one household in every four had at one time or another borrowed from a small commercial lender or pawn-broker. These confidential small-dollar loans were often sought when other credit avenues had been exhausted. With mounting concern over short-term loans and interest rates, Arthur Ham studied small-dollar lending while attending graduate school at Columbia University. His initial conclusions found high-interest short-term loans caused undue hardship for wage earners. As such, Ham became an early advocate against predatory lending.

In many ways, the research conducted by Arthur Ham and his activism resulted in usury laws that capped interest rates. Unfortunately, these laws closed many legal avenues to small-dollar loans and led to additional hardship as wage earners turned to loan sharks. Because of this, Ham altered his views and supported the development of small finance companies to serve the needs of the wage earner. In fact, his efforts offer lessons to today's affordability program administrators. However, before turning to the future, let us first consider the past.

Granting credit and debt financing dates back to the earliest civilizations. You may find it difficult to believe, but consumer debt and even government protections are twice as old as Christianity! Hammurabi, King of Babylon, published a *Code of Laws* around 1750 BC to govern patricians, plebeians, and slaves. The Code of Hammurabi dealt with a broad range of societal issues. These included marriage, commercial contracts, consumer rights, negligence, fraud, and inheritance, among others. Of the 282 laws comprising the Code of Hammurabi, nine of them specifically address debt.[1]

In these nine laws, Hammurabi limits the assignment of debt, specifies penalties for nonpayment, and even offers forgiveness of debt where good faith has been demonstrated. While many of these codes are embedded in the laws that govern our land, the penalties have changed dramatically throughout history. During the reign of Hammurabi, a man's unfulfilled debt was repaid to the creditor through the enslavement of his servants, his wife, his children, and even himself.

While enslavement is considered barbarous by our current standards, these penalties may have been more humane than the debtor prisons used in Europe and early America. Under the Code of Hammurabi, all debts were retired after three years of service. In contrast, prisons left debtors without viable means to repay outstanding obligations. As a result, individuals could languish for many years or even die imprisoned for unmet financial obligations.

Today, we do not enslave or imprison our debtors. However, high debt loads can burden individuals with shame, guilt, and hopelessness…perhaps an equally timeless sentence. Individuals in financial distress often falter and engage in a cycle of destructive behavior. Even solid and otherwise satisfying employment can become an unbearable burden. How long could you remain productive if every dollar earned was spent on basic necessities, and your family still remained in need?

Accounts receivable extend beyond the balance sheets of the public utility, and bad debt extends beyond the income statement. Behind the financial ratios, real people and businesses are struggling to meet financial obligations. Chronic payment troubles are often associated with the low-income population. Even so, a growing number of middle-class wage slaves struggle with rising costs-of-living and a seemingly insatiable social ambition.

Social pressures can and will destabilize the utility service territory. Relevant issues must be addressed within the context of long-term fiscal responsibility. For the public utility, shareholder expectation and ratepayer concern demand a better understanding of consumer payment behavior. Payment terms and pricing strategies must reflect the realities within the utility service territory. Concessions are required to ensure utility service remains affordable to all constituents. Otherwise, ratepayers must absorb far greater costs as local economies erode, stranding assets that result in operational inefficiencies. Luckily for both the utility ratepayer and shareholder, cost-effective affordability programs are available.

KEY CONCEPTS

Time constraints

A number of public and private organizations offer assistance to the low-income, elderly, and disabled. Yet, accessing these programs can be problematic for intended recipients. Most programs require written applications, in-person interviews, eligibility verification, and frequent recertification. As a result, program participation requires efficient time and resource management.

Given the breadth of need and limited available resources, assistance programs often operate seasonally and serve only a fraction of the total need. During peak heating and cooling seasons, accessing energy assistance becomes a competitive endeavor. As such, proper timing of individual applications is equaled only by the demonstration of need.

To successfully access energy assistance, the enrollment process must be completed before government quotas are exhausted.

Individuals must be well informed of, organized around, and responsive to program funding cycles. How can we expect this of households struggling with financial distress, family crisis, unreliable transportation, aging, utility termination, and eviction. Even as an industry professional, monitoring state programs and private assistance programs proves problematic.

To make matters worse, each form of assistance comes with added responsibility. To access state welfare programs or unemployment assistance, individuals must make efforts to find employment or risk losing public assistance. To demonstrate effort, relevant activities must be tracked daily and reported regularly. When work is found, income eligibility must be recertified.

While these reporting requirements are necessary, data tracking and submission requires time, effort, and understanding. Individuals may spend hours preparing an application only to find a single omission requires a repetition of effort. Unreliable transportation can result in missed appointments. Job insecurity can exclude in-person interviews. When these individual restrictions are tallied, time constraints within our target population can challenge or even prohibit program participation.

For many low-income families, cumulative program requirements become so overwhelming that a single ill-timed crisis could disrupt the flow of assistance. When program requirements are taken in total and acknowledged by service providers, low-income assistance is clearly time-consuming and demanding.

Special needs

Each consumer has a unique set of driving factors and constraints that influence their actions. For the low-income, elderly, and disabled, even seemingly trivial barriers are difficult to overcome. Without reliable transportation, employment opportunities are limited, even where public transportation is available. Likewise, getting to and from program service centers requires coordination between friends, family, community action agencies, and/or faith-based organizations.

Even without transportation issues, individuals may have other unforeseen needs. The English language can be an issue for immigrant populations. Even individuals conversant in English may feel uncomfortable filing applications or signing agreements written outside their native tongue. To overcome this concern, individuals may rely on trusted companions to review and advise them on actions. Because trusted companions often lack experience and training with the available assistance programs, nuances in service offerings may be difficult to communicate. Therefore, even simple negotiated payment options may be viewed with suspicion. And just when you begin to earn their trust, the media will air a story on an unscrupulous marketing scam.

Still, more serious barriers exist for the low-income service provider. Literacy, education, and access to technology are often lower within the target populations. Additionally, domestic violence and drug addictions may displace individuals from their homes temporarily. As a result, effective outreach can be difficult.

Even after the message is received, current domestic circumstance can prevent household consensus or reveal more pressing matters. For example, families dealing with domestic violence, drug abuse, mental illness, or debilitating illness may not prioritize financial matters. In such a case, even the most generous utility assistance program will not improve the family's financial circumstance.

In short, a number of special needs exist within our intended audience. These needs must be considered and carefully integrated with service provisioning. Acknowledging individual need and recognizing third-party supporters are important aspects of efficient service delivery.

Access to credit

Low-income families and other disadvantaged populations lack access to conventional banking. Instead, they rely on small dollar loans to meet unforeseen expense and seek expensive vendor financing for household purchases. Because favorable credit terms are unavailable to those in financial distress, ordinary household expenses are much higher than would be expected.

An individual with pressing financial obligations may require cash within the typical three-day hold placed on checks by most banks. As a consequence, the individual may utilize a check-cashing agency that charges a processing fee. This processing fee can range from 2% to 7% of the check value. When the check is less than the financial obligation, the individual may require a payday loan with an effective annualized interest rate exceeding 300%. This is, of course, just one example. The use of check-cashing agencies and other predatory lenders can result from pure convenience to absolute need.

Improved credit terms can be arranged for larger loans; however, significant assets must be pledged. A pawnbroker may be willing to loan $500 on a car worth $3,000. The interest charged averages 10% per month on the original loan amount. If the customer requires six months to repay the loan, the interest on a title loan will be $300; more than one-half of the loan principal. While the effective interest rate remains well below that of a payday loan, title loans appear usurious when compared to unsecured credit terms offered by commercial banks.

While commercial lenders are willing to loan large sums, they typically require them to be 80% collateralized by tangible and appreciating assets, such as stocks, bonds, and homes. Individuals seeking less than $1,000 are usually granted unsecured lines of credit based on their work history and monthly income. Unfortunately, individuals with low incomes often have no accumulated assets. They may be new to or retired from the workforce. As such, commercial lenders are unable to serve their financial needs at any level. Unfortunately, high-cost credit is the only realistic financing vehicle available outside utility affordability programs.

SURVEY OF
BILL REDUCTION PROGRAMS

Oddly enough, a multibillion dollar predatory lending industry has evolved to serve the specific needs of low-income wage earners. Meanwhile, public utilities are left to finance unpaid bills through a series of specialized affordability programs. These programs offer improvements over traditional collection activities. However, they do little to resolve reoccurring expenses associated with marginal service affordability and the continued accumulation of debt. To understand the scope of utility attempts to resolve service affordability, we will examine current industry practices.

Utility fee waivers

Fee waivers have been used to improve service affordability for families and individuals in need. Following deregulation, additional and larger fees have been sought throughout the industry. Even with regulatory oversight, a disturbing trend has been observed.

According to annual surveys compiled by the LIHEAP Clearinghouse, a steep decline in utility waivers occurred between 1997 and 2001. In 1997, 13 states offered $64.3 million in utility fee waivers. In 1998, 11 states offered $46.2 million. By 2001, utility support for fee waivers dropped again, with 12 states offering just $35.1 million. This represents a 45% decline in low-income fee waiver support.

While utilities added $9 million in fee waivers in 2002, they also have raised existing fees and gained approval for new fees. For instance, one utility (Bay State Gas Company, 1992) now charges a *warrant fee* of $35 where warrants are required to disconnect service.[2] Other examples include proposals for in-field payment fees, bill nonpayment fines, and meter-error claim charges. Noting this trend, consumer advocates intervened to protect disadvantaged populations. Utilities have responded by waiving fees for selected populations, such as the low-income, elderly, sick, and disabled.

Affordable housing waivers. A number of incentives are provided for developers wishing to construct, refurbish, or maintain low and fixed-income housing. Developer incentives include financing options, tax credits, and fee waivers. While most of these programs remain governmental initiatives, utilities as well as other private industries benefit. Rehabilitating abandoned property and revitalizing deteriorating neighborhoods bolster utility revenue growth. At the same time, they promote energy efficiency and service affordability.

Tallahassee. The city of Tallahassee waives impact fees, speeds processing, and provides technical assistance for developers of affordable housing. To qualify for these incentives, developers must sell 30% of the total units at 1.6 times the area median income.[3] Although this places an upper limit on the sales price, the remaining units may be sold and occupied according to market conditions. Therefore, developers retain some flexibility in their pricing strategy while enjoying financial assistance from local and state governments.

Chicago. The city of Chicago offers a range of developer services to address the many aspects of affordable housing. The following is a list of programs offered by the Department of Housing Services:

- Chicago Partnership for Affordable Neighborhoods
- Class 9 Property Tax
- Class S Property Tax
- Donations Tax Credit
- Empowerment Zone Building Preservation
- Home Start Program
- Joint Lenders
- Low-Income Housing Tax Credit
- Multi-Family Loans
- Multi-Family Mortgage Revenue Bonds
- New Homes for Chicago[4]

Given the variety of programs, resulting benefits are difficult to summarize. However, the city of Chicago provides a small list of developer benefits. These benefits include city-owned vacant lots sold for $1, reductions in various building and utility connection fees, perimeter site improvements, and a $10,000 subsidy per home. Other benefits include a $30,000 subsidy for two-flats, a $30,000 purchase price subsidy for qualified buyers, and development funding up to $220,000.[5] In short, both financial and marketing assistance through the city of Chicago are available to developers of affordable housing.

Although local and state governments provide affordable housing incentives, utilities may find viable strategies within these programs to revitalize local housing stock. In addition, utilities can promote energy efficiency, improve service affordability, and simultaneously bolster revenue growth.

Connection/switching fee waivers. Utilities often charge connection fees for households wishing to establish service. These connection fees represent a substantial burden to households without significant cash reserves. This is especially true for consumers with outstanding utility debt. In addition to connection fees, utilities may request security deposits plus payment of outstanding balances. The situation is exacerbated upon entering a new premises because each energy, telecommunication, water, and cable provider has similar fee structures.

For the low-income consumer, utility connection and switching fees often deplete or exceed available cash reserves. Because of this practice, access to utility service may be prohibitive for the low-income tenant. To accommodate their needs, regulators have authorized connection fee discounts and waivers for the low-income, elderly, and other disadvantaged populations.

In July 2001, southern Texas experienced regional flooding that forced families from their homes. Southwestern Bell Telephone Company offered affected customers an opportunity to enroll in relevant call forwarding features without installation charges. In addition, service fees were waived for the first month. Although some restrictions applied, consumers could reestablish existing telephone service without additional charge. By easing the burden of unexpected financial and emotional stress, Southwestern Bell Telephone Company provided a valuable community service while returning customers to their lines as quickly as possible.

Riverside Public Utilities in California currently offers free installation of water and electric service under the We Care program. As a result, low-income households and homes with senior citizens or disabled residents can access utility service without delay. In addition, Riverside Public Utilities can leverage energy efficiency and consumer education to improve service affordability for We Care participants.

Utility service discounts. In place of waivers, discounts may be used to lower access charges and improve the affordability of utility services. In accordance with federal legislative action, Oklahoma's Link-Up America Program provides a 50% discount on installation services to qualified low-income families. Once connected, low-income families receive preferential rates for basic landline services via the Oklahoma Lifeline Program.

Similar discounts are now available in every state. To qualify, individuals must be enrolled in any one of the means-tested low-income assistance programs, including Food Stamps, Medicaid, SSI, TANF, or Head Start. For residents of former or current tribal lands, additional incentives are available via the Enhanced Lifeline Services. In fact, basic telephone service may be available for less than $5/month. This is significantly less than the $20/month or more fee for standard telephone services.

Customer charge waivers. Once utility service has been accessed, low-income initiatives may waive the monthly customer charge. Entergy Texas offers one such program with the added benefit of automatic enrollment. Describing their efforts, they explained that "Entergy Texas has an approved tariff in place that allows low-income customers to benefit from a waiver of the monthly customer charge, but historically it was necessary for customers to request the rate and provide proof of eligibility. Our effort this year enrolled thousands of low-income customers who did not have to ask."[6]

Other southern states have adopted similar waivers of the monthly customer charge. The customer charges represent the cost of line maintenance, metering, and billing. This is typically $6–$8/month.

In Georgia, the monthly charge is waived for low-income persons over age 65. Mississippi provides a similar benefit to senior citizens who also receive means-tested assistance, such as TANF, SSI, or food stamps. Alabama waives the monthly customer charge for ALL low-income customers receiving means-tested assistance. The cost of the program in Alabama is recovered through the residential rates (4¢–6¢/month).[7]

In states where rate discounts are available to the low-income and elderly, the monthly customer charge waivers are less common. However, the state of New York adopted a provision to freeze the customer charges for low-income persons. The resulting $5 monthly customer charge was one-half of the $10 charge applied to other residential accounts.

Customer charge waivers are also used to ensure service reliability standards. The state of Illinois adopted Service Reliability Standards that require the waiver of the fixed monthly customer charge for customers whose service fails to meet the reliability standard.[8] Similar reliability standards were adopted in Michigan, where restoration of service must occur within a reasonable period. (This could be 16–120 hours, depending on the circumstances.) Otherwise, the greater of $25 or the monthly customer charge shall be credited to the account.[9]

Tax exemptions and incentives. Once a customer accesses utility service, various usage charges are accumulated based on volume. State and local governments often tax utility sales. The collected revenue is allocated through the general budgets to fund government services. Because the intended use of these funds is to support community needs, disadvantaged populations are often granted discounts or exemptions from utility sales taxes and usage fees.

In a recent survey conducted by the LIHEAP Clearinghouse, several states provided tax relief to customers receiving public assistance.[10] Qualifying customers receive waivers, rebates, or refundable tax credits to lower home energy burdens. Iowa and New York offer sales tax exemptions, while Maryland provides rebates on utility sales tax. Similarly, Virginia offers a sales tax waiver on deliverable fuels such as propane.

In cases where outstanding balances exist, utilities must examine the rationale for late payment fees before applying them to low-income customers. In many cases, limitations or waivers of late payment fees serve the interests of both parties.

Tax credits may be found outside the low-income framework. Missouri offers a residential utility tax exemption for all residents of apartments and condominiums.[11] Incentives are sometimes targeted at organizations assisting selected populations. The state of Washington excludes usage taxes on public utilities that provide service to Indian tribes or disabled persons.[12] Washington also allows public utilities to claim a tax credit for assisting low-income customers. One-half of the qualifying discounts and contributions made to assist a target population can be taken each year by the utility.[13]

Late payment fee waivers. Low-income and special-needs customers are often exempt from late payment charges. For example, Entergy Mississippi is working with the Department of Human Services to qualify low-income assistance recipients for late payment fee waivers.[14] With only 18% of its low-income population exhibiting high-risk payment behavior, Entergy prefers to find mutually beneficial billing practices to assist customers through temporary financial distress.

Some companies charge a monthly late fee of 5% on all outstanding balances, similar to the approach used by Southwestern Public Service Company in 1993.[15] At these rates, outstanding balances can easily double in just two years, which is an annualized interest rate of nearly 80%. Such tactics can devastate consumers with limited financial resources, large energy burdens, and a demonstrated inability to pay. As such, a number of actions should be taken by stakeholders to limit the scope of late payment fees.

Consumers are advised to solicit waiver of all late fees and negotiate acceptable payment arrangements before falling behind. In cases where outstanding balances exist, utilities must examine the rationale for late payment fees before applying them to low-income customers. In many cases, limitations or waivers of late payment fees serve the interests of both parties.

Sometimes utilities forego such restraint and apply charges as a percent of outstanding balances. Advocates then may intervene on grounds that utility late payment fees must be cost-based and serve the interest of relevant stakeholders. Researchers have published guidelines on the applicability of these fees and build convincing arguments for fixed-dollar fees to compensate expenses incurred by the utility.

One such resource can be found at the Web site of the firm of Fischer, Sheehan, and Colton, who maintain this resource at *http://www.fsconline.com/lib/lib.htm.* Individuals interested in consumer law as it relates to public utilities are advised to read through the various documents, especially those dealing with universal service and service affordability.

Rate discount programs

The energy burdens placed on low-income people are much higher than those experienced by higher income households. A family of three existing at the federal poverty guideline in 1997 would earn $12,859 per year, with utility bills averaging $1,338.[16] The resulting energy burden for this household would be 10.4% as compared to 3.6% for a family living at the national median income level. Consequently, this family is three times more sensitive to the cost of home energy than is the average family. For impoverished households, energy burdens can exceed 25%, making these households vulnerable to rising utility costs.

Many states have authorized rate discount programs and bulk fuel purchases to reduce the energy burdens placed on low-income households. The rationale behind these programs is to lower energy costs. They ensure the variable costs of fuel are covered by payments from the beneficiary along with some contribution towards the fixed system costs. Where customer payments exceed the marginal cost of fuel consumption, all remaining ratepayers are better off than if these customers were removed from the system. Whereby ancillary improvements in payment behavior are also realized, additional savings can result from reduced collections activity, avoided service calls, and improved cash flow.

These arguments have been adopted by many states, resulting in a variety of rate discount formulations. Relevant strategies are highlighted in the text that follows.

Straight discounts. Under straight discount programs, the entire utility bill is reduced by a fixed percentage. Since the discount is available to all qualified customers, administrative requirements are minimal. The utility need only identify those eligible for the discount and adjust the bill appropriately.

Typically, utility bills are discounted between 15% and 40%. In 1991, Mass Electric Company requested and gained approval for a straight discount program. In this program, LIHEAP-eligible customers qualify for a 35% discount on their electric bills.

However, utilities may tailor the discount program to meet unique market conditions or to integrate with existing programs. Toledo Edison and Cleveland Electric Illuminating exemplify the latter. In addition to the standard low-income rate discount, an additional 2% discount is available to customers enrolled in Ohio's Percent of Income Payment Plan, integrating two distinct discount programs.

The availability of broad discount programs can dramatically reduce the cost of home energy for eligible populations with minimal administrative costs. For example, the state of West Virginia offers a seasonal discount of 20% to seniors receiving SSI, WV WORKS assistance, or Food Stamps during the winter months. For the typical household, this discount could reduce heating costs by as much as $300 per year.

As such, straight-rate discount programs may be the most viable and cost-effective approach for the immediate resolve of low-income energy burdens. However, these programs do little to address specific requirements of the low-income household.

As a consequence, ratepayer advocates may object on grounds that straight-rate discount programs do not maximize the collection of debt from low-income customers. Roger D. Colton expressed concern with respect to straight-rate discount programs. Colton said, "There are legitimate reasons not to endorse a straight-rate discount in lieu of other alternatives. The purpose of a low-income rate should not simply be to provide rate relief to all low-income customers. Rather, the purpose of such a rate should be to recognize in advance those households who will likely find it impossible to pay their utility bills on a regular, timely basis and to collect the maximum amount of revenue from those households in the most cost-efficient and cost-effective way possible."[17]

It is true that alternatives to the straight-rate discount programs realize greater efficiencies. However, most alternatives require larger investments in both financial and personnel resources. State and federal funds may be needed for these alternatives to demonstrate ratepayer cost-effectiveness. As such, straight-rate discounts may prove the only viable first step for utilities seeking to stabilize low-income payments and improve continuity of utility service.

Limited discounts. Under the limited discount model, rate reductions apply only to the usage charges and employ an inverted block rate to encourage conservation. The general format for a limited discount program includes usage tiers, discounted by a fixed percentage based on household income levels.

For example, customers of Philadelphia Electric Company living in poverty are given a 50% discount on the first 500 kWh. Customers living between 101% and 150% of poverty received only a 25% discount over the same block of energy. In contrast, National Fuels Gas offers a fixed 29% discount off the standard usage charge to participants of their Low-Income Residential Assistance (LIRA) program.[18]

While we discuss these programs from the low-income perspective, many states have adopted similar rate incentives for industrial customers. In those cases, utilities sought to maximize revenues, as opposed to minimizing uncollectibles. They chose to offer discounted rates to businesses having viable alternative fuel sources. Similarly, large employers are offered rate incentives to create and retain a large workforce. In fact, industrial rate incentives are simply the opposite side of the same coin.

Both incentive programs seek to retain valuable customers who contribute efficiencies to the distribution systems. The end result is a net benefit to all ratepayers. When structured properly, these limited discount programs should find a broad base of support from all internal and external stakeholders.

Tiered rate discounts. Although tiered rate structures have been introduced as low-income initiatives, inverted block rates are commonly implemented across the entire residential class. Regardless of the intent, tiered rate discounts offer lower rates for the first increments of energy use and progressively rise as consumption levels increase.

For example, Arizona Public Service (APS) offers a tiered discount rate structure for persons requiring medical equipment in their home (see Table 5–1).

Table 5–1 Arizona Public Service's Medical Equipment Care Program

	Discount
0–800 kWh	30%
801–1400 kWh	20%
1401–2000 kWh	10%
Above 2000 kWh	

These rates are targeted for the disabled. However, similar structures can be used across the general residential class for both gas and electric utilities. The discount would be replaced by a fixed cost per unit of consumption.

The advantage of the tiered-rate structure is that it can be implemented across the entire residential rate class. Since low-income customers tend to use less energy than their higher-income counterparts, target populations are served without administrative overhead or regulatory constraint. Given that economic incentives for energy conservation are embedded in the rate structure, potential overuse by target populations is of less concern.

While this approach would serve 100% of the targeted low-income households without added marketing costs, the tiered-rate discount has certain deficiencies as well. With this structure, individual needs are not addressed. Although the general low-income population is well served by the tiered-rate structure, extremely high-use households are effectively penalized without regard to their ability to pay.

A large family would generally occupy more square footage than smaller families of similar income. Consequently, their overall housing expense, including rent and utilities, would be greater as a percent of their income. For these low-income families, homes tend to be larger, older, and less energy efficient than those of smaller families. The resulting energy burden may be substantially higher than that of other low-income families. As a result, the tiered discount program would effectively reduce the amount of assistance for the family with the greatest need.

When a tiered discount program is chosen by a utility, care must be taken to address extreme cases within its target population. For example, a tiered-rate structure might be used for the general population, with a straight-discount exception for families with energy burdens in excess of 20% of household income. Additionally, limited discount programs could be used for customers caught in the middle. There are many benefits of tiered-rate structures, and they are easy to implement. Consequently, utilities should not exclude these models when restructuring or applying for new rate tariffs.

Lifeline rates. While our focus is primarily on gas and electric utilities, other public service companies must address and serve disadvantaged populations. The telephone industry initiated the Lifeline program in 1985. Included in the Lifeline rates are many phone features. These include single-party voice quality switched network access, DTMF signaling, and 911 emergency services. Other features are directory assistance, operator assistance, and access to long-distance. Although access to long-distance service is included, Lifeline rates do not apply to long-distance charges. However, the federal government is considering assistance for a minimal amount of long-distance service. Where Lifeline households accumulate long distance charges beyond their ability to pay, provisions exist to block or limit access to long-distance service while maintaining local phone service.

Later, the Telecommunications Act of 1996 amended and strengthened the Lifeline program with a statutory universal service goal. However, many low-income households still consider basic phone service a luxury.

As of July 2001, less than 87% of homes with annual incomes below $10,000 had active telephone service. This is far below the mandated 100% penetration sought by the FCC. In fact, of the 43.5 million households eligible, only 6.2 million households participate in the Lifeline program.[20]

To increase participation rates, several states have adopted automatic enrollment policies. By sharing data with other low-income providers, telephone companies were able to boost enrollment significantly. For example, Cincinnati Bell Telephone doubled its participation rates immediately following automatic enrollment in June 1999. Similarly, Verizon Ohio more than doubled its Lifeline participation rates. Participation increased from 10,740 customers before the use of automatic enrollment to 39,065 customers shortly thereafter.[21]

While the positive outcome from automatic enrollment is encouraging, utilities and the FCC should consider other program modifications to boost enrollment. States are now considering extending benefits to households earning twice the federal poverty guideline to help an emerging class of the working poor move from welfare to work.

While access to essential phone services is the foundation of the Lifeline program, customers also receive additional benefits to improve the affordability of phone service. Customers participating in Lifeline are exempt from a number of federal taxes and qualify for reduced subscriber line charges. To fund this initiative, the federal government offers up to $7/month per line and piggyback assistance with Link Up America. Together the Lifeline and Link Up programs account for $512 million of the estimated $4.5 billion in annual universal service charges.

While the Lifeline programs are often discussed in the context of telephone utilities, a number of municipalities offer similar programs for water, sewer, and drainage. The city of Kent, Washington offers seniors, disabled, and low-income customers discounts from the normal usage rates. Monthly charges for sewer are $31.27 for the general residential population versus $28.65 for Lifeline participants.

Similarly, storm drainage is also discounted for Lifeline partici-pants. Within the city of Kent, water consumption is billed on a two-tier system, with rates dependent on seasonal use and location. The city of Kent charges customers between $1.30 and $2.58 per CCF depending on various factors, making budgeting difficult for those without discretionary resources. Consequently, Lifeline participants receive a simplified billing of $0.48/CCF inside the city limits or $0.50/CCF outside the city limits.[21] As can be seen from this example, the Lifeline programs with water and sewage utilities resemble the rate discount programs offered by gas and electric utilities.

Heating fuel discounts. Deliverable fuels, like liquid propane and heating oil, are used for residential heating in forced air, hot water, and steam systems. While deliverable heating fuels are used throughout the United States, heating oil customers are more prevalent in the Northeast. Liquid propane is more common in southern and midwestern states.

The Energy Information Agency estimates that approximately 15% of U.S. households in 1997 heated with either liquid propane or heating oil at a cost of $3.8 billion annually.[22] To offset winter heating costs, state LIHEAP agencies may distribute fuel funds or government appropriations to qualified customers using deliverable fuels. The strategies commonly employed are advanced purchases, volume discounts, negotiated margins, and fuel recycling programs.

Mass Energy Consumers Alliance has a heating oil discount program available to all consumers. By negotiating margins with regional vendors, Mass Energy Consumers Alliance can offer retail discounts that typically range between 15¢ and 30¢ per gallon of heating oil. In January 2004, the average retail cost of heating oil was $1.57/gal. Members of the Mass Energy Consumers Alliance were able to purchase heating oil at $1.40/gal. As such, members can expect savings between 10% and 20%.

More typical of low-income assistance are advance and bulk purchases of home heating fuels through state appropriations. For example, state LIHEAP offices in Minnesota and Vermont received advanced appropriations to purchase heating fuels in the summer, while prices and demand are low. By prepurchasing fuel in bulk, qualified LIHEAP recipients receive heating fuel at significantly lower rates.

Nonprofit organizations and other limited-use agencies may reclaim unused heating oils for distribution to low-income families. For example, homes changing from heating oil to natural gas may have tanks with remaining fuel, which represents a potential environmental contaminant. To reclaim excess fuels, organizations arrange for the collection and distribution of unused heating oils. Fuel reserves are accumulated over the summer cooling months and distributed during peak heating months, serving as a valuable resource for families in crisis.

OTHER BILL REDUCTION PROGRAMS

Within deregulation, a number of payment and service alternatives were expected. Yet service options remain remarkably unchanged even in the most liberal regulatory environments. Instead, deregulation has yielded markets in which the incumbent local distribution company still enjoys a natural monopoly, despite the introduction of competitive energy suppliers. To date, deregulation has largely failed in its promise to lower utility service charges and address the diverse needs of individual ratepayers.

> *"According to Richard Wight,*
> *President of Energy Market Solutions,*
> *consumers want choices*
> *within their utility,*
> *not choices between utilities."*

Deregulation is often synonymous with customer choice and universal service provisions. These allow individuals to choose between energy suppliers and be assured access to an energy provider. While a viable first step in deregulation, utilities must eventually adopt more sophisticated pricing models, service options, and technological adaptations to meet growing consumer demand.

Oddly, the North American utility industry will turn to third-world economies to exemplify service innovations where loyalty programs and prepaid metering services have been successfully adopted. However, even within our reregulated framework, options still exist for segments of our population.

Account aggregation

Consumers have varying degrees of flexibility through which lower fuel prices, competitive discounts, and service options can be accessed. *Account aggregation* provides one such avenue to access preferential rates.

For decades, volume discounts and customized rates were limited to regional industrial accounts. However, in the late 1980s through the 1990s, a number of national accounts conducted the requisite research to access preferred rate tariffs. Efforts initially came from large box retailers with 24-hour operations, like those of Target and Wal-Mart. These stores have relatively flat demand profiles, desirable power factors, and a large employment base. Consequently, utilities were inclined to customize rate tariffs to attract these accounts into their service territory. The resulting economic stimulus more than justified the investment by utilities.

Following the early success of national accounts in obtaining rate discounts, many national franchisees looked to lower utility costs.

The avenue for these discounts was to aggregate the demand for all franchise holders into a single billable account. By increasing the usage base, account power factors were notably improved, thereby opening discussions for preferential rates. Such aggregation was not widely adopted by the utilities, because distribution costs were not impacted. Also, the infrastructure to support emerging tariffs was not cost-effective. Instead, account aggregation focused on the acquisition of fuel from competitive suppliers.

Following deregulation in the late 1990s, some municipalities and state agencies began to aggregate fuel purchases. The resulting savings were passed on to selected residential consumers, largely the low-income and other disadvantaged households. Today, you can find investor-owned utilities aggregating fuel purchases for their low-income customers.

Columbia Gas of Ohio successfully piloted one such program, later expanding the program into neighboring Columbia Gas of Pennsylvania. In these programs, customers participating in Percent of Income Payment Plan (PIPP) were pooled into a single purchasing group. Columbia Gas then requested that energy suppliers submit bids for the aggregate low-income class. The resulting bids successfully lowered expected fuel costs by 12%, and the cost of utility service by 7%.[23]

Similarly, National Fuel Gas formed a low-income gas aggregation program with help from state and community agencies. The Public Assistance Cooperative for Energy (PACE) enrolled public assistance households in two New York counties, Erie and Chautauqua. By pooling customer load and placing it out for competitive bid, PACE secured savings approximating 9% annually.[24]

Fuel-switching programs

Also following deregulation, *fuel switching* has been used to reduce low-income energy costs. Green Mountain Power, Puget

Sound Energy, and Consumers Power have explored the conversion of electric water and space heating to gas as a potential energy-savings measure.

Northgate Apartments in Burlington, Vermont announced that it would prepay HUD loans and raise rents to market levels. The resulting increase was to displace low-income tenants from the 336-unit complex. Following a successful grassroots campaign to purchase the property, Northgate Non-Profit agreed to maintain the existing income mix. They also agreed not to displace existing residents and to rehabilitate the complex with a focus on energy efficiency.

Among the chosen retrofits was a $267,000 utility-sponsored switch from electric heating to natural gas. Prior to this retrofit, Northgate accounted for 5.2% of Burlington Electric's residential load. Following the retrofit, Northgate represented just 1.6% of the electric load.[25] So why would an electric utility sponsor a switch from electric to an alternative fuel?

"All that is needed to effectively serve the low-income household is a little unregulated thinking within the framework of deregulation."

In the case of Burlington Electric, the decision was largely economic. Burlington Electric Department was a winter-peaking utility in 1993, using heating oil to support peak demand. The inherent inefficiency of burning oil to generate electricity and converting electricity back to residential heat served no one. Utilities could not fully recover the cost of peaking generation, while consumers paid more for electric heat than they would otherwise pay for natural gas. As a result, Burlington Electric invested $3 million in the Heat Exchange Program, reducing electric use by nearly 12 million kWh annually.[26]

As can be seen from Burlington Electric, utilities can benefit under the right circumstances. Yet for most electric utilities, the potential revenue consequences and technical barriers jeopardize shareholder support for fuel-switching initiatives. Likely, fuel-switching programs will need to be integrated with other programs to demonstrate their effectiveness as a low-income service affordability measure. Such programs might include state weatherization programs and Assurance 16 initiatives. The important point here is that a once-taboo subject of fuel switching has proven a reasonable option for lowering the energy burden of disadvantaged households. All that is needed to effectively serve the low-income household is a little unregulated thinking within the framework of deregulation.

The use of advanced metering technology

Technology advancements have lowered metering costs substantially. Looking back just a decade, interval level data was available only with significant investments in specialized metering technology. A whole-premise meter would cost several thousands of dollars in the early 1990s. Today a metering device with similar function would cost just a few hundred dollars.

This 10-fold decrease applies to size as well as cost. In the past, the metering technology was housed in a metal cabinet about the size of a fuse box. Today, interval data is captured *under glass,* a term indicating the technology is integrated with the standard usage meter. As such, advanced metering technology can replace the standard premise meters while supporting a variety of utility practices. These include manual and automated meter reads, demand forecasting, time-of-use rates, home energy loyalty programs, and prepaid metering services.

These technological advances coupled with deregulation have allowed a number of experimental tariffs to be tried within the residential sector. Households with behavioral patterns significantly different than the general population may be able to use energy during nonpeaking hours. For example, a retired couple may have more flexibility with respect to their energy use than would a dual-income family with school-age children. As such, a time-of-use rate could encourage desirable energy consumption patterns through economic incentives. Populations able to monitor and adjust home energy use throughout the day are likely participants in residential time-of-use programs.

Wisconsin Public Service has implemented one such tariff (see Table 5–2). At the time of writing, the standard electric rate for Wisconsin Public Service is 8.535¢/kWh. Those opting for the time-of-use rates save during nonpeaking hours and are penalized for use during regular peaking hours.

Table 5–2 Wisconsin Public Service time-of-use prices

	Price During Time-of-Use Electric Savings Hours
3.843¢/kWh 45% of standard rate	Winter Option 2: noon–4 PM, 10 PM–9 AM Summer Option 2: 8 PM–10 AM
	Time-of-Use During Peak Usage Hours
16.179¢/kWh 189% of standard rate	Winter Option 2: 9 AM–NOON, 4 PM–10 PM Summer Option 2: 10 AM–8 PM
8.535¢/kWh	Standard Utility Rate

(As published on the Web site of Wisconsin Public service http://www.wisconsinpublicservice.com/home/tou.asp)

The proposed rate structuring is interesting in that the time-of-use rate structure is equivalent to the standard utility rate for a 24-hour demand profile with no variance. Under the proposed tariff, a 1-kW load left on for 24 hours in the winter would cost $2.03/day under the time-of-use rate schedule and $2.04/day under the standard rate.

However, time-of-use rates can change usage costs significantly. Let us say a 1-kW load is active just nine hours a day. Under the Wisconsin Public Service's standard rate, this daily energy use would cost $0.77/day. Under the time-of-use rate structure, the identical load could cost anywhere between $0.35/day and $1.46/day. As can be seen, the difference can be substantial. Therefore, careful monitoring of home energy use is necessary to realize the benefits of time-of-use rates. For some low-income households, time-of-use rates could lower utility billings and improve service affordability.

Another emergent trend supported by advanced metering technology is prepaid metering. Long distance pricing options that were once limited to time-of-use rates now include prepaid calling cards and cellular minutes. Because use is paid in advance, utilities offering prepaid services can remove the risk of nonpayment, thereby improving receivables. As such, the cost of service is lower for those using prepaid metering.

For some target populations, prepaid metering represents a viable billing alternative. Customers experiencing only marginal service affordability issues may be able to receive discounted service by choosing prepaid metering. Even where price discounts are unavailable, immediate in-home feedback may warrant a premium. In many pilot programs, prepaid metering has lowered home energy consumption between 15% and 20%, thereby offsetting any premium charged for service.

Despite its promise, prepaid service within electric, gas, and water companies is still an emerging trend. So additional study will be needed to determine if this pricing option is viable within the low-income population. The first step needed is to determine what drives the observed energy savings. Is it the technology that allows for behavioral change, or is it unrecorded service terminations? By answering this single question, the industry can make wide inroads for the use of advanced metering technologies to facilitate a range of pricing options.

Survey of Payment Stabilization Programs

In addition to bill reductions, service affordability can be enhanced through payment negotiation and convenient payment options. One trend that evolved during the 1990s was the consolidation of service centers. While this arguably led to improved utility operations, many communities lost convenient utility service centers. Another trend that emerged was the development of individualized payment plans, budget counseling, and debt forgiveness programs designed to stabilize payment behavior.

Payment options

One fundamental factor in the success of any business is the collection of accounts receivable. As such, the number of payment options appears to grow each and every year. With recent technological advances, electronic payment processing has grown both in depth and breadth. Today, individuals can wire money from one continent to the next via a simple e-mail account. Within the utility industry, a number of advanced payment options are available, including electronic account drafts, pay-by-phone, online bill payment, and credit card authorizations.

With the advanced payment options available, managing bill payment has become easier for most of us. Yet, for the low-income customers without a regular checking account, bill payment options have actually been reduced. Community utility service centers have been consolidated, effectively removing the in-person payment option. Cash payments are no longer accepted by many utilities, and check cashing is left to the pawnbroker. In addition, households without basic checking accounts often lack access to consumer credit. As such, low-income customers are often left with just one payment option: buy relatively expensive money orders. As a result, making a utility payment can be both time-consuming and costly. In an effort to reduce payment barriers, utilities are exploring a number of payment options.

Preferred cycle dates. Perhaps the simplest and least costly mechanism to improve bill payment is to assign convenient due dates. Bills arriving at times when households have the greatest discretionary income should lead to improved payment behavior. For example, the first of the month may require rents, mortgages, and car loans to be paid. These large-ticket items can easily deplete available funds. By establishing a midmonth billing cycle, conflicts with other necessary expenditures can be avoided.

In recognition of this fact, many credit card companies allow individuals to specify preferred payment cycles. Unfortunately, billing cycles within the utility industry are often tied to meter reading routes, making preferred cycle dates an operational issue as well.

To avoid this complication, AmerenEnergy employed a simple and effective strategy: allow customers receiving retirement benefits or disability payments to delay paying their energy bills for up to 10 days. By extending a grace period for utility payments, AmerenEnergy effectively shifts the payment to another income cycle, thereby easing payment constraints. Another option to assign preferred cycle dates without operational constraints is to install automated meter reading or advanced metering devices. By doing so, the meter read can be effectively separated from the meter reading route.

The minimum amount due. Minimum payment amounts have been employed by credit card companies to ease payment requirements. While financial institutions have differing motivations than would a utility, consumers may require flexibility to manage household expenses. Establishing a minimum payment amount provides this needed flexibility.

For those with limited financial resources, the minimum payment allows prioritization of monthly bills while encouraging timely and regular payments. While most utilities do not escalate collection activities when a contribution has been made toward the current bill, AmerenEnergy formalized this policy. MPAY allows customers to make smaller payments when the entire balance cannot be paid in full. MPAY asks customers to pay one-twelfth of their outstanding utility balance, plus a levelized billing payment. By doing so, customers have a year to catch up on previously missed payments without experiencing late charges or past-due notices. By allowing customers to make smaller payments when necessary, AmerenEnergy acknowledges that unexpected household expenses may arise from any number of uncontrollable events.

Bill payment centers. Bill payment centers have replaced many regional utility service centers. These payment centers are now located within grocery stores, convenience marts, check cashing centers, and commercial banks. While some individuals may demonstrate a preference for in-person payments, many low-income households do so out of necessity.

Verdi & Company reported that more than one-half of the low-income participants indicated a preference for using a company drop box or authorized payment centers.[27] Verdi found that "these lower income customers who pay in person…may do so not out of convenience but of necessity, a factor that often necessitates an energy company's provision of in-person payment options."[28] In fact, the report is so telling we encourage its review. It can be found online at *http://www.verdico.com/acrobat/DSU_5_UtilityBill PaymentBehavior.pdf.*

The bottom-line is that low-income and elderly persons prefer to make payments in person. As such, closing community service centers may negatively impact payment behavior. Many utilities have outsourced bill payment centers to businesses able to process personal checks and cash transactions. These include banks, grocery stores, pawnshops, and other small-dollar lenders.

"Without proper attention, bill payment centers may lose the confidence of those who most depend on them. In fact, one utility is currently dealing with a payment center that declared bankruptcy with $10 million of accrued payments that had yet to be received by the utility."

As with any outsourced activity, operational issues can arise unexpectedly. For example, the District of Columbia Office of the People's Counsel issued a consumer alert warning of unfair consumer practices at bill payment centers. The alert warned that cash payments are not necessarily received by the utility on the date of payment. For those facing late-payment fees and disconnection, the use of bill payment centers may not stop imminent collections activity.

Without proper attention, bill payment centers may lose the confidence of those who most depend on them. In fact, one utility is currently dealing with a payment center that declared bankruptcy with $10 million of accrued payments that had yet to be received by the utility. As a result, utilities must now consider the risks associated with the practice of outsourcing bill payment centers.

Analyzing payment preferences. It is important to remember that credit/debit card payments, bank drafts, and automated payment solutions are often unavailable or undesirable options for the low-income consumer. Money orders can be an expensive, yet necessary, option for many low-income consumers without checking accounts. Additionally, wire transfers, like those offered by Western Union, may be relied upon during times of financial distress. The cost of these activities can accumulate to unmanageable levels for low-income households. Utilities should consider analyzing payment preferences of their low-income population. They then can develop strategies to ease the burden of bill payment before investing in additional collection methods.

Budget billing plans

In 1926, John Wanamaker authored a 30-page illustrative manual, *The Budget Credit Book.* In his book, Wanamaker describes budget credit as follows, "A budget account is a savings plan which permits the satisfaction of possession first and accepts payments in convenient sums—as the money is saved."[29] In principal, utility budget billing plans work in a similar fashion. Annual utility bills are estimated and amortized over a 12-month period. Utility customers make equal payments throughout the year. Excess payments during off-peak months are banked to ease the financial impact of higher seasonal on-peak billings.

Utilities offer these plans to help customers avoid monthly fluctuations in utility billings, thereby making household expenses easier to manage. Because of this convenience, utility budget billing plans have been widely adopted. Nearly every utility in North America offers a levelized payment plan to consumers at all income levels.

A fixed monthly utility expense is a valuable and desirable option for many families. Yet, an inappropriate budget amount can negatively impact consumer payment behavior and undermine the value offered by budget billing plans. When budget amounts are set too high, the affordability and the convenience sought by the consumer are jeopardized. On the other hand, budget payments set too low result in unreasonably high annual adjustments, introducing large undesired seasonal bill variance. In both cases, low-income consumers would experience difficulty in raising the necessary reconciliation amounts. This, of course, increases the likelihood of arrears.

Where the budget amount is proven inappropriate, corporate liability becomes another issue for the utility. Consider a budget amount set higher than the actual annual billing. In such a case, the customer would bear expenses higher than were actually incurred. At the end of the year, the utility would owe the remaining balance. To reconcile these overpayments, utilities must either print a check or issue a bill credit to the customer. However, this assumes the budget amount was paid in full and represents the best circumstances. Where the utility seeks unreasonable adjustments at the end of the year, customers may feel misled and angry. The customer assumes the utility is monitoring actual use and can fairly estimate future use.

Whether true or not, the legal concept of *detrimental reliance* may provide the framework for legal action. To avoid this, the New York Public Service Commission's *Rules of Practice* says budget billings are subject to regular review for conformity with actual use. Where this practice is not followed, utilities can be found negligent and therefore forfeit the legal right to collect monies for the energy used. Managing consumer expectations goes a long way towards managing corporate risk.

Deferred payment plans

For those already behind in their payments, a combination of payment plans may be needed. One arrangement must address past due balances, while another addresses future energy use. Plans like this are known in the industry as *deferred payment plans.*

In their most basic form, the past due balance is amortized over a fixed period of time, typically one or two years. In addition to this amount, a budget payment amount is established for the next 12-month period. The combined amount represents the monthly minimum utility payment for the coming year.

These deferred payment plans are often better suited for those with lower energy burdens than are typically seen in the low-income population. Customers struggling with service affordability are unlikely candidates to succeed when monthly amounts exceed the average monthly billing. As such, a number of low-income programs have been developed. The following programs are important variants of deferred payment plans.

Percentage of income payment plans

Instead of arrangements based on the current billings or accumulated arrears, a number of states are now employing an income-sensitive repayment schedule. This approach was the first to recognize that low-income families were contributing a significant portion of their income to utility bill payment. The average energy burden for an average household may be 3%–9%. In contrast, a low-income family can have energy burdens in excess of 30% of their total household income.

State regulatory offices began to wonder if utility service was affordable at these levels. To normalize energy burdens placed on the low-income population, states encouraged utilities to accept a *percent of income* as payment in full. To offset utility revenue shortfalls, states would direct federal energy assistance grants to program participants and adopt system benefit charges. These programs became known as PIPPs.

Standard PIPPs. In the early 1980s, the state of Ohio created one of the industry's first PIPPs. Supported by a systems benefit charge, the state of Ohio Public Utility Commission allowed income-eligible customers to lower their energy burdens. This was accomplished by directing a percent of their income towards home heating.

The program requires customers to contribute 10% of income to home heating and an additional 5% to secondary energy providers. In effect, the program asks customers to pay the gas utility 10% of household income and the electric company 5% of household income. Where a home is electrically heated, then the electric company would receive 15% of household income. For families living deep within poverty, below 50% of federal poverty guidelines,

PIPP payments are based on 3% of household income. To maintain eligibility in PIPP, the state required customers to recertify and apply for home energy assistance each program year. Customer participation in home weatherization was also encouraged.

As one of oldest programs, the Ohio PIPP serves as a model for implementations in other states. One distinction of the Ohio PIPP program is an established exit strategy. Customers removed from the Ohio PIPP become eligible for the Arrearage Crediting Program.

The program allows customers to maintain their PIPP payment level for 12 months. The shortfalls are accumulated in arrears and accumulate until the third year following PIPP participation. At this time, customers are allowed to pay the arrears at $20 per month. This component of the Ohio PIPP allows customers time to acclimate as they move from government assistance to self-sufficiency.

Percent of Bill Payment Plan (PBPP). A variant of the standard PIPP is the PBPP. Like the standard PIPP, the PBPP starts with household income. A fair energy burden is set, typically around 10% of household income. The affordable energy burden is then converted into an annualized dollar amount and compared to the customer's average annual energy use. The resulting fraction is expressed as a percent of the customer's average energy use. Customers are then asked to pay a fixed percent of the energy bill.

To exemplify this, let us consider a household earning $15,000 a year with an average utility bill totaling $2,500. This household would have an energy burden near 17%. Choosing a 10% energy burden as affordable, the customer would be expected to pay $1,500 towards the utility bill. To calculate the desired percent of bill, we divide the $1,500 PIPP amount by the $2,500 average utility bill. The resulting percent of bill is 60%.

In this case, the PBPP customer would be asked to pay 60% of the actual utility bill each month. For convenience, the PBPP payment amount is often levelized so the amount remains fixed throughout the year. Since the payment amount is tied to energy use, an economic incentive is provided to reduce energy consumption. By tying payment amounts to energy use, market forces absent with the standard PIPP are in place under the PBPP.

Fixed credit model. The fixed credit model (FCM) also employs an economic incentive tied to household energy use. As with all PIPPs, an affordable energy burden is first established. Like the PBPP, household income is compared with annual energy consumption. Using the example above, annual customer payments are expected to total $1,500, while the actual revenue billings would be $2,500 annually. The $1,000 difference would be the credit for the year. In the FCM, the customer would see a credit of $83.33 appearing on his monthly invoice. Instead of adjusting the billing amount, the FCM simply applies a fixed credit effectively lowering the amount due.

Customer assistance programs

You will note that all PIPPs require some interaction with the program participant. To establish household income, check stubs and/or federal tax returns are used to verify eligibility and to calculate payment amounts. Since an in-person interview is required for enrollment, the industry began to consider the value of additional factors influencing payment behavior. These factors could include household expense, medical circumstances, educational attainment, and other socioeconomic factors.

In the early 1990s, the state of Pennsylvania mandated that utilities develop programs to address growing affordability issues. The resulting programs are the Customer Assistance Programs (CAPs) and Customer Assistance and Referral Evaluation Services (CARES). Together these programs represent a case management approach similar to that used in social welfare programs.

The goal of these programs extends beyond simple payment arrangement. The intake center, typically a community action agency, reviews the family situation to coordinate support services via CARES. Where appropriate, referrals are made to agencies outside the utility industry. For example, a low-income family may be informed of TANF assistance or disability benefits under SSI.

The focus of CARES is to ensure factors impacting utility bill payment are addressed. A CARES participant is not only informed of available assistance programs, but may be directly enrolled in those programs taking applications.

For example, households in economically repressed areas may receive information about available CARES programs through utility bill stuffers, neighborhood canvassing, or public service announcements. Respondents schedule an in-person interview during which they share information regarding income, household expense, medical condition, and home heating/cooling habits. The CARES agent then screens the customer for program eligibility. Applications to LIHEAP, fuel funds, and home weatherization are filed through CARES.

In addition, CARES agents provide CAP services, establishing affordable customer bill payment. Generally, one of the PIPP methodologies is used to estimate an affordable monthly payment. Household expenses are then considered during budget counseling to arrive at a mutually agreeable payment amount. The result is a utility payment amount that is certain to fit the household budget.

The objective of CAP is to secure regular and consistent long-term utility payments from program participants while leveraging available home energy assistance. From these programs, utilities realize predictable payment flows, improved operational effectiveness, and guaranteed revenue recovery via regulatory mechanisms. In turn, the participant receives a lower monthly energy bill, improved control over household expenditures, and long-term financial incentives for good payment behavior. The only question that remains is whether these programs are good for the ratepayer.

Initial studies suggest that CAP program participants are served at lower costs than similarly situated nonparticipants. However, definitive studies have yet to quantify ratepayer benefits in excess of the system benefit charges. With many of these programs under development, it will likely be another 5–10 years before the industry can corroborate ratepayer cost-effectiveness. Yet, one can be certain that CARES and CAP give the participant a chance to regain self-sufficiency. Ratepayers and society benefits would far outweigh current program costs.

GENERAL CONSIDERATIONS

Many of the programs were developed through regulatory agreements as utilities sought deregulation. Regulators and advocates sought to ensure that affordable utility service is both accessible and affordable to the populations in greatest need. Practices witnessed after the deregulation of other industries demonstrate that continued oversight will be required.

Fee increases following deregulation

Following the deregulation of the banking industry in the 1980s, record revenue growth resulted from skyrocketing consumer banking fees. These fees placed an unfair burden on the middle- and low-income populations. In 1999, the U.S. Public Interest Research Group conducted a survey of bank fees. They concluded, "In our view, the rise in fees and the increasing complexity of the fee system have created a burdensome and consumer-unfriendly banking system that places huge costs on the middle class and prices lower-income people out of the federally-insured banking market. For these consumers, the only alternative may be even higher-priced check cashing stores."[30]

Following deregulation, banks employed three strategies to boost consumer fee revenue. They increased existing fees, invented new charges, and made it more difficult for consumers to avoid fee events by unbundling services. "According to the FDIC, continued strength in noninterest revenues, particularly fee income, is a critical part of commercial bank income. For example, noninterest income accounted for 44% of net operating revenues in the fourth quarter of 1999."[30]

The trends observed in the banking industry also appeared in the utility industry. During the 1990s, familiar terms emerged as utilities considered pending deregulation. Industry trade journals were using words such as *unbundling, fee-for-service,* and *wire charges.* All suggested increasingly complicated billing structures embedded with service fees.

Following deregulation across individual states, the pubic service commissions heard complaints of unsavory practices. Words like *slamming, cramming, consolidation,* and *defunct* crossed over from the telecom industry and became associated with gas and electric marketers.

During the late 1990s, the state of Georgia adopted a market-driven model with few consumer protections in place. A notable characteristic of Georgia's initial deregulation model was that customers had no direct relationship with the distribution company. There were no assurances of any provider-of-last-resort, and disconnections were authorized for the nonpayment of any portion of the natural gas bill.

The result was predictable. Market forces led to aggressive sales tactics, attracting customers to emergent energy providers without the technical or fiscal infrastructure to manage the growing volume of customers. As the number of energy providers eroded, 94% of the residential market was left in the hands of just three companies. As a result, the anticipated competitive forces were not in place to protect retail customers.

According to Phil Nowicki, GA PSC Consumer Affairs Director, customer complaints grew 40-fold immediately following deregulation. Complaints rose from a pre-deregulation low of 208 in 1998 to a post-deregulation high of 8,596 in 2001. Throughout late 1999 and 2000, the GA PSC received 15,281 complaints against marketers. These included 2039 billing complaints, 179 service complaints, and 13,063 alleged deceptive marketing practices.[32] To address these concerns, new legislation was adopted. Customer protections were set into place. Protections include limitations on connection fees and deposits, billing standards and disclosures, publication of comparative rates, and the adoption of low-income protections.

Regulators and interveners in other states took preemptive actions. In 1997, the Energy Cents Coalition argued that Minnesota Power's proposals would exacerbate already overwhelming problems confronting the low- and fixed-income customers.[33] The proposals included reconnection fee changes, late payment charges, deposit requirements, and use of estimated final billings. Although Minnesota

Power gained authorization to raise its fees, low-income and elderly customers were excluded from the new tariff. Without an active consumer lobby, these charges may have passed without notice.

Consumer awareness and ease of enrollment

Consumer education must accompany new legislation if the intended benefits are to be realized. "More than 600,000 families, most with low incomes, missed out on $238 million in tax refunds in 2001," reported the *Washington Post*.[34] Although this tax credit was unrelated to utility sales and use taxes, the event highlights the challenge facing proponents of waivers, rebates, and discounts that require self-enrollment.

Even relatively simple enrollment methods may fail in light of the overwhelming demands placed on the disadvantaged. Back in the early 1990s, an interview with a welfare recipient was broadcast on National Public Radio. Her comments made a lasting impression. Speaking from experience, her opinion mirrored that of Willem de Kooning, a Dutch-born painter living in the United States. He said, "The trouble with being poor is that it takes up all of your time." Listening to the rest of her story, you began to understand what she meant.

Every form of assistance offered, every contact with a creditor, and every unexpected event had an associated chain of demands. While one can appreciate the difficulty of an unexpected medical emergency, she highlighted many seemingly trivial events that resulted in additional hardship. Simply missing her normal bus cost her at least an hour's wage. Missing her bus a couple of times cost her more than a single job. Standing in line to get a money order, the only acceptable form of payment for an overdue bill, resulted in a loss of one-half day's pay. She noted that even store coupons have an expiration date!

Without a reliable car, accumulated savings, or job flexibility, she was understandably overwhelmed and discouraged as so many opportunities passed by her. We must realize that being poor does require a lot of time spent in planning, prioritizing, and coordinating. Low-income initiatives will fail to reach those most in need unless the services are well publicized, convenient, and without excess demands.

Applicability of late payment fees

Copying trends that followed deregulation in the banking and telecommunication industries, utilities have sought and successfully imposed late payment fees. Historically, two arguments have been made to justify these fees. First, utilities seek compensation for direct expenses related to the outstanding debt. Second, utilities impose these fees to shorten current payment cycles.

In 2002, the New Hampshire Public Utilities Commission approved a 1% late payment fee for Unitil Energy Systems (Unitil). Although the commission approved the fee structure, a decremental cost analysis was ordered in place of the embedded cost analysis used by Unitil.[35] By doing so, the commission required the cost of collection associated with the late payment fees to be less than the cost of collection without them.

The National Consumer Law Center supports the use of decremental cost analysis but cautions that even within these constraints, a limit on late payment charges is necessary. The following excerpts from their legal practices series, *Access to Utility Service* (2nd edition), help illustrate their point. The Center notes "it is a legitimate inquiry as to whether the level of the late payment charge bears any relation to an acceleration in payment dates." They also note "limits need to be placed on the level of late payment fees. Given the fixed dollar nature of out-of-pocket expenses, late payment charges calculated as a percentage of the bill might be challenged on this ground."[36]

These arguments are particularly salient within the context of our target populations. One cannot add new charges to a household unable to pay current bills with a realistic expectation that these new charges will be paid in full along with the current liabilities.[37] In many cases, the imposition of a late payment fee would neither lead to a more prompt payment nor lessen the cost of credit and collection.

When one considers legislative protections for some classes of customers, late payments may be counterproductive. For instance, Roger Colton concluded, "Late payment charges are often inappropriate for low-income customers because of the special credit and collection protections established by state Public Utility Commission (PUC) regulations. Under many PUC rules, utilities are prohibited from seeking to collect a bill through the disconnect process."[38]

Windfall tax revenues on rising fuel costs

With recent increases in gas and electric prices, windfall revenue may result from utility taxes. In those instances, local governments may choose or even be required to return the windfall revenue to the consumer. According to Howard Fine, "Councilman Robert Holbrook introduced [a] proposal, which calls for capping utility taxes at levels before the big price run-ups and returning any excess to the ratepayers."[39]

The article from the *Los Angeles Business Journal* tracked efforts of San Jose, Burbank, and Culver City to expand exemptions to the low-income and elderly following a steep increase in fuel price. Some of these cities have in place double-digit utility tax rates that generate a large proportion, as high as 25%, of the city's tax revenue. Consequently, city administrators are reluctant to offer tax exemptions that could become permanent following the energy crisis.

The solution was to offer rebates to all residential customers, returning windfall revenues to the ratepayer. However, the results varied between cities. For example, Culver City exempted low-income senior citizens from the utility tax, thereby expanding current exemptions. Other cities adopted expanded exemptions, as well as providing a one-time rebate. Still other cities took a more cautious approach and were still debating if such windfall revenues really existed.

The lesson is clear: tax incentives raise complicated issues that must be addressed in advance of legislative initiatives. It should also be noted incentives are provided at all levels of government and extend well beyond the utility framework. Although resources originate outside the utility framework, windfall tax revenues can be leveraged to raise assistance for those families struggling to meet their energy burden.

Residential aggregation

In the truly competitive markets, price incentives are offered to increase sales volume and to stabilize revenue streams. Large purchasers of a commodity benefit from decreased per unit costs because the supplier benefits from decreased costs per unit delivered. A simplistic justification of this practice stems from the fact that it is less expensive to deliver a large quantity of goods to a single location than to deliver the same quantity of goods to many separate locations.

Similar justifications have been used to offer discounts to very large energy consumers. The practice was based on a number of factors but revolved primarily on lowered costs of service. For example, an industrial plant may build its own substation in order to eliminate normal electric fluctuations from sensitive manufacturing processes. In such a circumstance, the utility clearly avoids the expense needed to refine electric service for this specialized end-use.

With decreased metering costs, enhanced software, and a rise in end-user sophistication, bill aggregation offers other users the opportunity to request special discounts. National accounts and municipalities have sought, and in some cases successfully negotiated, discounts based on aggregated load factors rather than traditional cost-of-service reductions. The justification for these discounts is derived from the argument that ratepayers are better served by the utility with the aggregated load than they would be without the aggregated load. Such arguments succeed on volume because load factors are improved as base energy use increases.

Today, we see similar arguments being used to aggregate residential accounts. With advances in technology, any individual premise can be aggregated into a group. This is done much the same way that individuals are grouped within a credit union to obtain preferred insurance rates. However, residential loads demonstrate both seasonal and daily peaks that betray load factor improvements. Sales volume arguments fail because the costs to serve are not lowered without a consolidated point of delivery.

Residential aggregation appears as a double-edged sword for the low-income. On the positive side, the low-income lobby has successfully argued for rate discounts and even made bulk fuel purchases on behalf of its clients. This establishes a precedent providing a convenient point of aggregation. However, these actions are largely political rather than economic.

Aggregating low-income accounts may lower fuel acquisition costs, but this does not necessarily lower the overall cost to serve. Although some daily operating expenses are avoided when affordability is improved, the cost of delivering energy to the home is not. Without a single point of delivery, the same utility assets are required to move the energy through the community into the home. Consequently, the incentive to aggregate volume discounts for the low-income relies on socioeconomic conditions and political support. It does not rely on operational improvements in local energy distribution or savings from bill processing.

To illustrate the potential problems with residential aggregation, let us consider the following question. What will happen when developers of large high-end communities begin to aggregate residential loads behind a single communal meter with a single billing entity? For the answer, we can look at properties with consolidated water and sewage.

Consolidated water bills represent a two-fold revenue stream for the property manager. First, property managers are able to purchase water and sewage at bulk commercial discounts, while passing only a percentage of those savings on to the end-user. Second, monthly administration fees help offset the salaries of maintenance staff used to read the meters, bill the end-user, and support the delivery infrastructure. Many times these fees are based on market prices instead of the embedded costs to maintain these services. Although state and local legislation protect against replicating this practice for gas and electric services, such protections can change with the political climate.

The issue of residential aggregation remains important when discussing energy assistance. Today, low-income customers benefit from negotiated rate discounts and home weatherization, as well as energy assistance. However, as low-income customers lose their identity behind an aggregator, eligibility for energy assistance may be challenged.

Where private homes are included in residential account aggregation, who will bear the cost of income verification? Consider a municipality that chooses to aggregate electric and gas services for its members. The township takes delivery at a single point where the commodity enters the township. This enables the township to negotiate favorable bulk fuel rates and lower usage rates. But how will the utility charges be allocated to individual homes and businesses?

This question is largely decided by the governing entity. One strategy would be to incur all the costs for the community and levy taxes to cover the expense. A more common strategy is to use the existing meters, allowing the distribution companies to report individual use. This leaves yet another question—who will bear the cost for this new reporting requirement? The simplest strategy would allow the utility to bill and collect payments for each premise. However, with this approach, utilities do not realize any cost savings. In fact, such practices may be even more costly for the utility.

In order for residential aggregation to yield significant cost savings, a single billing entity and reduced delivery points must result. Under this scenario, individuals are lost behind the aggregator. Aggregation would likely include a mix of public and private housing of varied income levels. Challenges will arise to ensure low-income energy assistance and the requisite protections are not prevented by the residential account aggregator.

TAKING ACTION

The low-income utility

Universally affordable utility service may be more of a myth than an achievable result. When serving a very broad audience, inevitable market forces will result as ever-increasing service requirements result in higher operating expenses. Private corporations often target services at the middle class, leaving service gaps for individuals and households at the extremes of the population. Expectations naturally rise as the middle class becomes aware of improved technologies and the introduction of added service options. Any escalation in middle-class service expectations will invariably raise the basic cost of service. This will ultimately raise the cost of service beyond the means of lower income households.

The health industry provides an example of this. In the early 1900s, communities were happy to have a doctor in their neighbor-hood. Today, the standard family practice has an X-ray machine, multiple patient rooms, a nearby pharmacy, and consolidated group of medical professionals. As such, physicians rarely open practices outside a medical center. Similarly, hospitals compete to ensure the latest diagnostic equipment and the best medical staff are available to the community. Despite a growing number of medical professionals and increased competition, the cost of health care has risen to historic highs. So much so that medical insurance is unaffordable to more than 43 million households.

The same escalation of expectation is also seen within education. As individuals move up in social status, higher and higher levels of service are demanded of our educators. Grade school teachers today are required to have a master's degree from an accredited university to teach our children basic reading, writing, and arithmetic. Is this really necessary? Well, the debate is over, and the requirements are reinforced by our expectations.

To accommodate these rising expectations, organizations are forced to expand service offerings, accept the added costs, and raise market prices. While we see this with education and health care, the same can be seen in every regulated market: transportation, telephony, banking, and others.

Persons seeking only basic service levels have nowhere to turn. In many cases, the infrastructure costs to meet broad demographic demand add to the cost of even the most rudimentary services. As such, the payment-troubled and impoverished are denied access to basic medical care, post-secondary education, and utility service. The low-income population must be insulated from broad market demands that define service options. By focusing on the unique characteristics of the low-income and payment-troubled populations, energy marketers can serve disadvantaged populations at acceptable profit levels.

For universally affordable utility service to become a reality, a low-income utility must emerge. The only question is what structure will be used to form the low-income utility and when such an entity will emerge.

The unique characteristics of those at the extremes of our society will require services unappreciated by the middle class. For the social elite, specialty companies have emerged to cater to their whims. Similarly, the poor are provided government services. However, the scale between societal norms and societal extremes is contiguous rather than discrete. No fixed demarcation exists between the poor and the lower middle class. Rather, the classes blend across indis-tinguishable boundaries. This makes service provisioning difficult, even for a specialized service entity.

The very poor request a lower level of service and desire to pay much less than the average consumer. Unfortunately, this option is unavailable. The infrastructure required by the large middle class has a fixed cost component that must be covered regardless of the level of service requested. This presents a problem for low-income utility customers. How can they access lower service levels at a reduced monthly cost?

The only means of achieving this is to disaggregate low-income utility services from those services demanded by the general population. In the end, a low-income utility must emerge to serve this extreme segment of our population, much like the secondary resellers of phone services. However, unlike the secondary phone service resellers, the low-income utility must be able to provide basic utility at a reduced cost. Otherwise, the low-income utility simply pools those customers at greatest risk into a single entity under a guise of improved service.

Yet the value of a low-income utility is in the operational efficiencies gained through specialized services. For example, the customer service center within the low-income utility would deal only with low-income issues. The center would be familiar with the low-income provider network and would naturally provide referrals to other government programs.

The low-income utility could serve as the provider of last resort, and all federal assistance could flow through a single entity. This would reduce administrative costs associated with LIHEAP, HUD, and Community Service Block Grant, CSBG. This would, in turn, free monies for those in need and simplify the provider network. Lastly, the low-income utility would seek to minimize service options resulting in a deflationary pricing model with widening operating margins.

In the meantime, the only reliable method to improve service affordability for the low-income population is to improve the socioeconomic conditions across the entire utility service territory. By providing opportunities to households in financial distress, those in poverty have a chance to rise into the middle class. They then can realize the benefits of utility service affordability.

Automatic enrollment

Accessing data from low-income service providers, utilities are able to reach a larger percent of the eligible population. Entergy Texas is just one example of utilities boosting program participation through automatic enrollment. Qualified customers opting out of state and federal programs may still receive discounts by contacting the utility and certifying eligibility directly. Program managers looking to improve cost-effectiveness must consider shared data access and automatic enrollment. Similar initiatives within the telecom industry have doubled Lifeline participation rates and raised penetration rates several percentage points.

Integrated service delivery

Another strategy to lower service costs is to integrate service delivery. Because affordability programs are carefully monitored, regulatory reporting and data collection requirements raise the cost of service provisioning. While this is a necessary expense to ensure consumer protections, many programs build redundant delivery infrastructures.

Separate facilities, differing administrative staff, and distinct information technologies raise program costs to extremes. A better solution is to centralize data collection and reporting while distributing processing to each unique implementation. Today, technology is available to do just that. Browser-based solutions are just one example. So-called thick clients offer all of the advantages of Internet applications with the richness of a desktop application. In addition, peer-to-peer networking applications generate efficiencies without loss of the unique functionality required by regional implementations.

Universal service centers

To address the unique characteristics of low-income and payment-troubled persons requires informed and specialized support. The low-income population lacks the resources available to the general population. Many do not have checking accounts, access to credit, or reliable transportation. As such, the services convenient for the typical consumer are often prohibitive and unavailable to many fixed and low-income families. For example, online payment and electronic fund transfers simply do not apply to those with limited financial means.

Consequently, typical utility support centers are ineffective at dealing with low-income needs. Even worse, the payment options and arrangements offered simply do not improve affordability. As such, the low-income feel disenfranchised and maltreated. The $1 Energy Fund is just one organization attempting to resolve this problem with specialized low-income service centers. With 200+ member agencies across Pennsylvania and New Jersey, $1 Energy Fund implements affordability programs for a dozen utilities.

Still, this is just the first step in the process. Low-income customers require access to specialized services like check cashing and government assistance. Until program enrollment is both convenient and encompassing, the low-income population will remain on the fringe of society, settling for whatever services are offered.

A better approach is to unify low-income services and conveniences under a single roof. Then customers could cash personal checks, use cash to pay their bills, speak with representatives authorized to negotiate payment arrangements, or request crisis assistance. They also could access affordability programs from banks, telephone companies, energy providers, healthcare, and government agencies.

Such universal service centers have yet to emerge. However, they appear to be a natural evolution for utility programs providing referrals to social service agencies, private foundation grants, and even tax credits.

NOTES

[1] *http://www.wsu.edu/~dee/MESO/CODE.HTM.* 1996. As translated by L.W. King (1910) and edited by Richard Hooker of Washington State University.

[2] National Consumer Law Center. 2001. Access to Utility Service, (2d ed.), p. 140.

[3] City of Tallahassee. 2000. *Certification of Affordable Single- and Multi-Family Developments Policy.* City Commission Policy 1104. *http://www.state.fl.us/citytlh/treasurer/policy /cp 1104.html.*

[4] Chicago Department of Housing. 2003. Developers Services. *http://www.ci.chi.il.us/Housing/ developers.shtml.* Web site can now be accessed at: *http://egov.cityofchicago.org/city/webportal/ jsp/content/showDynamicContentItem.jsp?BV_ SessionID=@@@@0929940341.1091332100@@@@&BV_ EngineID=cccdadcmdgkhkhecefecelldffhdffn.0&print=true&top ChannelName=Homepage&contentOID=536903547&conten TypeName=1006.*

[5] Ibid.

6 Entergy Texas. 2003. Entergy's Customer Service Policies.
   http://www.entergy.com/corp/ lowincome/policies.asp.

7 Virginia's Consumer Advisor Board. 2000. Other States'
   Low-Income Energy Assistance Program and Electric Utility
   Restructuring (Sept.).
   http://dls.state.va.us/groups/elecutil/ cab/othrstts.htm.

8 State of Illinois 90th General Assembly. 1997–1998. 90_HB1537
   220 ILCS 5/8-209: Amends the Public Utilities Act.
   http://www.legis.state.il.us/legislation/legisnet90/hbgroups /hb/
   900HB1537LV.html.

9 State of Michigan Public Service Commission. 2002.
   Methods to Improve the Reliability of Electric Service.
   http://www.cis.state.mi.us/mpsc/orders/electric/2002/
   u-12270e.pdf.

10 LIHEAP Clearinghouse. 2002. FY 2001 State Leveraging
   Summary. *http://www.ncat.org/liheap/pubs/01stlvsm.htm.*

11 Missouri Department of Revenue. 2002. Residential Utility
   Exemption Certificate.
   http://www.dor.state.mo.us/tax/business/sales/forms/4438.pdf.

12 State of Washington. 2002. Public Utility Tax Exemption.
   http://dor.wa.gov/Docs/forms/ExcsTx/ExmptFrm/PublicUtil
   TxExmptFrSvcsPrvdToIndnTrbesAndPrsns_E.pdf.

13 State of Washington. 2002. Public Utility Tax Credit Application:
   Low Income Assistance.
   http://dor.wa.gov/Docs/forms/Misc/PublicUtilTxAppLwIncm
   Assis.pdf.

14 Entergy Corporation. 2003. Entergy's Customer Service Policies:
   Low-Income Exemption from Late Payment Fees in Mississippi.
   http://www.entergy.com/corp/lowincome/ policies.asp.

[15] Southwestern Public Service Company. 1993. Residential Late Payment Rider. Electric Tariff Number 1010.3.

[16] Energy Information Administration. 1999. A Look at Residential Energy Consumption in 1997 (Nov.). *http://tonto.eia.doe.gov/FTPROOT/consumption/063297.pdf.*

[17] Colton, R. D. 1995. Models of Low-Income Utility Rates. FSC Online (June) *http://www.fsconline.com/downloads/MODELS.pdf.*

[18] National Consumer Law Center. 2001. *Access to Utility Service* (2d ed.), pp. 215–216.

[19] Arizona Public Service Company. 1996. Medical Care Equipment Program: Electric Rates. *http://www.aps.com/images/pdf/e-4.pdf.*

[20] Travieso, M. J. 2002. Comments of NASUCA in the Matter of Federal-State Joint Board on Universal Service. National Association of State Utility Consumer Advocates, Sect. II.

[21] Ibid.

[22] City of Kent. 2003. Utility Billing—Lifeline Program. *http://www.ci.kent.wa.us/Finance/CustomerService/lifeline.htm.*

[23] Energy Information Agency. 1997. Consumption and Expenditure: Fuel Tables. *http://www.eia.doe.gov/emeu/recs/byfuels/byfuels.html.*

[24] LIHEAP Clearinghouse. 1999. Gas Aggregation and Low-Income Customers. National Center for Advanced Technology (Apr).

[25] Ibid.

[26] Patullo, C. 1993. Making Low Income Housing Affordable: The Northgate Retrofits. *Home Energy Magazine* Online (Mar./Apr.).

[27] Ibid.

28 Fehevari, K. 2000. Utility Bill Payment Behavior. Delivery Strategy Update (Oct.), p. 3.

29 Ibid. p. 5.

30 Wanamaker, J. circa 1926. *The Budget Credit Book,* p. 2.

31 Mierzwinski, E., et al. 2001. Big Banks, Bigger Fees 2001: PIRG National Bank Fee Survey (Nov.), p. 12. *http://www.stopatmfees.com/bigbanks2001/PDFs/ banks2001final.pdf.*

32 Ibid.

33 Alexander, B. 2002. An Analysis of Residential Energy Markets in Georgia, Massachusetts, Ohio, New York and Texas, p. 6. *http://neaap.ncat.org/experts/PartOnePDF.pdf.*

34 Marshall, P. 1997. Comments of the Energy Cents Coalition in the Matter of Minnesota Power's Petition for Authorization to Amend its Electric Service Regulations (October). *http://www.energycents.org/RegulatoryPrecedings/Minnesota%20 Power%20Fee%20comments.pdf.*

35 *Washington Post.* 2002. Tax Credits Unclaimed By 600,000 (Thurs., Oct. 3), p. E01. *http://www.washingtonpost.com/ac2/ wp-dyn?pagename=article&node=&contentId= A35339-2002Oct2&notFound=true.*

36 NH PUC (DE 01-247). 2002. Order Approving Implementation of Residential Late Payment Fee Pursuant to Phase II Settlement Agreement (Nov. 22).

37 National Consumer Law Center, pp. 145–146.

38 *PA PUC v. Columbia Gas Company of Pennsylvania.* 1990. Direct Testimony and Exhibits of Roger D. Colton, on behalf of the Office of Consumer Advocate. Docket No. R-891468 (Apr.).

[39] Colton, R. D. 1994. Determining the Cost-Effectiveness of Utility Late Payment Charges. *http://www.fsconline.com/downloads/LATE-FEE.pdf.*

[40] Fine, H. 2001. Local Cities Reaping Tax Windfalls From Energy Crisis. *Los Angeles Business Journal* (Apr. 16).

6

MARKET TRANSFORMATION PROGRAMS

STATEMENT OF OPPORTUNITY

To slow the escalation of home energy costs, individuals can invest in energy efficiency. Improving energy efficiency of home appliances and heating systems can significantly lower utility bills and raise property values. For the homeowner, this is a win-win strategy. Home improvement results in long-term capital appreciation, while lower utility expense generates cash. With home lending institutions offering energy efficiency incentives, you may wonder why market transformation programs exist at all, let alone dominate demand-side management initiatives. Why should utilities spend millions to lower energy sales?

Perhaps it is easier to first address the regulatory perspective on energy efficiency. With the obligation to protect ratepayers, the public utility commission can easily demonstrate the cost-effectiveness of residential energy efficiency programs. It is true that improved property values and lowered household expenses result. In addition, market transformation projects require the purchase and installation of energy efficiency measures that generate broad regional socioeconomic impacts.

Installed energy efficiency measures have cumulative impacts that span decades. As such, the consumption of natural gas, electricity, home heating fuels, and other fossil fuels is significantly reduced. This can help to address political, environmental, and conservation mandates. Consequently, energy efficiency projects are supported by state and federal agencies in response to regulatory mandate and legislative action.

Still, there remains the question of shareholder value of energy efficiency projects. After all, improved energy efficiency leads to lower energy sales per household. In a mature market, a decline in per-household revenues can lower top-line revenue growth. This could slow or even reverse stock appreciation. So why should utilities invest in energy efficiency and alternative fuels?

This question has added significance as utilities consolidate and seek investment capital from Wall Street. Just as large retailers like Wal-Mart, Starbucks, and McDonald's are rewarded for improvements in same-store sales, utilities could benefit from increased household energy consumption. The rationale for market transformation programs is fairly straightforward: to improve or maintain the health of the utility service territory.

Simply stated, utilities whose service territories are exhibiting robust economic activities and population growth will outperform utilities

"Rising commodity prices coupled with unbridled consumer demand can challenge the solvency of any utility. Every decade, a utility in great financial standing is caught off guard and is forced into bankruptcy, often due to unsustainable fuel costs."

located in recessionary economies with declining populations. For this reason, utilities may utilize energy efficiency programs to stimulate local economies, improve key financial ratios, meet emission standards, and appease regulatory pressures.

A utility may also implement load management programs to avoid expenses associated with peak energy production costs. Electric utilities are particularly sensitive to this issue. Electric utilities facing unexpected demands for electricity may find energy costs well above the average retail price, thereby resulting in negative gross profits.

Additionally, electric utilities may have infrastructure constraints that jeopardize service reliability. This is especially true in older areas and regions experiencing exceptionally high growth. In these cases, load reduction and appliance cycling programs are used to manage consumer demand for electricity. For utilities in such circumstances, energy efficiency avoids the high cost of meeting excess demand and improves service reliability without costly infrastructure investments. As such, energy efficiency contributes directly to utility profits.

Let us briefly explore how market transformation initiatives can impact profit margins. Utilities faced with increasing consumer demand must secure stable long-term energy supplies. Prior to deregulation, large baseline demands were met by building generation plants or expanding storage facilities. These additions cost hundreds of millions or even billions of dollars to construct. As a result, supply-side alternatives required careful long-term financial planning.

When unexpected demand triggered these investments pre-maturely, utilities were unable to access capital on favorable terms, thereby raising the cost of capital.

To avoid this uncertainty, utilities chose to divest from power generation and instead entered into purchasing agreements with energy providers. This divestiture separated the financing of supply-side projects from the daily operations necessary for distribution. Still, the local distribution company must understand and reliably forecast consumer demand to avoid higher cost energy supplies.

The potential liability resulting from the improper management of consumer demand can be staggering. Rising commodity prices coupled with unbridled consumer demand can challenge the solvency of any utility. Every decade, a utility in great financial standing is caught off guard and is forced into bankruptcy, often due to unsustainable fuel costs. Because of this inherent risk, utility executives carefully monitor consumer demand. Yet, many utilities are unwilling to leverage shareholder funds to manage consumer demand.

Instead, ratepayers are left to fund market transformation programs. Emerging programs are funded via systems benefit charges that are seen as line items on the customer bill. As such, utility energy efficiency programs are given greater scrutiny than they were when program funding was embedded in the standard usage charge. Regardless of the funding mechanism, energy efficiency programs have passed regulatory scrutiny. Market-transforming energy efficiency programs provide a wide range of impacts, especially when offered in the context of a low-income initiative.

Jerrold Oppenheim and Theo MacGregor conducted an economic analysis of low-income energy efficiency programs. They concluded, "Low-income energy efficiency is one of the most cost-effective investments a utility can make from the standpoint of program participants, non-participant customers, and society as a whole."[1] The report estimates that a 1-mill per kWh electric efficiency investment across the United States would generate many participant benefits for each funded year. Some benefits include reduced customer bills ($6.9 billion), reduced homelessness (1.1 million households), avoided moving costs ($540 million), and net wage gains ($1.4 billion).[2]

These benefits result from targeting services at low-income households. However, other benefits cited for low-income electricity efficiency investments would likely result even if the measures were installed in the homes of the general ratepayer. Such benefits include reduced electricity consumption (84 billion kWh), net employment (75,303 jobs), and CO_2 emission reductions (540 million tons). Other benefits could be increased property value ($8.9 billion) and a net GDP gain ($280 million).

These quantifiable benefits when added to the operational efficiencies realized by the utility illustrate the economic value of energy efficiency for industry participants. Still, a number of economic development and incentive programs also have market trans-formational impacts. These effects arguably lower utility operating costs and slow utility rate increases. As such, the following text highlights a range of market transformational programs that may or may not be adopted by the low-income household.

The programs highlighted in the following text represent the range of market transformation programs available. Program managers are encouraged to consider these programs as possible low-income initiatives. For example, low-income families are unlikely to be recipients of developer incentives for energy-efficient new home construction. However, these homes could be built near areas of concentrated poverty. Then low-income persons could benefit from these programs.

Jobs would result from the new construction project, and the surrounding community would benefit from the long-term economic stimulus from regional redevelopment. Low-income families taking advantage of these emergent opportunities could then occupy the homes through incentives from organizations such as Fannie Mae or HUD. Market transformation programs targeted at the low-income population tend to have added benefit streams. Even programs serving the general population can have a positive impact for the public utility and its service territory.

KEY CONCEPTS

Despite the benefit streams resulting from energy efficiency and market transformation programs, resistance to these initiatives is still found within the industry. For this reason, several key concepts must be understood and successfully conveyed by those developing or operating market transformation programs.

Market transformation perceptions

Those of you participating in the industry during the late 1980s and the 1990s will link demand side management (DSM) to energy efficiency; more precisely, load-reduction programs. Prior to deregulation, load-building programs were often developed as marketing programs. Load-reduction, peak-shaving, and peak-shifting programs were earmarked as DSM initiatives. In fact, the differentiation between marketing and DSM programs was further exacerbated by departmental segregation. Load-building programs were offered by the marketing group, peak-shaving programs by the load research group, and DSM initiatives by regulatory/consumer affairs. For many utilities, this delineation still lingers today.

While DSM theory includes load-building programs as well as load-reduction programs, this may not hold true in practice. Because of this, *market transformation programs* is a better description. This class of initiatives results in long-term qualitative improvements across the utility service territory. Home weatherization, appliance replacements, housing standards, appliance sales, and fuel-switching programs alter home energy consumption over an extended period of time. Therefore, all are market transformation programs.

This is important to understand because some market transformation programs were thrust upon the utility by aggressive regulators. While not necessarily a true representation, many utility professionals still hold this belief. Consequently, utilities may be reluctant to invest in market transformation programs. The most common rationale used is that market transformation programs reduce top-line revenues and add operational costs. Both inhibit stock price escalation. Often no thought will be given to the resulting utility benefits, most notably, the benefits of avoiding capacity constraints, the reduced peaking demand, and the load-building initiatives.

To overcome this bias, we must disassociate the market transformation from home energy consumption and focus on the qualitative market improvements. Instead of discussing energy efficiency and energy savings achieved through these initiatives, we must highlight economic stimuli, improved competitiveness, and increased property values. Who could say no to programs that improve the overall health of the utility service territory? After all, the quality of the utility service territory is one of the fundamental factors in utility stock valuation.

Overcoming market barriers

Today, barriers to energy efficiency exist both in the consumer market and in targeted delivery channels. Consumers and property owners benefit from energy efficiency investments. However, neither consumers nor owners fund large energy efficiency upgrades without incentives, despite broad public awareness and support for energy conservation. To exemplify this point, ask the weatherization field technicians if they would pay for a crew to install measures at their own expense. How many would be willing to spend the $3500 for comprehensive home weatherization? Despite their knowledge of the benefits and job security, few would invest in energy efficiency without favorable financing options or incentives.

The same is true within the general residential and commercial sectors. People are uncomfortable with large cash outlays, even when immediate and modest monthly returns result from the investment. For example, comprehensive home weatherization could reduce energy costs by 25% per year. For the average household, this reduction would generate savings of $450 per annum or $9,000 over the 20-year measure life. This is an annual percentage yield of 4.8%. Homeowners also benefit from improved resale values, thereby tipping the scale in favor of energy efficiency over other investments of similar risk.

While similar arguments could be made for the commercial sector, property owners have the ability to pass energy costs on to their tenants. Low-income tenants lack mobility and are susceptible to rate increases. As such, landlord investments in energy efficiency are rare. On the other hand, the low-income lobby has significant pull on legislators. Government agencies that subsidize low-income households often establish energy efficiency standards or cap utility allotments to encourage energy efficiency investments by property owners. HUD attempted the latter. Instead of triggering energy efficiency investment by property owners, these caps simply increased the energy burdens of the occupants.

As a result, government agencies are exploring effective strategies to remove barriers to low-income energy efficiency. In the delivery channel, the public utility has been tapped to sponsor market transformation programs. Energy ratings, appliance rebates, home weatherization, and financing options have been implemented with success because of the available recovery mechanisms provided.

Utility bill riders have been used to fund special purpose entities. In 1999, the Vermont Public Service Board (VPSB) established guidelines for *distributed utility planning.* This allowed market transformation programs to be used to avoid significant investments in transmission and distribution. Efficiency Vermont became the first statewide energy efficiency utility. Operated by Vermont's Energy Investment Corporation (VEIC), Efficiency Vermont conducts the state's energy efficiency and distributed generation projects. Efficiency Vermont offers technical guidance and financial incentives towards raising statewide energy efficiency.

With broad societal benefits resulting from energy efficiency, government support to remove market barriers is a practical solution. Unfortunately, at what point will these subsidies cease? Will the market ever adopt energy efficiency as a viable investment vehicle? The answer is likely to be yes. Already, many lenders recognize the added purchasing power created through investments in energy efficiency. Still, the government's exit strategy has yet to be revealed.

Until these guidelines are published, utility ratepayers will continue to fund energy efficiency upgrades through utility surcharges and personal income taxes. With today's *no new taxes* sentiment, many viable programs will remain underdeveloped. To overcome market barriers to energy efficiency, a series of impact assessments will be necessary. These must be conducted to demonstrate the market transformational effects of energy efficiency that extend beyond simple BTU reductions and reductions in greenhouse gases. Market transformation programs must also demonstrate socio-economic improvements to warrant increased spending. A number of relevant studies can be found on the Web site of Democracy and Regulation, *http://democracyandregulation.com/issues.cfm.* Yet, still more research is needed.

Improved cost-effectiveness

Managers are facing executive pressure to improve program cost-effectiveness. Many times this translates to expense reductions. However, cutting program expenditures can dramatically reduce program effectiveness. As such, great care must be taken with cost-cutting initiatives.

Having a library of impact assessments upon which to base your decisions will be necessary. Short of recent cost-effectiveness studies, managers should seek experienced individuals to review program operations. Still, managers must ensure the resulting recommendations are not simply lifted from other utility programs. A successful resolve must be crafted to fit the specific needs of the utility and its service territory.

One such strategy involves the analysis of customer payment behavior. While this is a good first step for many utilities, segmentation of the utility service territory on any single factor is likely to fail. In the following sections, we recommend a strategy to improve cost-effectiveness by segmenting populations on several factors. Such factors include socioeconomic conditions, emerging payment behavior, and service delivery constraints.

Integrated service delivery. One proven strategy to raise program effectiveness has been integrated service delivery. Utilities that leverage state home weatherization assistance programs in the delivery of utility-sponsored load-reduction programs have demonstrated added cost-effectiveness. This is accomplished by sharing administrative expenses and leveraging existing resources, such as regional training centers. With notable results in several states, added service integration will undoubtedly result in improved cost-effectiveness across all program components. To date, most integration has been associated with program intake and service delivery. Few states have sought to integrate program outreach, evaluation, and reporting. This will be an emergent trend of undeniable benefit.

Alternative energy sources. Most utilities fail to recognize the most effective load-reduction measure: fuel switching. Once taboo, fuel switching is a viable option in many deregulated states. Both Vermont and Michigan have tested the viability of fuel-switching programs. The programs looked at switching customers from electric to gas. In Vermont, the focus was on home heating, while Michigan piloted switching fuels on hot water heating. While these programs are demonstrative, switching from electric to gas does not realize the scope of available options. Southwestern states may find viability in switching to alternative fuels, such as wind and solar. Similarly, distributed generation could also relieve infrastructure constraints.

Following deregulation, state agencies and utility program managers should explore opportunities that best address program goals. Regulators driven by societal pressures will adopt fuel-switching strategies presented by utilities. While these programs may require government subsidies to overcome technical barriers, any program that lowers the energy burden of low-income households will ease financial distress and result in more affordable utility service.

SURVEY OF EXISTING PROGRAMS

To effectively transform a marketplace, demand for higher standards must be present, along with an adoption of those standards by a majority of participants. The classic demand versus supply mimics a classic paradox: which is to come first, the chicken or the egg?

Investing in a market not yet established has many imbedded risks. Significant investments sailing on untested waters can be sunk during their maiden voyage. Yet the rewards for the first entrant are substantial, often well beyond anyone's imagination. A driving factor in market transformation is an individual's perception of risk. Buyers of technology are eager to adopt new features. However, they are less likely to pay for those features in the early stages. As such, suppliers often distribute emerging technology with little or no profit margins.

Often this is a necessary evil. Technology is of little value to users until an established base of early adopters understand and are able to communicate the value of the added features. When my father bought a reel-to-reel voice recorder for our home, callers were often surprised and disoriented by the stale interaction of this big green machine. As such, this primitive answering machine was of little value for handling incoming calls. Yet my father found it a useful addition to his entertainment system and for use as a portable Dictaphone. However, once persons were accustomed to the magnetic greeting, the reel-to-reel voice recordings quickly demonstrated the machine's ability to ease communication. When I wanted to extend my after-school activities, I could do so without reprisal. My classmates soon wished their parents had such a device. This *cool factor* led to increased demand, added supply, and emerging distribution channels.

Energy efficiency is just another technology being introduced into the market. Consumer demand is now emerging, as are the supply channels. However, this technology is still considered expensive by the average consumer and property owners. Government incentives were installed to reduce the initial costs of adoption by consumers and to lower the risks for suppliers.

Public utilities have been reluctant proponents of these initiatives because top-line revenues are negatively impacted by energy efficiency initiatives. Until recently, many market transformation programs were judged solely on their energy impacts. However, utilities are now recognizing the value of transforming the residential marketplace. By raising housing affordability, homeowners are buying up in class. Homes have greater square footage than in the past, and the demand for gas and electric appliances has supported continued revenue growth. Despite rising energy efficiency standards over recent decades, utility revenue growth has been supported. A survey of existing market transformation programs will help to illustrate this.

New home construction

Until the housing industry accepts energy efficiency standards, the residential market cannot be successfully transformed. Recognizing this, utilities offer developer/builder incentives. Developers adopting high energy efficiency standards benefit from available appliance rebates, preferred financing options, and improved marketability of their properties. Incentives for these programs vary widely.

Florida Power & Light (FP&L) offers professional services to builders via the FP&L BUILDSMART program. Builders and developers receive free advice on the design of energy efficient electric homes. In consideration for these services, the utility is able promote the value and marketability of high-efficiency electric appliances. Consumers benefit from an enhanced building envelop, while gaining the convenience and reliability of modern high-efficiency appliances.

While most new home programs are targeted at the upper middle class, the construction of affordable housing alternatives targets lower-income families. NSTAR's Energy Low-Income New Construction Program partners with the Low-Income Energy Affordability Network (LEAN) and a number of similarly focused agencies to construct and renovate low-income tenant properties.

Other new construction projects are targeted at individuals choosing to install energy efficient heating/cooling systems and to adopt energy efficiency practices. These incentives are typified by rebates offered under the Energy Star label. Rebates often range between $700 and $2,500. PSE&G is just one of many utilities supporting the construction of energy-efficient homes and the creation of affordable housing through energy efficiency rebates.

Given the societal value of improved energy efficiency and rising consumer demand, both state and federal initiatives are developing. New York has adopted a wide range of incentives managed by New York State Energy Research and Development Association (NYSERDA). These programs have demonstrated energy efficiency improvements in excess of 600 MW and are expected to exceed 1 GW through additional investments. Similarly, Efficiency Vermont has supported statewide energy efficiency. Efficiency Vermont has lowered annual energy use by 38 million kWh for more 32,000 customers.

At the federal level, the House Ways and Means Committee has introduced a tax credit backed by the National Association of Home Builders. The House bill provides tax credits of $2,000 for homes 30% more efficient than the IECC standards. The committee also removed the provision of builder self-certification, a victory for the consumer. Instead, energy-service companies specialized in home ratings will have an opportunity to establish themselves in this growing market niche.

Home rating systems and on-site audits

A number of residential home rating programs and audit services have evolved to certify energy efficiency upgrades. Home energy audits that were once available only under state home weatherization programs are being offered to utility customers without regard to income. This supports energy efficiency financing and rebate incentives.

The El Paso Energy Efficiency Program provides free energy audits to residential homes. Similarly, Mid-American Energy does not screen applicants for income eligibility in their HomeCheck Program. Others are developing programs to fill gaps in available assistance. NorthWestern Energy developed the E+ Residential Energy Audit Program for customers ineligible for home weatherization programs. Residential energy audits are even extended to those using deliverable fuels for space and water heating. NorthWestern Energy also supports alternative fuel initiatives.

With growing appeal for residential energy efficiency, utilities are now offering audit programs as a value-added service. Customers of PacifiCorp's distribution company can obtain a Home Comfort Profile by submitting a self-audit form. The resulting profiles provide customized energy saving tips and may be accompanied by low-cost measures, such as showerheads, aerators, and/or window treatments.

Progress Energy offers a comprehensive residential energy evaluation program that provides customers with an analysis of energy consumption and recommendations on energy efficiency improvements. Similar tools have emerged online and can be accessed through the utility's Web site. Mid-American Energy, working with First American Bank, offers a residential audit program throughout the Midwest. Additionally, online libraries are available for customers researching energy efficiency technologies and available incentives. Mid-American Energy's ENERGYsmart

University is just one of many such examples. When offered in conjunction with home energy audits, energy libraries provide customers with a range of actionable alternatives.

Perhaps one notable program is the Shelter Audits offered by Iowa Power and Light. By targeting homeless shelters, added support is provided to those customers who have dropped from utility distribution lines. The economic burdens placed on low-income providers restrict participant offerings. Where monthly expenses can be lowered through energy efficiency, valuable resources are freed for individuals seeking self-sufficiency.

With the growing importance of home ratings, a national accreditation program has evolved. The Residential Energy Services Network (RESNET) worked with the mortgage industry and National Association of State Energy Officials. Together they developed the Mortgage Industry National Home Energy Rating System Accreditation Standard. To qualify for energy efficiency incentives, many lenders and utilities acknowledge ratings only from certified vendors. A registry of authorized home energy rating systems (HERS) is maintained by RESNET and can be found at the following URL: *www.natresnet.org/accred/registry.htm.*

Energy efficiency incentives for existing homes

While new construction is necessary for long-term market transformation, the existing home market offers significant short-term potential, especially within the low-income customer segment. As such, many incentives are available to those willing to invest in energy efficiency.

Families purchasing an existing home can often roll efficiency improvements into the mortgage. Many banks recognize the ability of energy efficiency investments to reduce living expenses while simultaneously raising property values. Both banks and consumers benefit from this duality. By financing energy efficiency, consumers can either pocket the savings or exercise their added purchasing power. In either case, the bank has an expanded loan base upon which to generate financing revenues.

Banks are not the only lenders in the marketplace. Utilities, mortgage companies, government agencies, and specialized nonprofit groups also fund efficiency. RESNET is one such nonprofit organization. "RESNET's mission is to qualify more families for home ownership and improve the energy efficiency of the nation's housing stock by expanding the national availability of mortgage financing options and home energy ratings."[3] Individuals seeking added information about national home rating standards and industry participants should first contact RESNET at 760-806-3448. They can also visit their Web site: www.natresnet.org.

The local distribution companies often support energy efficiency through unsecured loans and rebates to both builders and property owners. Conectiv Power Delivery offers tiered rebates for the installation of high-efficiency heating/cooling systems via the CoolAdvantage Program (see Table 6–1).

Table 6–1 Conectiv's CoolAdvantage equipment requirements and rebates

Rebate Level	SEER (Seasonal Energy Efficiency Rating)	Minimum EER (Energy Efficiency Rating)	Minimum HSPR (Heating Seasonal Performance Rating)	Heat Pump Rebate	Central AC Rebate
Tier One	13–13.99	11	8	$460	$370
Tier Two	14 and greater	12	8.5	$710	$550

(http://www.conectiv.com/cpd/your_home/cool_advantage_yh.cfm)

In addition to promoting the adoption of energy efficient technology, Conectiv also requires industry professionals to properly size heating equipment. HVAC dealers often size equipment upward to ensure adequate cooling capacity is present. While common, the practice causes systems to run at less-than-optimal efficiency and raises unnecessary economic barriers. Larger units cost more and have higher operating costs, especially when these systems are operated below their rated efficiency. For this reason, Conectiv requires vendors to submit sizing estimates in conjunction with the customer's rebate application.

Conectiv's CoolAdvantage Program is typical of industry appliance rebate programs. We found similar efforts across the country within both gas and electric distribution companies. With the EPA's Energy Star certifications, some utilities have adopted incentives for the purchase of appliances earning the Energy Star rating. Minnesota Power offers a $150 rebate when an Energy Star dishwasher, refrigerator, and clothes washer is purchased from any participating dealer. Minnesota Power also has incentives in place for the purchase of individual energy-efficient appliances, including hot water heaters, window air conditioners, dehumidifiers, and compact fluorescents.

While most programs are targeted at new purchases, Florida Power and Light has incentives to address other sources of efficiency. Florida Power and Light will test residential air ducts for leaks. Problems are documented and provided to the homeowner with a list of certified vendors able to complete the necessary repairs. Rebates up to $150 are offered to repair the ducts in single-family detached homes.

Even with these rebates, consumers may be adverse to the initial cost of energy efficiency measures. As such, utilities also provide financing options to overcome these market barriers. Backed by Fannie Mae, utilities like Progress Energy will finance home improvements that are energy efficient. Often these loans are unsecured and have some imbedded risk for the utility. For this reason, utilities are able to recognize revenues in the form of competitive interest rates.

Competitive interest rates add a potential revenue stream for utilities able to generate consumer interest in energy efficiency. The added revenue stream is necessary to compensate for the added risk associated with unsecured loans. However, utilities rely on operational improvements to justify participation in energy efficiency initiatives.

Fuel switching/alternative fuels

The value of reduced electric demand can be so important to system reliability and least-cost planning that a utility will even support fuel-switching and alternative fuel programs. While these programs are often driven by federal legislative actions, such as the Energy Policy Act of 1992, utilities realize operational efficiencies where these initiatives are properly targeted.

Efficiency Vermont provided $400,000 to analyze a fuel-switching component in a state home weatherization program. Green Mountain Power participated in this initiative, switching space and water heaters from electric to gas. The Northgate Retrofits took place more than a decade ago, but this project still represents a model case study for fuel switching. According to Chip Patullo, "In 1988, the owners of the Northgate Housing Project intended to prepay their U.S. Housing and Urban Development (HUD) loan ahead of schedule and convert the 336-unit complex to market level rents."[4]

Threatened with the displacement of 1,400 residents and the loss of affordable housing, the property was bought out and is now held by a nonprofit organization. Additional funds were used to renovate the property, lowering monthly home energy costs through energy efficiency measures. "The key energy retrofit was the replacement of old electric baseboard heaters and electric water heaters with 336 individual gas-fired boilers to provide both space and water heating."[5]

The technical aspects are of significant interest to industry professionals. However, we include the Northgate retrofits here because Burlington Electric agreed to contribute $267,000 to help them raise additional funding. Given that the retrofits occurred prior to deregulation, the timing of this statement by Alan Meier now mimics my sentiment of the marketplace 10 years later. He says, "Most electric utilities don't like to discuss fuel switching, but it is an increasingly popular money and energy-saving strategy."[6]

Today, alternative renewable fuel sources have become viable sources of home energy. With support for net metering, individuals can effectively sell excess generation back to the utility. Wind turbines and solar panels are typical sources for distributed electric generation, although fuel cells and microturbines are also available.

Nevada Power is one utility with an active solar rebate program. The first 50 customers to purchase and install one-kW photovoltaic systems in compliance with Nevada Power's net metering interconnection requirements will receive $3/kWh generated. This will be paid up to a maximum of $3,000. Like other rebate programs, the equipment is purchased by the customer, installed by licensed professionals, and certified by the utility. Following the submission of appropriate rebate forms, the customer simply has to wait for the rebate.

New Jersey also supports the use of alternative fuels. Individuals living in New Jersey receive financial incentives designed to lower the initial costs of renewable generation systems. New Jersey's Clean Energy Program provides incentives for the installation of solar, wind, and biomass generation systems. Incentives are provided for generation facilities of all sizes. However, 50% of the total incentives are reserved for small systems of 10 kW or less.

Incentive levels reflect this preference. Systems less than 10 kW receive between $3.00 and $5.50 per watt, up to a maximum of 70% of installed system costs. In contrast, larger systems qualify for incentives ranging between $0.15 and $3.00 per watt up to a maximum of 60% of installed system costs. While this provides a quick summary of the incentives, the availability of incentives periodically changes to reflect capacity requirements and allocations of funding. For the current status of incentives, readers should visit the New Jersey Clean Energy Program Web site at *http://www.njcep.com/html/2_incent.html.* For this program, a preinstallation application must be submitted to the New Jersey Public Utilities for technical review. It must be open to inspection after construction or installation.

Home weatherization programs

For existing residential properties, home weatherization is the most comprehensive and perhaps the most common service affordability program available. Given that the installed measures last decades, home weatherization is also a market transformation program. Supported through federal block grants, home weatherization has evolved into a broad range of initiatives administered by either state agencies or utility companies.

In the early years of home weatherization, low-cost measures were emphasized to provide seasonal assistance. Treatments were often limited to caulking, weather stripping, and plastic window barriers. Program administrators soon recognized the need for more permanent measures, such as windows, doors, and insulation. Over time, insulation standards increased and weatherization treatments evolved along with diagnostic equipment. By the late 1980s, HVAC system repair and replacement were added to a growing list of acceptable weatherization treatments. Cost-effectiveness studies supported the trend from prescriptive measures to audit-based recommendations. This fueled technological advances in available audit tools, allowing crews to individualize housing retrofits to maximize energy savings.

Today, home weatherization programs vary widely in the scope of installed measures and range of imbedded services. Some programs mimic early weatherization efforts that utilized prescribed measures, thus avoiding the costly but effective home energy audits. Other programs include sophisticated home energy audits, advanced weatherization techniques, extensive building envelope enhancements, and HVAC system upgrades. More recently, a number of weatherization programs now include energy education, budget counseling, payment negation, program referrals, and health and safety awareness.

As a result, cost-effectiveness has shifted from simple year-to-year energy savings to include other nonenergy impacts. In addition to energy reductions, home weatherization also lowers home energy costs. As a result, payment behavior and the accumulation of arrears are impacted. Following deregulation, these nonenergy impacts will grow in importance, as increased competition demands an assessment of program impacts on utility ratepayers and shareholders.

A survey of existing programs reveals a geographic disparity between program offerings. For example, southern states may focus on low-cost measures and conservation training, while northern states offer comprehensive weatherization programs that may even include experimental treatments.

Entergy Louisiana supplies weatherization kits through the Weatherization and Housing Revitalization Program serving TANF recipients. Similarly, Entergy Texas relies on conservation training and the distribution of caulking, hot water heater blankets, and compact fluorescents to help low-income customers improve home energy efficiency.

Comparing this program with Columbia Gas of Ohio's Warm Choice Program helps to illustrate the difference. The WarmChoice program leverages the state weatherization program, ensuring participants receive the most comprehensive treatments available. Advanced diagnostic equipment is used to identify needed retrofits and verify the effectiveness of installed measures over the course of several visits. Included in this list of equipment are blower doors, flue gas testers, and infrared video recorders. Through WarmChoice, a participant may receive home repairs, setback thermostats, added wall and attic insulation, and HVAC treatments totaling more than $3,000. In addition, participants will be referred to available energy assistance and receive on-site energy education.

You will also find programs like the Cool Roofs Initiative sponsored by the Housing Authority of Baltimore. This program replaces traditional tar roofs with light-colored acrylic skins, thereby reducing heat absorption and lowering cooling costs. Exelon Energy has piloted a Solar Hot Water Program to test renewable technologies to reduce energy use for low-income customers. Also, providers like the Energy Coordinating Agency of Philadelphia have developed enhanced energy education initiatives and successful weatherization techniques.

Southern states lag behind in program offerings, often mimicking the weatherization initiatives from the early 1980s. While one may be tempted to blame the utilities, the difference is rooted in a funding bias that discounts cooling degree-days when allocating resources. The result is that weatherization programs in cooler climates are allocated greater funds than initiatives in warmer climates. As a consequence, programs in the northern states had a 10-year head start.

With deregulation and increased attention to the funding bias, several southern states are making marked advances in home weatherization. Texas is one such state. Houston Electric and Entergy Texas both supplement the state's Weatherization Assistance Program. Refrigeration, air conditioning, heat pumps, lighting, and water conservation initiatives are being supported by utilities. This results in a comprehensive state weatherization program. Similarly, Florida Power and Light has added incentives for increased insulation standards.

Other notable changes include the extension of program benefits to increasingly higher income levels. PECO extended the Low-Income Usage Reduction Program to reach customers at 200% of poverty guidelines. Indianapolis Power and Light Company applied the same extension, offering the Residential Low-Income Energy Efficiency Program to customers with all-electric homes living at 200% of poverty.

However, not all trends in home weatherization were positive. Cuts in federal funding and delays in state appropriations have hampered state-run weatherization programs. As such, the escalation of national debt under the current administration and the funding of Homeland Security could jeopardize future funding levels. Even today, energy efficiency funding has been targeted for federal cost reductions. In the future, when added concern for a balanced budget emerges, federal funding of home weatherization may again be targeted. In addition, deregulation has led to increased mergers and acquisitions. As a result, utilities are paying close attention to the bottom-line.

The resulting scrutiny threatens to simplify home weatherization and return to prescriptive measures in an effort to lower per-unit costs. To avoid this regression, program administrators must do a better job of targeting program services and demonstrating program cost-effectiveness. Given the budgetary constraints of many home weatherization programs, funding for data collection and analysis must often take a back seat. However, this is a catch-22, as program impact assessments are often necessary to raise capital for both shareholder and government-funded initiatives.

Energy efficiency rebates

Utilities now offer rebates to recycle outdated appliances and replace them with high-efficiency models. Target appliances often include kitchen appliances, hot water heaters, clothes washers and dryers, heating and cooling systems, and even windows.

Appliance replacement and recycling programs target baseload reduction. Many homes have an old, and often unused, refrigerator in the basement that remains connected, adding to home energy use. To rid the home of these appliances, Utah Power will pay customers $40 to allow the company to pick up and recycle old refrigerators and freezers. The program has a uniquely identifiable name: See ya later, Refrigerator. It pays an incentive larger than many utilities. More typical of appliance recycling programs are incentives around $20.

Removing unused equipment is one thing, but there also exists an opportunity to replace inefficient appliances with high-efficiency units. Minnesota Power participates in the state's Conservation Improvement Program. Its primary function is to replace inefficient appliances through the state weatherization program. Pike County Light & Power targets aged refrigerators, whereby qualifying customers receive a similar-sized model via the Energy Savings Partners program.

Energy efficiency rebates are popular with the public utility because of their low administrative overhead, ease of implementation, and participation from established retail partners."

Other programs have recognized passive efficiency measures in the form of window replacements. Windows with a Solar Heat Gain Coefficient of 0.55 or less and have a U-Value of 0.40 or less often qualify for a $20 rebate. Customers are also encouraged to replace a minimum number of windows and to seek additional energy efficiency improvements.

Energy efficiency rebates are popular with the public utility because of their low administrative overhead, ease of implementation, and participation from established retail partners. Through the participation of large retail chains, sales agents can leverage added energy efficiency to up-sell consumers on household appliances. As such, appliance rebates are successful in overcoming many market barriers. Consumers benefit through reduced energy costs, and retailers benefit from third-party incentives. Utilities benefit from communal goodwill, improved energy efficiency, and the recovery of program costs via surcharges.

There are many positive influences from these energy efficiency rebates. Yet the question often arises whether or not participants would have purchased the efficiency upgrades in the absence of the rebate incentives. While the issue of *free-ridership* is a valid concern, managers must not forget that a business case already exists to justify the use of rebates to encourage desired behaviors. As such, managers should focus on removing market barriers, especially in the context of low-income initiatives. For low-income households, new energy-efficient appliances may simply be too costly to purchase with cash. In this case, additional incentives such as low-interest loans may be necessary to gain their participation.

Advanced metering technologies

During the summer peaking season, many electric utilities struggle with the simultaneous demand of residential air conditioning. Constraints in available electricity coupled with an overburdened distribution system create the need for direct load control.

Utilities often address this through residential appliance cycling programs. Louisiana Gas and Electric offers a $5 credit on bills from the months of June–September per installed load control devices. Mid-American Energy offers a similar program known as the SummerSaver Program. Nevada Power offers residential customers an Air Conditioning Load Management Program. Utah Power targets its Cool Keeper program to the Wasatch Front area, thereby focusing load reduction during peak periods to very specific areas of need.

While these programs effectively defuse costly extreme peaking conditions, appliance recycling programs have embedded inefficiencies. A monthly participation fee is often provided to the consumer year after year to ensure resources are in place for these relatively rare extreme peaking conditions. In addition, load control devices require regular maintenance and year-round installation to ensure critical load reductions are in place. Just a decade ago, appliance recycling programs were the only options available.

In the deregulated environment, utilities now have other load reduction techniques that could be applied. Rate incentives and time-of-use penalties can be supported with advanced metering techniques. Like the water restrictions used by the municipal water and sewer companies, gas and electric utilities are now able to structure similar incentives and penalties using whole premise load recorders.

Although widely untested, several states have introduced residential time-of-use alternatives. As we move forward, restricted use and time-of-use incentives may prove viable alternatives to appliance recycling programs. More importantly, advanced metering technology lays the groundwork for loyalty programs and other consumer-oriented billing structures.

Taking Action

An emerging market opportunity

With banks offering mortgage incentives for energy efficiency investments, a market is emerging for energy efficiency audits. To date, support for energy auditors has come from utilities and builders. However, more providers are getting requests from homeowners seeking methods to lower utility costs. Unfortunately, many homeowners are left frustrated by utilities and service companies that are unable to offer private housing audits. In some cases, a comprehensive home energy audit is simply too expensive. In other cases, the available workforce is insufficient to meet the unpredictable consumer demand in a timely manner.

With rising demand for housing audits, often required by housing mortgagers, a new market opportunity has emerged. Private companies organized around homeowner demand for energy efficiency will find a market ripe with significant growth potential. The residential audit provides a beneficial blend of energy efficiency and community development to leverage federal and state incentives. When supported by empowerment programs and SBA-backed loans, home energy services represent a viable business opportunity for disadvantaged entrepreneurs.

Targeting areas within the utility service territory

To improve cost-effectiveness, market transformation programs must be promoted in areas where a combination of socioeconomic factors, payment behavior, and infrastructure constraints co-exist. Targeting areas based on just one of these factors will not realize the desired efficiencies. For example, targeting areas of concentrated poverty is often effective and easily implemented.

Using widely available socioeconomic data, areas of repressed socioeconomic condition can be identified. Because low-income households are less likely to invest in energy efficiency measures, homes in concentrated areas of poverty may exhibit higher energy intensities ($BTUs/ft^2$). Likewise, residents living amidst concentrated areas of poverty may exhibit unique service affordability issues. As such, areas in socioeconomic decline require attention.

Unfortunately, areas of the lowest socioeconomic condition will require several decades of continued investment to generate significant improvements in overall conditions. Because of this, a viable business case for the utility shareholder is much more difficult to construct. While the community may benefit from added services, utility shareholders may consider a 30-year payback outside their investment horizon. As a result, concentrated areas of poverty are more frequently served by government redevelopment initiatives.

Similarly, a strategy of targeting those with poor payment behavior is also lacking in scope. Individuals with chronic need and overwhelming financial obligations may lack the resources to overcome present circumstances. As such, a more comprehensive resolve is needed. In these cases, shareholders may opt to distribute financial assistance to other individuals whose families could prosper from the utility investment.

Another simple strategy that would undoubtedly result in shareholder value would be to target service areas with infrastructure deficiencies. By doing so, local distribution of energy can avoid the need for rolling brownouts through aging urban communities. Because this practice appears discriminating, utilities may face litigation that demands both remuneration and substantial infrastructure upgrades. Still, shareholder returns can remain elusive because this strategy fails to address household need. Programs targeted by system constraint can fail to realize the necessary participation levels.

The only reliable means to target market transformation initiatives is to integrate multiple factors into a single comprehensive algorithm. Targeting customers with worsening payment behavior in areas of mild socioeconomic decay can yield positive results for all stakeholders. Since the most difficult case to justify is the shareholder investment, let us start there.

Shareholders must realize immediate and lasting returns to justify continued investment. Market transformation programs impact two vital factors used in utility stock valuations: quality of earned revenue and the economic health of the utility service territory.

Redirecting sales away from households struggling with energy affordability can lower outstanding receivables and improve the quality of revenues earned. The net impact of improved cash flows and a stronger balance sheet is to raise corporate valuations. Similarly, improving the quality of the service territory can also improve valuations, leading to enhanced share performance.

Catching worsening economies before they become critical is an important strategy. Utility revenues are tied to the socioeconomic health of the service territory. Therefore, reversing negative economic growth can trigger investor confidence. The combined result of improved fundamentals and growing investor confidence can spark renewed interest in a utility stock. For this reason, programs should be targeted to customers and regions with appropriate socioeconomic indicators, payment behavior, and delivery constraints.

Full integration of state, federal, and private programs

A number of states have successfully integrated the delivery of home weatherization services. Those programs that integrated service delivery often outperform independent state-sponsored and utility-sponsored programs. By leveraging existing programs, administrative expenses can be shared along with warehousing and specialized equipment. As such, the cost of service is reduced even as current offerings are expanded. For example, infrared cameras were (and still are for some) prohibitively expensive diagnostic equipment. By pooling resources, several programs can share emerging technologies without overwhelming investment. As a result, program performance can be enhanced while maintaining cost-effectiveness.

With demonstrated success integrating service, utilities are now looking to leverage the integration of program outreach, evaluation, and reporting. Where integrated programs exist, cofunded evaluation could lower both data collection and data analysis costs while promoting a more robust and informative study. Given that state WAP programs are funded through the U.S. DOE, the focus of state evaluations has been limited to measuring effectiveness and energy savings. Utility-sponsored evaluations are trending towards program cost-effectiveness and nonenergy impacts. Cofunded initiatives could spawn more comprehensive studies that include a wider stream of impacts for a greater range of stakeholders.

For example, several studies found energy assistance reduced following home weatherization. Is this an aberration or an unexpected outcome resulting from home weatherization? Answering such questions requires the integrated evaluation efforts between agencies. In this case, the DOE and the DHHS are involved. Both entities and the public utilities potentially could benefit by shifting LIHEAP appropriations to state weatherization programs!

Similarly, cost savings may be found with integrated reporting tools. Imagine a centralized database that was flexible enough to support multiple programs through a distributed client interface. Administrators could integrate program reporting without burdening agencies with cumbersome reporting requirements or standardized business processes. In addition, governmental agencies and implementation contractors could share the cost of data tracking. By reducing agency administrative expense, federal programs could redirect efforts to expand or improve low-income offerings, instead of reinvesting in technology.

For this reason, we now endorse integrated Web-based tracking systems developed to manage workflows, track program activity, and ease regulatory reporting. Vendors endorsed by our organization will support the full integration of program services and provide the business delivery infrastructure necessary for a range of implementations.

Employee participation pilots

Piloting new initiatives and messages within your own organization is a cost-effective study of market potential. In addition, employees often provide frank and expanded feedback. Employee comments can be leveraged to improve your efforts prior to public solicitation.

During my tenure at A&C Enercom, this strategy was used to promote appliance recycling programs. An employee enrollment pilot was expected to generate immediate interest and overwhelming participation rates. However, we found employees were fickle and often expressed concerns typical of that of the general population. As such, employee enrollment pilots soon transformed from a marketing effort to a research tool.

Employee participation pilots proved to be a good tool in the identification of market barriers and evaluation of promotional campaigns. Even in those programs targeted toward low-income consumers, employee participation pilots have merit. Low-income programs often require greater consumer involvement, especially in energy-efficiency programs. Offering services to a number of employees can reveal operational constraints in the proposed implementations. As such, employee participation pilots offer significant and valuable feedback for any proposed initiative.

Retroactive behavioral incentives

For decades, electric companies managed peak demand with appliance recycling programs. While these programs are more effective at meeting peak demand than peak-generation facilities, these programs are inherently inefficient. An appliance recycling program may run for years without activation.

The reccurring costs associated with direct load control (DLC) are like insurance contracts. Where the recycling programs are not activated, the cost of maintenance was unnecessary. Yet utilities cannot afford to be without some form of coverage due to the outstanding liability should system demands overwhelm available capacity. The question remains whether or not these programs are really cost-effective and whether or not DLC could be replaced by other initiatives.

Important in this assessment is the self-enrollment criterion. Consumers must opt into these programs. Consequently, switches must be added and removed at the will of the consumer. In addition, tenancy changes require costly premises visits. This makes one wonder if alternatives could be just as effective.

During times of extreme conditions, many public utilities have sought voluntary restrictions of service. Water companies have solicited voluntarily reductions in consumption and have placed statutory restrictions on end-use. Similarly, gas and electric companies often rely on consumer support during natural disasters. During the recent blackout in the Northeast, customers were asked to restrict appliance use to balance load, allowing utilities a chance to restore utility services.

Anecdotal evidence suggests a willingness of consumers to alter consumption patterns on behalf of communal needs. With advances in metering technology, individual premises can now be monitored for compliance with both voluntary and statutory restrictions. As such, economic incentives and civil penalties could be designed to replace DLC and other peak-shaving initiatives.

Utilizing free and effective media outreach, households could be instructed on behaviors that serve the community. In return, households could benefit from retroactive behavioral credits. For households where one or more adults remain at home throughout the day, voluntary response could shave system demand without programmatic costs associated with load cycling programs. Yet desired behavior will be rewarded with improved service affordability. In the deregulated marketplace, technological advances lower advanced metering costs and add to utility metering capabilities. Thus program managers must keep an open mind to available options.

NOTES

[1] Oppenheim, J., and T. MacGregor. 2001. The Economics of Low-Income Electric Efficiency Investment. *Democracy and Regulation* (Nov. 19).

[2] Note that other benefits were included in this study. See the citation above at p. 4 in the table of benefits for low-income efficiency.

[3] RESNET Lender's Corner. 2004. (Feb. 8). *http://www.natresnet.org/lenders/default.htm.*

[4] Patullo, C. 1993. Making Low Income Housing Affordable: The Northgate Retrofits. *Home Energy Magazine Online* (Mar./Apr.). *http://hem.dis.anl.gov/eehem/93/ 930308.html #93030818.*

[5] Ibid.

[6] Meier, A. 1993. Fuel Switching and Source Energy. *Home Energy Magazine* Online (Mar./Apr.). *http://hem.dis.anl.gov/eehem/93/930308.html#93030818.*

7

COMMUNITY DEVELOPMENT INITIATIVES

STATEMENT OF OPPORTUNITY

The public utility has long been a good corporate citizen, often helping local nonprofits with event sponsorship and foundation grants. Among the favorite charitable causes of the public utility are education, affordable housing, home energy assistance, and the arts. Other favorite causes include economic development organizations, small business development, energy efficiency, and employee participation in local empowerment projects.

All corporations have a vested interest in the local economies within which they operate. As such, large employers invest resources to ensure an employable workforce is available to support long-term strategic growth. The same applies for the public utility that relies on local talent to provide utility service. Yet, this is not the entire story for the public utility.

Unlike other corporations, the public utility has a vested interest in each and every other business. Each new business within the utility service territory is another customer with long-term revenue potential. Additionally, each new business provides jobs, attracting new residents to the territory or providing opportunities for existing residents. This economic stimulus builds utility revenues while simultaneously improving the quality of those revenues. The dual quality of revenue growth and revenue quality enhancement improves the overall health and economic well-being of the surrounding community, adding to shareholder value.

Despite this vested interest, utilities cannot invest in just any popular cause. Instead the utility must consider the size and long-term potential of all investments for existing shareholders. For many low-income initiatives, the necessary quantitative methods have not been developed to adequately translate societal improvements into utility revenue estimates. Yet, utility ratepayers and shareholders do benefit as communal ills are nurtured back to health.

Instead surrogates to revenues are often used to qualify the impact on utility revenues. One such factor is the number of utility customers by segment. Because utilities must monitor home energy use for billing and demand forecasting, revenue contributions from active accounts are easily identified. This provides a convenient measure to estimate the impact of various initiatives. Similarly, the number of active customers is a valuable surrogate for the direct calculation of revenue impacts. Household income is yet another.

The relationship between household income and consumerism is represented by demand curves. For discretionary goods, as income rises, more items of a given price will be bought. Conversely, when income falls or the price of the item increases, the number of items purchased will lower. This relationship shows an inherent elasticity based on price and income. For the energy industry, energy consumption has been considered inelastic, suggesting changes in income and energy prices do not affect demand. The rationale behind this inelasticity is that a minimum amount of home energy is required to maintain an acceptable level of comfort.

Yet, utilities are recognizing the existence of some inherent elasticity in the use of home energy. During electricity shortages in California, a number of electric customers felt a responsibility to do their part to reduce energy demand.[1] As a result, consumers took actions to reduce electricity demand.

A number of studies have documented higher home energy use among households with higher incomes. The reason for this is that higher income families often have larger homes with a greater number of appliances. Yet, even similar-sized households demonstrate increased energy use as incomes rise. Research finds higher income families tend to have higher energy requirements than do their lower income counterparts.

Utilities willing to track a modicum of data will be able to identify shareholder impacts from varied communal improvements. In the following pages, programs that focus on the health, safety, and economic development of communities are highlighted for your consideration. In many cases, these programs are not limited to the low-income. However, community development programs designed to assist and attract new business often provide the requisite opportunities for those unemployed and disadvantaged.

Utilities wishing to expand customer base, increase cash flows, improve regulatory relations, or simply wanting to spur economic growth will inevitably find strategic initiatives intertwined with low-income issues. As such, any community program will have a substantial political component.

Only through the integration of low-income programs with economic development activities will the utility shareholder realize the desired return on his investment.

Key Concepts

Given the charitable nature of many community development initiatives coupled with unquantifiable returns, utility support of these initiatives has not been questioned. This lack of critical debate means few key concepts have evolved. However, several concepts are presented for your consideration. The key concepts reveal the business rationale for community development efforts and affirm continued support by utility shareholders.

Protecting the service territory

One fundamental factor in the valuation of a public utility is the quality of its service territory. When economic times are good, consumer optimism will drive production levels higher, stimulate job growth, and attract new businesses to the area. The result is an increased customer base that drives utility revenues. In addition, improved economic conditions also strengthen the quality of utility revenue.

"During recessive economies, lowered productivity levels, stunted job growth, and business closings have the opposite effect. Operating margins are reduced, and revenue growth is slowed. As a result, shareholder value is challenged."

Business entities and individuals can explore opportunities for added income and leverage resources to access capital. Under these conditions, regular monthly expenses are more easily met. For the utility, improved circumstances can translate to improved payment behavior and reduced collection activity.

The combination of increased utility revenues and lowered expenses will generate shareholder value through enhanced share price and cash dividends. However, all economic trends must eventually cycle out of favor. During recessive economies, lowered productivity levels, stunted job growth, and business closings have the opposite effect. Operating margins are reduced, and revenue growth is slowed. As a result, shareholder value is challenged.

The perpetual nature of this cycle places a great burden on senior management. During economic upturns, senior management will focus on expanding the service territory and adding new customers. During economic downturns, senior management must focus on protecting the service territory. This is true of any corporate entity.

Under difficult circumstances, businesses of marginal profitability may require the support of their energy provider. Lower rates may be available to sustain employment levels and prevent business closures. In addition, payment terms may be negotiated, in effect extending favorable credit terms to struggling operations at times of great need. These concessions during economic downturns can weigh heavily on shareholder value. Yet, without these concessions, business closures and workforce reductions could lead to even more devastating impacts. In the final analysis, utilities must fight to keep existing customers during times of economic recession and to add customers during economic booms.

Regional economic condition

Macroeconomic cycles impacting the entire service territory can be forecasted, allowing business leaders to minimize shareholder impacts through collaborative efforts. However, microeconomies are less predictable. Even under the most favorable economic conditions, utility service territories have pockets of recessive microeconomies. Inverse relationships between competitive industries perpetuate a dichotomy of regional economic condition.

The introduction of competitive forces further threatens the incumbent utility's customer base. As such, senior management must protect microeconomic as well as macroeconomic cycles. Mark Dempsey, President of AEP-West Virginia, commented on these challenges during an interview in July 2003. West Virginia is a state whose population has declined 39.7% during the past 50 years (1950–2000), and it has only recently stabilized (1990–2000).[2] Consequently, Mr. Dempsey faced challenges unfamiliar to his peers who enjoyed robust economic growth over a similar period. Naturally, the protection of the utility service territory was paramount to maintain shareholder value.

During our discussion, Mr. Dempsey shared a few strategies used to secure shareholder value. His first strategy was aimed at competitive pressures. With deregulation pending in West Virginia and active in other states, AEP sought the status of least-cost energy provider. In those states where competition has been allowed, utilities with the lowest rates have retained a dominant market share.

The second strategy was to promote economic development activity within existing properties. By doing so, AEP avoids the cost of line extensions, recognizes revenues from once-abandoned buildings, and targets job creation in areas having the greatest need. One cannot argue this strategy.

His third strategy was to investigate various rate structures and payment arrangements to provide options within the utility. By offering choices within the utility, consumers need not seek service options through a competing enterprise. This focus on consumer desires will undoubtedly serve shareholder and ratepayer interests.

While Mr. Dempsey highlighted other initiatives, the discussion resonated with a clear focus. His aim was to protect the service territory through a variety of integrated efforts and place the organization in the best possible position to compete should the West Virginia Legislature pass laws allowing statewide utility deregulation.

Corporate responsibility

Every successful business participates in the community, either directly or indirectly. At a minimum, corporate income and property tax fund local initiatives. As such, businesses with profitable operations contribute funds used for societal enhancements. Where products and services are offered by businesses directly to the consumer, community involvement is a key success factor. This symbiotic relationship between provider and consumer is a source of communal harmony. No business can sustain itself without the community.

"Every business and every individual must rely on the public utility to deliver essential services. For this reason, public utilities do indeed have a responsibility to those communities in which they operate."

Likewise, no community exists without supporting businesses. In fact, a society without this codependence is incomprehensible.

As mentioned earlier, the public utility is more vested in community development than almost all other businesses. Every business and every individual must rely on the public utility to deliver essential services. For this reason, public utilities do indeed have a responsibility to those communities in which they operate. For a public utility to argue that all programs providing a societal benefit remain outside their purview is indefensible. In taking this stance, a utility must believe that its operations will remain profitable regardless of the economic condition across its service territory.

Why then do utilities insist on regulatory tariffs that provide relief from rising fuel cost? The answer is simple. Without these regulatory protections, the public utility would have to assume a great deal of added risk. In the face of deregulation, even ratepayer-funded initiatives have a risk component that must be considered. Where competitive interactions exist between energy providers, proven investments in energy efficiency can be stranded when customers choose a new energy provider.

Advocates of low-income initiatives often view shareholder investments as low-risk because the underlying cash flows generated by the utility minimize the probability of a business failure. However, risk has two dimensions: probability and magnitude. The enormous capital investments required for the distribution of energy means the utility has a significant risk component.

The electric crisis in California is a recent reminder that utilities can and will go bankrupt. In the past two decades, many seemingly healthy operations found their way into bankruptcy. Without government loans, community support, and legal protections, the short-term viability of these bankrupt utilities was threatened.

In the final analysis, the public utility only prospers in a healthy economic community. Because of this, utilities must participate and support the regions in which they operate. If initiatives can improve the overall health of the utility service territory, then the utility must do so!

Constructive intervention in regional economies is in the share-holder's best interest. Low-income initiatives must not be discarded by the utility without the appropriate due diligence. By the same token, corporations must expect some long-term benefit from their investments, even investments in charitable causes and ratepayer-funded initiatives. At times, community development activities require a value judgment rather than a simple cost-benefit analysis.

In those cases, the investment must not represent a substantive expense. Utility executives understand this well and still support many community development initiatives that create jobs, enhance earning potential, provide affordable housing, or simply promote related services. Who would argue the long-term shareholder value resulting from these investments? As long as the expenses are kept at reasonable levels, ratepayer and regulatory concern will not arise. However, low-income and ratepayer advocates have not been sympathetic to shareholder concerns in this area. Therefore, regulators have not rewarded shareholders for corporate responsibility.

Responsive thinking

Utilities will support a number of internal and external initiatives to assist members of the community. With each manager having a discretionary budget, the sponsorship may not be well coordinated. While this decentralization is necessary to avoid bureaucratic bottlenecks, larger initiatives require greater coordination to ensure a positive outcome. In fact, most utilities have management controls in place to coordinate charitable giving and direct economic development activities. However, few utilities develop low-income programs, assess economic development options, evaluate charitable contributions, and fund governmental lobbies in relation with one another. Instead, departments act independently to secure shareholder value amidst regulatory mandate. While beneficial outcomes for the utility are often synthesized from these activities, one must wonder if this practice is good enough!

A recent survey of program managers found initiatives were largely driven by regulatory mandate or settlement. One must wonder why the utility did not initiate these programs. Was the program not in the utility's better interest? Would the program adversely impact ratepayers? If so, then why would regulators support the initiative? Inevitably, programs mandated by the regulator must have demonstrative value to ratepayer and societal interests. Responding to inquiries, evaluating proposals, and reacting to regulatory initiatives have long been passive endeavors. If the utilities take a more proactive stance, could the cost of regulatory activity be reduced? Could a more palatable and timely resolve be found to address low-income issues? Could utilities better support economic growth within their service territory? Of course, the answer is a resounding *yes.*

By monitoring regional socioeconomic conditions in conjunction with individual behavioral patterns, utilities are better able to target community development initiatives. At the end of this chapter, we discuss the value of responsive thinking and recommend utilities adopt the practice of *collaborative strategic planning.* Several progressive utilities have demonstrated the value of this approach.

Exportation of American jobs

As of the 2000 census, 280 million individuals live in our country. Of the total population, 209 million are between the ages of 18 and 65. That means nearly three-quarters of the population are of working age. Yet, only 64% of Americans participate in the labor force, leaving 70 million at home. Add to this number the 8.3 million unemployed and the 1.7 million disenfranchised, and we have 80 million individuals without jobs.

While many of these individuals choose not to work or are simply unable to work because of age or circumstance, we know from the Bureau of Labor Statistics that at least 10 million have sought but could find no work. The real question is, why do individuals choose not to work? Is it because of their family values or because the appropriate opportunities are not available?

Matching jobs to the available population could result in an unexpected resource pool. If telecommuting was a viable option or flexible hours allowed them ample time to fulfill family obligations, stay-at-home parents might choose to reenter the workforce. What proportion of our 30 million disabled would opt to work in roles that fit their disability? How many of the 38 million individuals living in poverty would refuse viable careers within their community? How many individuals respond to unsolicited Internet ads seeking work-from-home options, only to be further discouraged by distasteful predatory action?

Open borders conflict with the exportation of jobs to low-wage countries. In the past, manufacturing and industrial jobs provided long-term economic security for those seeking the American ideal. When the dream was elusive, subsequent generations learned that a strong work ethic would provide increased opportunity.

Individuals working in retail, hospitality, and agriculture industries have only limited opportunity without a formal education or the chance accumulation of wealth. These employment cul-de-sacs offer no viable progressions in responsibility. Without visible and tangible prospects, a notion of entitlement soon replaces opportunity in their vision of the American dream. Subsequent generations witness continued despair in the face of workforce enslavement. Only the roll of two individual die can determine their fate.

America has just two choices. We can either create revenue opportunities for all or we can subsidize the existence of nonworking Americans. With advancements in technology and the economic diversity within our country, no individual should be without an endeavor worthy of some financial compensation. Yet, 80 million individuals have opted out of our economy. Imagine the impact on our economy if just a fraction of these individual returned to the workforce.

SURVEY OF
EXISTING PROGRAMS

Within the context of poverty and public utility, a number of programs have been tried and continue today. We have looked at household subsidies, payment stabilization efforts, and market transformation programs within the utility industry. In the following pages, we focus our attention on the development of local economies as well as public health and safety. While deregulated utilities appear unwilling agents of social policy, community development initiatives emerge as utilities exercise a vested interest in the local economy.

Community councils

One cannot underestimate the value of listening to those in the community. Convening community leaders to discuss critical social pressures revitalizes an ancient tradition of elder councils. While age is not a prerequisite for participation, community councils are comprised of influential business leaders, respected advocates, and sympathetic politicians. This pool of diversity reflects the social ills for diagnosis and healing. Coupled with consumer panels and private research, council members serve as generals leading a valiant militia to expel poverty from the contiguous territories.

The Economic Development Council of Avista Corporation calls upon cross-functional leadership to promote regional growth. Utilities working with economic development groups retain, recruit, and expand employment opportunities by supporting regional industries. Yet job stimulus is only a partial solution. New jobs must also be accessible to those in need. To accommodate this need, the Beacon Council of Miami-Dade encourages business development in poverty-stricken locations through economic incentives.

Realizing the latent potential of vacant properties, Illinois Power carries property listings on its Web site. The Available Property Program found at *www.illinoispower.com/ed* lists industrial properties located within the utility service territory. But without an available workforce solution, such revitalization efforts are futile. To promote renewed and continued prosperity, the Broward Alliance Education Workforce Development Committee supports local businesses. They do this by cataloguing desired skills, designing compliance curricula, and orchestrating educational support.

Important in these efforts is the recognition that special populations often have special needs. The Low Income Forum on Energy is administered by the New York State Public Service Commission (NYSPSC) and New York State Energy Research and Development Association (NYSERDA). It draws the attention of participants from community groups, government agencies, and energy companies toward the resolve of low-income need. Similarly, the Aging Consortium Counsel of Duquesne Light identifies, develops, and delivers services for seniors in need.

Representing one of the most comprehensive councils active today is the South Ward Neighborhood Partnership. Public Service Electric and Gas (PSE&G) works with 123 organizations to enhance economic development, environmental quality, and public education. They also aid affordable housing and other quality-of-life issues for residents and businesses in targeted communities. Participants include law enforcement agencies, secondary schools, faith-based institutions, local residents. and others. PSE&G's holistic model of community development illustrates the feasibility of collaborative strategic planning to direct communal resolve.

Community trusts

A natural evolution from community involvement is the formation of trusts and charitable foundations. A number of utilities allocate shareholder funds to support individuals and community action. The Newark Asset Building Coalition supports individuals and families seeking self-sufficiency through member local businesses, community groups, government agencies, and faith-based organizations. Likewise, DTE Energy Foundation, PacifiCorp Foundation, and Keyspan's Economic Development fund support a broad base of initiatives to strengthen communities.

Low-cost financing and infrastructure grants are the most common foundation efforts. In addition, operational grants may be used to publicize government resources, stimulate job training, or fund continued education. The focus of today's community trusts centers around civic betterment, performing arts, cultural activities, public health, human services, and education.

Tax credits are given to Florida corporations participating in the Corporate Tax Credit Scholarship Program. With this program, companies can receive up to $50 million in tax credits by creating scholarships for low-income students attending school. Through the scholarship program, low-income students are able to choose private schools that would otherwise be unaffordable.

Companies like Florida Power & Light benefit from the tax credits, but more importantly, they provide individuals a chance to move from poverty to prosperity. When an individual succeeds in this endeavor, society and the public utility reclaim their investments as the student moves from a subsidized existence to become an active member in the local economy.

Lobbying efforts

The value of a professional lobby is often underestimated. Given the societal impact of poverty and the regulatory nature of the utility industry, professional lobbies are necessary. They help to inform politicians, regulators, and the general public of pending issues and funding requests. Given the complex nature of the industry, the ability of lobbies to establish a position from one perspective in relation to that of another perspective can be instrumental in a negotiated resolve. Similarly, lobbying efforts can resonate with the public, allowing politicians a base for legislative support.

Legislative staff receive frequent updates ensuring assistance programs are given due consideration on the House and Senate floor. On the other side, Energy Arkansas' Grass Roots Initiative provides information to low-income advocates and participating providers. With supporting lobbies representing both the low-income and the utilities, lawmakers hear informed opinions from many sides of a single issue. The information provided via these lobbies balances individual bias, providing a base for an equitable resolve to emerge.

Impact assessments are critical for effective policy change. The Colorado Energy Assistance Foundation (CEAF) and the American Association of Blacks in Energy (AABE) participate in Xcel Energy's Low-income Energy Forum. The forum highlights the impact of energy costs on those struggling near poverty. If your state is considering utility deregulation or simply would like a greater allocation of federal funds, a professional lobby could be beneficial.

The lobby can balance shareholder need with low-income advocacy and overcome many legislative barriers, setting in motion regulatory and legislative bodies via public sentiment.

Moratoriums and utility restrictions

Many states in the Northeast forbid utility disconnections during the winter months. Southwestern states may forbid utility terminations during the summer. However, the goal to protect consumers during periods of extreme temperature remains the same.

Utility reconnection and access are also regulated by the state. Where extreme seasons are common, the use of credit scoring and deposit requirements may be disallowed or greatly limited. For example, Louisiana Gas and Electric offers a one-month waiver on utility payment to individuals of demonstrated need. In Philadelphia, the use of utility deposits may not prohibit access to electric and gas service.

Moratoriums on utility disconnections and other restrictions on the public utility require alternatives. The Pennsylvania Public Service Commission has authorized a suite of programs designed to offset the impact of utility operational restrictions. These programs include CARES, CAPs, and the Low-Income Usage Reduction Programs (LIURP). Together they seek to mitigate the impact of poverty on utility operations, while protecting individuals in need. Even so, the commission actively considers available options that balance low-income need with utility requirements.

Affordable housing foundations

Foundations focused on the low-income need not seek funds from public sources or utilities. In fact, many organizations are funded through private donations, either by individuals or corporations. Private foundations often focus on infrastructure development, such as equipment, land, housing, and other tangible property. Foundations that assist in the purchase of property can have positive impacts on surrounding residents. Revitalization efforts provide immediate, mid-range, and long-term impacts. Short-term construction jobs provide immediate opportunities. Retail positions open as the property nears completion, and jobs emerge as residents or businesses inhabit available property. As such, both the public and private sectors heavily favor property development.

The St. Louis Equity Fund develops affordable housing projects throughout the city, while CenterPoint Energy Minnegasco develops energy-efficient housing alternatives for low-income families. Other organizations include Habitat for Humanity, the Greater Metropolitan Housing Corporation, Project for Pride in Living, and the Minnesota Department of Commerce. These are just a few of the partners for the development of energy efficient low-income housing.

Collaborative efforts

To effectively address low-income issues, a collaborative approach is required. Like the rest of society, those living near poverty face competing demands for financial resources. For low-income persons, even basic necessities can drain financial reserves. For this reason, both long-term and short-term assistance are often needed to move those in poverty to prosperity.

The Urban League provides a number of services via community outreach centers. Low-income families receive food, furniture, clothes, appliances, heaters, fans, as well as other items to meet everyday circumstances. Yet, during extreme weather conditions, low-income families are at even greater risk. In recognition of this, Ameren shares information and coordinates assistance for low-income families via Operation Weather Survival.

With public and private resources stretched by the overwhelming need of those living in poverty, organizations seek to allocate resources to as many families as possible. Community organizations may use databases to avoid duplications in service. Ameren supports one such database, ROSIE. Likewise, Conectiv works with social and government agencies to coordinate low-income services in Maryland, Delaware, New Jersey, and Virginia. It provides call center training through its Community Outreach program.

Utility support of community-based organizations is often needed to orchestrate system-wide benefits. While low-income providers are well informed of local and national issues, multistate concerns and specific utility priorities may elude these organizations. With utility support and training, an established low-income provider network will be better positioned to distribute support, achieving corporate and regional development objectives.

Case management programs

Utilities recognize the complex and varied circumstances leading to payment trouble. For this reason, a number of utilities throughout the country now have social workers on staff or have contracted similar services from community-based organizations. DTE Energy has a case management group handling payment negotiation, referral services, and follow-ups to low-income families.

During times of crisis, DTE Energy refers families to Michigan's State Emergency Relief (SER). The Family Independence Agency administers the SER, providing cash assistance to individuals and families whose health and safety are threatened. Rent and mortgage payments may be subsidized to avoid homelessness and forestall foreclosures. State Emergency Relief also includes home repair and utility bill assistance. For victims of fire or family death, funding is provided to assist with appliance replacement, refurnishing, or burials. Yet even with notable programs in place, the Family Independence Agency continues to collaborate with regional utilities to extend government services.

By referring customers to state and local agencies, consumers may receive assistance for other household items, freeing resources for utility bill payment. El Paso Electric has the Gate Keeper Program. Working with a number of state and county agencies, customers with special needs receive care via social service agencies.

Recognizing the value of referral programs, state regulators have authorized cost-recovery for utility case management programs. New Jersey Comfort Partners provides arrearage forgiveness and payment negotiation, allowing customers to remain current on their utility bills. Duquesne Light offers budget counseling to the low-income population through the Consumer Credit Counseling, a nonprofit debt management advisory service. Also included are referral services, home weatherization, and utility bill assistance.

Avista Utilities offers a program that illustrates this concept. Their CARES program has trained representatives to recognize need and provide for the following: budget counseling, payment negotiation, home weatherization, and social service referrals. "CARES representatives make every attempt to reach a solution that is beneficial to both the customer and the company. Through this interaction, CARES representatives can better help Avista Utilities to be aware of future customer needs."[4]

This recognition of customer need and the value of a cooperative resolve led to increased participation in case management programs by utilities across the nation. With growing support for case management initiatives, many utilities now seek to integrate low-income services to construct a more comprehensive resolve. Once reactive to customer need, utilities are now anticipating emerging need and coordinating support for a number of special services.

To make consumers aware of these programs, a convenient reference is necessary along with public awareness campaigns. Baltimore Gas & Electric has compiled a list of assistance programs throughout its service territory. The publication is known simply as *The Purple Book* and is available online at *www.bge.com/CDA/Files/ 20032004_pb_eng.pdf* or upon request from Baltimore Gas & Electric. Nevada Power has a similar publication, known as *Helping Hands for Adults,* which makes it easy for individuals in need to find support within their community.

Examples of proactive community involvement can be seen across the nation. For example, Empire District Electric has the Gatekeeper Program. The program identifies elderly members experiencing a decline in independent function. By coordinating assistance with the Area Agency on Aging, Empire District Electric ensures the aged receive requisite care.

Other examples of proactive intervention are exemplified in many programs, including ComEd Helps Activated Military Personnel (CHAMP). ComEd works in conjunction with the U.S. Department of Defense and the Employee Support for the Guard and Reserve (ESGR). They provide payment plans, budgeting, and cash grants to families of activated military personnel. ComEd recognizes the potential earnings loss associated with military deployment and attempts to resolve payment difficulties before the actual accumulation of arrears.

Green Mountain Power assists with back rent and security deposits where the need arises via the Emergency Assistance Housing Program. The Manatee County Economic Development Council has a "Trailing Spouse Program." This program helps find employment for the spouses of those who have relocated to the area.

Keyspan Energy employs social workers, called consumer advocates, to assist consumers with home energy. They provide information and referral services as well as more in-depth individualized services. Through their Customer Assistance Programs, social services agencies provide social workers to help customers one day per week during the heating season at local customer offices.

PPL has the Double Notice Program. Shutoff and late-payment notices can be forwarded to friends, family, clergy, or other community agencies assisting a customer. PPL also serves the visually and audibly impaired via Braille Bills and TDD services.

Perhaps the most innovative and exemplary service provided is Illinois Power's program, A Hand Up, Inc. Illinois Power created A Hand Up to assist individuals in financial distress. Individuals can perform community services to pay rent, utilities, or other bills. By matching skills and job openings in a number of charitable organizations, individuals can establish an employment history while paying down utility debt, past due rent, and other bills. The service offered by A Hand Up promotes personal responsibility through allowing individuals to earn credits through work and/or schooling.

Empowerment programs

Rising beyond poverty to prosperity requires new skills for many individuals living near poverty or outside the workforce. We often relate needed skills with job training, literacy, and education. Yet basic life skills are lacking, such as stress management, strategic decision making, communication, and financial planning.

A number of utilities recognize this and offer assistance in a broad range of initiatives. Many programs are targeted at individuals. However, a number of programs assist providers. To begin, let us first look at programs addressing individual need. It takes only one inspired moment to significantly alter behavior. Because these moments are different for every individual, increased exposure to fresh perspectives, sincere faces, and powerful voices enhance the likelihood of positive change. One such source is a utility's Speakers Bureau.

Many utilities have speakers to address relevant community issues. Generally, the speakers are utility employees and recent retirees looking to give back to the community. You may find these speakers giving presentations at schools, churches, public events, or private workshops. Favorite topics include career choice, energy safety, personal responsibility, and education, just to name a few. While inspiration and perspiration remain the agents of change, the economically disadvantaged may need more direct assistance.

The creation of individual development accounts by Green Mountain Power and Entergy provide very real returns for positive change. These utilities match individual contributions to savings accounts by low-income families. With a 1:1 match, even very low-income families find ways to reduce expenses and direct some monies toward their future. With an immediate return on their deposits, families are able to build assets to fund home ownership, housing repairs, and education. These simple deposit accounts can return the so-called unbanked to the financial mainstream.

Minnesota Power helps customers to understand their utility bill and provides advice on energy efficiency and the resulting bill reduction. Through the Salvation Army's Money Management Program and

First Time Home Buyers Club, low-income customers can better address the financial pressures that have long haunted them.

One basis for resolving chronic financial distress is to return these individuals to the workforce. Illinois Power created A Hand Up, Inc. to do just that. As we highlighted in the previous section, A Hand Up, Inc. provides jobs with local nonprofits. However, an equally valuable component is the compensation individuals receive for attending classes and earning credits toward their GED. The concept of earning while schooling is innovative, allowing individuals to address everyday expenses while enhancing their long-term earnings potential.

Southern California Edison also has an innovative community development initiative. Southern California Edison has a 10-week program to prepare the unemployed, underemployed, and welfare recipients for entry-level jobs within the company. The strategy of helping yourself while helping others is fundamental to defining an everyone-wins scenario. By moving the disadvantaged into the workforce, Southern California Edison also benefits from a highly motivated employee who will use energy wisely and make timely utility bill payments. Remedial training addresses basic math, conversational English, and computer use. Recipients also benefit from advanced training that includes self-esteem and confidence building, budgeting, time management, resume writing, goal setting, and interview techniques.

Job training is also available through federal and state initiatives. With the modernization of welfare via TANF, moving individuals from subsidized living to workforce participation is a national priority. Project Self Sufficiency of Larimer County, Colorado, assists low-income, single parents to build and maintain strong, healthy families. It also helps them achieve economic independence and become free from community and government assistance. Through career planning, program referrals, and counseling, program alumni are able to find work, housing, and transportation. By participating in the workforce, program participants also become eligible for earned income credit that effectively adds to household income.

While individual assistance is needed, local providers also find support from the public utility. CenterPoint Energy, in conjunction with the University of Houston, developed a one-day conference preparing nonprofits for success. The program, known as Power Tools for Nonprofits, addresses risk management, program marketing, professional development, fund raising, as well as other skills needed for successful administration of a nonprofit organization.

Assistance also comes in the form of cash grants. First Energy provides foundation grants for community development initiatives. Empire District Electric has the School/Business Partnership with the Joplin Chamber of Commerce to provide resources and funding for local schools. Illinois Power's Bright Ideas supports nonprofit groups assisting low-income individuals with professional clothing, transportation services, school supplies, etc. Illinois Power also offers small grants to teachers helping students with special needs, such as school supplies and clothing. Also common are grants for continuing education.

PSE&G organizes a number of empowerment initiatives and volunteer efforts. The most notable is the Books in a Bag Drive that collects new books for children in Head Start programs. Similarly, the Make a Difference Day Book Drive encourages reading among the youth. PSE&G also organizes the Tools for School drive, collecting supplies for needy children. Baltimore Gas and Electric participates in the Bentalou Elementary Mentoring Program, assisting third and fourth graders with reading.

Empowerment programs target personal development as a tool for self-sufficiency. Critical to workplace participation is literacy. A number of utilities sponsor adult literacy programs. Lunch Buddies is one such program. Volunteers read books to low-income families over their lunch hour. By stimulating interest and providing one-on-one help, both children and adults can learn to read. Puget Sound Energy goes a step further, offering in-house translation services where English is a second language.

Perhaps overlooked in many programs is the application of literacy in consumer awareness. Individuals are exposed to ads with fine print, promotional literature, and other messages designed to encourage spending. In addition, consumers must verify credit card statements, review monthly bills, and balance their checkbook. In recognition of this, Baltimore Gas and Electric supports the Carroll County Financial Literacy program. The program helps individuals create household budgets, establish personal savings accounts, manage debt, and define strategies to reduce household expense.

Workforce development initiatives

While empowerment programs prepare individuals for the workforce, no amount of training will suffice when opportunities are limited. With utility shareholder performance linked to regional economic conditions, workforce development initiatives benefit both the low-income community and the utility.

Attracting and retaining large employers is supported by most utilities. Houston Electric participates in economic development initiatives, helping communities address key corporate issues such as site selection, networking, marketing, strategic planning, and mapping. CenterPoint Energy partners with the Bay Area Houston Economic Alliance, Baytown Economic Development Corporation, and Brazoria Economic Development. Thus CenterPoint Energy is in a position to coordinate electric and gas service for economic development projects.

To attract industrial and large commercial accounts to their service territory, utilities may offer rate incentives. ConEdison has business development rates available to organizations that sustain or create jobs, occupy vacant properties, or expand operations into target areas. The New York City Energy Cost Savings Program provides further rate incentives for businesses and nonprofits locating within the city.

Conectiv has economic development riders and negotiated contract rates allowing eligible new or existing large commercial and industrial customers to access discounted rates pending commission approval. The presence of these tariffs helps Conectiv address competitive concerns, fuel switching, facility relocation or expansion, production shifting, and the potential for physical bypass. Because these issues also impact communities, state and local governments provide assistance to companies poised for job expansion. The Redevelopment Authority of Allegheny County does just that. Allegheny County also provides free assistance to emergent small business entities via the Small Business Development Center.

Often targeted for economic stimulus are low-income communities. The South Florida Community Development Coalition initiates activities designed to revitalize low-income neighborhoods. In fact, their Web site is a good source of information regarding community development and local legislation. This Web site is *www.floridacdc.org/mainpage.htm.*

Areas of concentrated poverty often emerge as jobs are relocated outside urban centers to surrounding neighborhoods. Without the requisite mobility to fill these jobs, inner city occupants are left stranded. The Brookings Institute published a report on urban land reform in October 2002. The authors found that "across the largest 100 U.S. metropolitan areas, only 22 percent of people...work within three miles of the central city."[6]

NSTAR economic development rates are available to customers who increase employment in targeted areas. The Urban Development Initiative works with state governments in redeveloping five older industrial areas.

These incentives can yield substantial energy savings for qualifying entities. Progress Energy has a redevelopment rider offering a 50% power discount to companies relocating in North Carolina, South Carolina, or Florida.

In addition to financial support, many utilities can guide emergent businesses through the revitalization of target areas. PSE&G provides a "Community Resource Guide" to interested parties. The guide provides an analytical overview and step-by-step tour through each phase of neighborhood development. Business development groups can be an invaluable resource for the young start-ups on the verge of expansion.

Energy education programs

Virtually all utilities offer some form of energy education. The tools used range from bill inserts to Web-based software, and the interactions range from in-home visits to televised public service announcements. While the topic is relatively simple, the implementation of energy education varies greatly. As such, the references highlighted in the following text are meant to demonstrate current methods rather than highlight select success stories.

In general, energy education is meant to inform customers across all segments on the value of energy efficiency, energy conservation, and the resulting impacts on utility billings. While industrial and commercial accounts receive advice on energy use, our focus will be on methods used in the residential segment.

Mid-American Energy promotes energy efficiency awareness through advertising campaigns known as ENERGY action and Save some Green. Mass media campaigns are often used to promote appliance cycling and rebate programs to the general population, only indirectly supporting low-income initiatives. These ad campaigns can be cost prohibitive for programs with strict income eligibility. However, public service announcements provide a cost-effective alternative for the use of mass media. Public service announcements have been used to support a wide range of community-based initiatives and to extend awareness into remote communities.

While state regulators serve as watchdogs for the consumer, few do more than print brochures and maintain informational Web sites to promote their initiatives. To date, most PUC-sponsored education dealt with utility choice and consumer fraud. However, the Pennsylvania Public Utility Commission (PA PUC) took proactive steps to warn consumers of escalating energy costs. With higher energy costs, the PA PUC anticipated growing affordability issues.

In November 2003, with support from utilities, the PA PUC hosted the "Be Utility Wise Fair." This provided utility education and networking opportunities to health and social service agencies. The fair, meant to educate the educators, was also open to the public and news media free of charge. Participants obtained information on utility access, consumer protections, available services, and emerging trends. In this example, we see a commission that actively supports its regulatory action.

A number of private entities also sponsor fairs supporting local service providers. Utilities, of course, are active at community fairs and public events across the nation. During these events, utilities provide information to the general public, thereby raising public awareness and increasing indirect referrals to available programs. Public events can also be used to support program intake. Baltimore Gas and Electric holds community assistance fairs, providing direct referrals to various assistance programs.

Similarly, retail outlets such as Border's Books and Music will host book signings, sidewalk sales, and community awareness events. Authors may be invited to discuss topics of local interest, such as poverty, energy conservation, aging, health, or public policy. While these events are used to draw traffic and promote in-store sales, participating community service providers can leverage these events to expand outreach and boost program participation.

Less general in scope are the workshops. In this format, a large number of participants can benefit from specific training. Entergy Louisiana invites individuals to participate in energy conservation training at churches and community action agencies via the Winter WRAP program. This program, like other energy conservation workshops, instructs participants on the use of low-cost measures and proven behavioral modifications designed to lower energy consumption.

In Arkansas, Entergy goes even further, organizing volunteers to assist in the weatherization of low-income homes via a program known as SWEEP, or Sharing Weatherization Efforts with Elderly People. These volunteer programs lack the comprehensive measures available in state weatherization assistance programs. Yet, volunteer programs could be of practical value to utilities in cases where fuel source is not a major contributor to the home energy burdens.

In certain communities, scholastic programs may be considered low-income initiatives. PacifiCorp has created a curriculum for middle schools that addresses electric generation, safe energy use, meter reading, and other skills needed for intelligent energy use. Because of the large number of children living near poverty, Pacifi Corp considers the in-school program a long-term investment in the community. They provide future generations with strategies that can be tested at home.

In similar vein, Florida Power and Light provides secondary schools with an "Electrifying Experience." This program demonstrates the science of electricity while promoting a healthy respect for safe energy use. Nevada Power has an educational partnership with the Community Service Agency and Nevada's Fair Housing Commission. They offer a similar learning experience for mature adults at various senior centers and low-income housing complexes.

Within many comprehensive home weatherization programs, individualized training addresses bill payment, energy conservation, and energy efficiency. Ameren distributes the "Clean Slate Weatherization" video to help participants achieve affordable home energy. Entergy Mississippi provides hands-on training at local community-based organizations to demonstrate simple weatherization techniques via the "Powerful Solutions Tour." Rockland Electric Company participates in the Comfort Partners Program that adds personalized customer energy education and budget counseling to its energy efficiency programs.

Mid-America Energy combines community development with energy efficiency in its Trees Please program. Through the program, Mid-America Energy encourages individuals to plant trees. These are beneficial as windbreaks and for shade, while beautifying parks, roadways, and other common areas.

For those highly motivated individuals, online resources are available from nearly every utility in North America. These resources range from basic informational pages to interactive software applications. You can find industry level data, home energy tips, and comprehensive home energy audits at many utility Web sites.

Public health and safety

Utilities often support a number of community-based initiatives targeting disadvantaged populations. Seasonal support for the low-income, elderly, and unemployed can offset

"Programs that help the low-income population with self-esteem may provide the inspiration needed to lift individuals from poverty. Seemingly small gestures can have lasting impacts on the youth."

likely household expenditures. As winter approaches, many homes must attend to natural gas pilot lights. In many areas, shutting down the gas furnace and turning off the pilot light during summer months is still practiced. With increasing frailty, this simple task can become problematic for those aged experiencing vision loss, unsteady hands, or reduced mobility. As a result, pilot lighting programs may be sponsored or run by the local energy provider. While lighting the pilots, a system check is often required to ensure proper functionality. Therefore, many pilot lighting programs embed a system clean and tune.

The Gatekeeper Program at Puget Sound Energy is another program to help the elderly and disabled. Employees of Puget Sound Energy identify and assist at-risk customers who may require the services of a social service agency. While not designed specifically as a low-income initiative, the Gatekeeper Program provides valuable referrals to financially distressed individuals.

In older homes, a number of risk factors may remain. PSE&G supports the Clinton Hill Health Initiative to abate lead poisoning of preschool children. Parents are provided information to identify and remove toxins from the home, while the children are screened for specific toxins and immunizations. In addition, PSE&G also supports the Newark Health Renaissance, a two-year action plan addressing a number of health concerns. Working with hospitals and other health service professionals, the program intervenes to combat diabetes and cardiovascular illnesses through behavioral modification.

One area of particular concern for families living in poverty is hunger and malnutrition. Without proper nourishment, individuals and households are at risk. Meal programs provide seniors, disabled, and low-income children with food and funding. Houston Electric and Houston Gas conduct drives to raise money and goods for existing food banks. Illinois Power supports Meals on Wheels with both donations and volunteers. Buckets for Hunger, Meals on Wheels, and school lunch programs are just of few of the programs supported.

To raise funds for these programs, corporations may use raffles, sporting contests, public events, and regional canned food drives. Participation in community events raises corporate goodwill and helps utilities identify community partners engaged against poverty. NSTAR helps low-income families by facilitating enrollment and renewal of school lunch programs.

Volunteer services

Utilities are a great resource for volunteer programs. With an established employee base throughout the service territory, utilities can often support volunteer programs in even remote locations. This is important, because poverty is not limited to inner-city communities. In fact, the majority of the nation's poor live in remote rural communities.

Programs that help the low-income population with self-esteem may provide the inspiration needed to lift individuals from poverty. Seemingly small gestures can have lasting impacts on the youth. Oprah Winfrey talks of one Christmas morning in her youth that served as a catalyst to her success. Her family lacked the resources to provide gifts to their child, so Oprah prepared herself for the worst. What would she tell her classmates when each of them showed up with new clothing, and she arrived with nothing new? At age 10, she considered herself to blame. Luckily, she never had to address this fear.

A small group of Catholic nuns knocked on her door and presented her family with gifts for the holidays. Overwhelmed by this, her outlook spanned the gap between the stark poverty of that moment and the boundless hope in knowing that someone was looking out for her well-being. With a renewed spirit, Oprah Winfrey overcame poverty and inspires others to prosperity.

MinneGasco partners with a variety of social service agencies to purchase gifts for low-income families throughout the holiday season. Illinois Power operates two programs throughout the winter season. A Time for Sharing and Operation Warm Winter coordinate an annual effort to present food baskets, coats, and gifts to individuals and families nominated by their employees. While we tend to think of children through the holidays, seniors are particularly vulnerable, especially if they live alone without family support. Empire District Electric has a partnership with the Area Agency on Aging. Their Christmas Elf Program provides gifts to seniors who may no longer have nearby family or friends.

Throughout the remaining months, utilities do not forget the value of community involvement. Houston Electric and Houston Gas provide volunteers to HomeSavers and the Houston Urban League to assist low-income and senior citizens with home repair. Progress Energy participates in a Day of Caring, allowing employees to help with low-income home improvements and to collect food for local food pantries. Entergy's Call-a-Thon provides volunteers to raise funds for Project Care, a home energy assistance program.

This is just a small sampling of volunteer programs supported by the utilities. Nevertheless, we recognize the respect utilities have for the community and the support they are willing to provide.

TAKING ACTION

Utilities are supportive of community development initiatives. With little opposition from ratepayer and low-income advocates, few critical issues have emerged. Because of this, you may believe little opportunity exists for improvement. In fact, this is not the case. Broad support for utility-sponsored initiatives is evident. However, we hope to point out that more can be done to secure long-term enhancements to the utility service territory, enhance shareholder value, and document resulting impacts.

Collaborative strategic planning

The first logical place to start is to develop a corporate strategy for community development. Recognizing that utility revenues are closely tied to the local economies served, we can readily deduce that what is good for the community is also good for the utility. Utilities thrive in broad economic booms, where businesses flourish, population surges, unemployment is minimized, and expansion seems inevitable.

Yet, even in the best economies there are pockets of economic repression. All too often, these areas remain the same for decades. Areas of concentrated poverty may resist economic growth for decades. In these communities, you find families and individuals stranded, without significant opportunity for improvement. By the time the government recognizes the decline, the neighborhood is in a broad state of disrepair. Areas of poverty dispersed across rural America suffer a similar fate.

The cycle is predictable and stubborn. It starts when a large employer cycles out of favor or is acquired by a competitor. The company is then forced to lower employment levels and transfer jobs out of the surrounding areas. Those able to move do so and find other opportunities. In contrast, those unable to move often regress under worsening conditions. Within a short decade, a low-income community becomes entrenched and disenfranchised. When this happens, efforts to stimulate the local economy may displace low-income individuals from their homes. As such, lobbies form to protect the areas. Unfortunately, this is a trap.

Without economic stimulus, the community passes its plight to yet another generation. Therefore, the only viable solution is to provide jobs to those in the community and to ensure housing options exist for those displaced. Not only does this cost money, the politics involved often delay development projects for years. Because of this, a long-term view must be taken for areas already established and impoverished. We must ask, can the cycle be avoided?

Fortunately, some warning signs exist. Through collaborative strategic planning, utilities and community action agencies can work together to address emergent trends. When signs of regressive economies emerge, a coordinated action can save the community. Often state and federal incentives will be necessary. However, the utility also has a role to play.

Utilities have the advantage of owning data associated with energy use and payment behavior. Using this data, economic trends can be foreshadowed, allowing utilities to intervene proactively. By inviting emerging businesses to target areas, the resulting jobs can stabilize or reverse regressive economies before individuals are significantly impacted. Local agencies can play a significant role through job training, budget counseling, household subsidies, and targeted economic stimulus.

Through a customized *segmentation matrix,* utilities can detect these recessive communities and coordinate the actions of both internal and external resources. As we learned as children, an ounce of prevention is worth a pound of cure. With limited resources to address communal ills, utilities and government agencies must constantly prioritize efforts. Collaborative strategic planning involving many stakeholders is but the first step in preventive community care.

Community-based outsourcing

We are accustomed to the juxtaposition between socialism and capitalism. While the theoretical motives underlying each do suggest a clear distinction, the concept of regulating corporate activity already merges these concepts. Health care, banking, insurance, transportation, energy, and utilities are just a few industries that already operate within such an environment.

Using the public utility as an example, for-profit entities provide basic communal needs: energy, telephony, and water. Each is essential for the economic health of the community and safety of the individual. For this reason, utilities have been regulated since their inception with the goal of providing reasonable rate of return for utility shareholders in exchange for safe, reliable, and affordable utility access.

It is often assumed that each utility shareholder, each utility employee, each government regulator, and each utility customer understands this delicate balance between shareholder return and public service. However, such an understanding does not exist. The inherent diversity of utility industry participants ensures some disagreements will arise as to the exact purpose of the public utility.

I recently asked a room full of 150 or more people whether or not the existing low-income population could be profitably served by a utility serving only this single community. Not one person felt it possible. After I explained the premise of *community-based outsourcing,* a few converts began to appreciate the possibility. And even if it were not possible to profitably serve only the low-income population, many felt opportunities did exist to better serve the low-income customer.

To illustrate this possibility, state weatherization programs can serve as a model. Instead of contracting private for-profit entities to install weatherization measures, a group of community-based organizations were involved. They could do the same task with greater efficiency and at lower costs. Similarly, specialized call centers can more effectively address low-income needs, again at greater efficiencies and at lower costs. Extending this concept across the entire utility company, we can envision a for-profit energy marketer serving low-income customers through a closely monitored and tightly administered collaboration of nonprofit community action agencies. The resulting community-based outsourcing model lowers operational costs while providing jobs to those areas in need. As a result, utilities can provide more affordable service at even greater profit margins.

Can the low-income population be served profitably by such an organization? Only time will say for certain! Would existing utilities consider giving away their low-income customers? If not, then there must be some inherent profitability in serving this population. By outsourcing functions to low-income communities across the service territory, utilities can lower operational costs. At the same time they can provide an economic stimulus within their service territories. As such, community-based outsourcing could provide the most effective outsourcing option available to the public utility.

Evaluating the impact of community development initiatives

One reason that community development initiatives have not demonstrated quantifiable benefits to participating utilities is that the industry has not agreed on the appropriate measures to track. Current metrics focus on participant outcomes and broad governmental statistics. Few have taken the time to translate these impacts into a language of fiscal managers.

"Until community development initiatives are translated into utility revenue and operational expenditures, community development initiatives will be treated as charitable gifts and costs-of-doing business. Therefore, even sympathetic executives cannot invest substantially in the community."

Communal prosperity is thought to translate to utility revenues. However, few programs convert jobs, public health, or personal income into utility revenues. While any proposed algorithm will be criticized, the need for this metric is clear. It is as valuable to the utility executive as the CPI and census are for the Senate and House appropriation committees.

Until community development initiatives are translated into utility revenue and operational expenditures, community development initiatives will be treated as charitable gifts and costs-of-doing business. Therefore, even sympathetic executives cannot invest substantially in the community. Corporate governance demands a return on all expenditures.

If utilities are to do more, convincing evidence must demonstrate shareholder impacts. With a global investment market, we are not at liberty to assume an improved standard of living for our country's poor is of any value or interest to a foreign shareholder. Therefore, specialists who evaluate community development initiatives must create and adopt standards of practice. These must demonstrate program impacts on the utility shareholder while having a positive impact on the program participants.

A return for corporate responsibility

Regulators can authorize a return on a range of utility expenditures. The question often boils down to whether or not these expenditures have a direct shareholder benefit. Assets associated with the distribution of utility service and the management of those assets provide a return for the shareholder. Conversely, charitable contributions often do not. If the results of community development initiatives were quantifiable, a reasonable case could be made for the inclusion of these expenditures in the rate base. If regulators wish to encourage corporate responsibility, the ratepayers and community action groups must recognize that utilities deserve some compensation for their efforts.

Following deregulation, a new component of risk entered the equation. Customers receiving services could take those assets to a competing entity. As such, even ratepayer-funded market transformation initiatives now have an embedded risk. Take for example a weatherized home funded through a utility-sponsored initiative. The newly weatherized home was an investment by ratepayers who expect some distant return. However, should this household change utility energy providers, then the investment is now offering returns to a different set of ratepayers. Is this fair for the utility ratepayer who invested in the property? Certainly some compensation is required for the utility ratepayer and shareholder who funded the original project. As such, a return may be required to entice utility shareholders to act responsibly given the existing regulatory framework.

Returning jobs to those in need

Competitive pressures also force corporations to lower production and operational costs. Outsourcing is one such strategy. With advances in technology, even service jobs can be effectively transferred to distant lands. The benefits of job transfer can be substantial: lower wage requirements, relaxed environmental regulation, and eased labor relations. All these reduce corporate costs, ultimately improving the short-term shareholder returns. Yet the danger of this outsourcing often lingers below the waterline. Each job transfer outside our border entails some risk.

Financially, production cost savings may be diluted by increased distribution costs, higher insurance premiums, and complex management controls. However, even greater risks exist for long-term investors. These include political climate, currency destabilization, import/export restrictions, and changes in commodity prices that can adversely impact the shareholder return.

Additional risks linger here at home. Transferring valuable trade secrets, intellectual property, and critical operations outside an organization can devalue company stock by raising competitive pressures. Overseas outsourcing can even halt corporate mergers. Where a firm has most of its operations overseas, suitors interested in an American corporation may even shy away from the deal.

More relevant to our concern is the resulting decrease in employment levels and reduced market for unskilled labor. There are 40 million individuals at or near poverty and another 10 million looking for employment opportunities. Extra-border outsourcing will increase the number of individuals requiring subsidized living. Even more detrimental is the lack of opportunities for those with limited educations, poor work histories, or gaps in employment. Without significant opportunity, these individuals are excluded from our workforce, drawing upon already limited resources.

While job training seeks to change this condition, not everyone can gain new skills or even desires them. Having labored for a lifetime, a middle-aged plant employee may not be satisfied working behind a desk or even remotely interested in grazing on data bits amidst a vast cubical farm. Transforming our job market to fit the American white-collar model excludes a host of immigrants labors greeted by the Statue of Liberty as they pass into Manhattan. Essential for the American dream is opportunity. Each service transferred oversees reduces the opportunity for those invited to our land. Even worse, it isolates those unemployed and further alienates those already disenfranchised.

The solution is not job training. Rather, it is job creation. Proponents of global solutions highlight the impact that lower-cost goods had on our economy by pointing to the stock rally. Proponents of a self-governing market cite rising average personal incomes despite fewer jobs. Looking at the jobs data as half-empty, could we not say that lower wage jobs were simply cut from our economy? It would be interesting to study whether or not those who were laid off or retrained found higher paying jobs.

So what can be done? Perhaps, utilities could set an example for all corporations by evaluating outsourcing options in areas of demonstrated need. Why not target energy efficiency projects in rural America where job loss, payment troubles, and home energy intensities are substantially higher than in other areas? Similarly, could we hire inner-city youth to read meters in and around their neighborhood? Could utilities encourage celebrities to move their fashion empires to inner-city warehouses, providing jobs to those living in the surrounding poverty?

Shifting production jobs and outsourcing options to motivated individuals within the utility service territory protects corporate concern and bolsters local economies. This provides the stimulus for utility revenue growth.

The Purple Book

If nothing else is done, the low-income provider network must be documented. Creating something like *The Purple Book* for each utility service territory and providing referrals can help. It could help social service agencies with the difficult task of community outreach and program intake. A minimal investment to promote, support, and raise funds for our community providers is a basic tenant in the provision of affordable and profitable utility service to those in need.

NOTES

1 Hungerford, D., et al. 2002. Conservation Understanding and Behavior among Low-Income. Electric Education Trust Consumer Education Project. *http://www.energy.ca.gov/papers/2002-08-18_aceee_presentations/PANEL-08_HUNGERFORD.PDF.*

2 State of West Virginia. 2002. A Look at West Virginia's Population by Decade, 1950–2000. HSC Statistical Brief No. 8 (May).

3 Based on an informal survey conducted by KMDR Research, Inc. of utility program managers in January 2004.

4 CARES Program. 2004. (March). *http://www.avistautilities.com/products/assistance/cares.asp.*

5 Project Self Sufficiency Mission Statement. *http://www.ps-s.org.*

6 Brophy, P. C., and J. S. Vey. 2002. Seizing City Assets: Ten Steps to Urban Land Reform. The Brookings Institute (October).

SECTION III

~

DEVELOPING YOUR
LOW-INCOME INITIATIVES

8

ASSESSING YOUR SITUATION

OVERVIEW

The final section of the book will help you put into practice those ideas uncovered in previous sections. No prescription exists to cure the economic plight suffered by the low-income population. However, a number of preventative measures can be implemented to immunize your organization from the secondary impacts of poverty. Before preventative measures can be taken, a complete and thorough diagnosis is required.

In this chapter, we will review the fundamentals of situational analysis relating to utility service affordability. The analysis begins with an understanding that a corporation is a living entity. The corporation has stages that include infancy, adolescence, a very long maturity, and in some cases, even death.

Recognizing this life cycle, you can better appreciate that corporations require the attention, nurturing, and commitment of trained professionals. Even then, these entities will periodically require specialists to diagnose and treat conditions that threaten an organization's fiscal well-being. Because of this, the medical analogy introduced is appropriate here.

To become a family physician, you first study the anatomy and the biological processes of the healthy human. Once your understanding is sufficient, you are able to recognize abnormalities. These abnormalities are carefully noted and categorized into a library of known illnesses and conditions. When an individual's physical well-being is threatened, treatments are sought to normalize the biological processes.

Unfortunately, physicians do not exist to treat corporate fiscal abnormalities. When the fiscal well-being of your organization is challenged, an all-too-familiar sequence often results. First, middle management will attempt to resolve local manifestations of systemic problems. When that fails, senior management will put in place management controls to stop the bleeding. Committees are developed to implement operational controls that serve as tourniquets. While this may stabilize the situation, the underlying abnormalities are left largely untreated.

Having treated only the symptoms, systemic problems grow to unmanageable levels, often necessitating the amputation of noncore assets and existing staff. Although survival rates from these interventions are good, corporations rarely reclaim the revenues lost from years of stunted growth.

If physicians existed for the corporation, regular fiscal exams would be required, latent illnesses would be cataloged, and known cures would be documented. Beneficial calisthenics would be designed to prevent future ills. It is true that generally accepted accounting practices establish standard measurements of fiscal well-being. Comparative financial ratios help identify abnormalities. However, little has been done to catalog these abnormalities, and even less has been done to package treatments. Because of this, program and corporate managers are left to treat their own children. With powerful financial and emotional ties to their organization, objective assessment and critical thinking are understandably absent.

In the following pages, the fundamentals of situational analysis will be applied to the public utility. While you will not become a trained corporate physician after reading this section, you will be able to act as a responsible parent. You will be better equipped to recognize abnormalities in your organization and then can seek expert assistance under appropriate situations. Luckily, corporate specialists are available for house calls!

Understanding the Fundamentals

To diagnose problems that may exist within your organization, you must first define *normal* within the context of your industry. To accomplish this, one must look at statistics of similar companies. One inexpensive source of data may be surprising: the Internal Revenue Service (IRS).

The U.S. IRS classifies returns by industry. For example, you can download composite filings for all major SIC codes. To illustrate the value of this data, you should download the composite utility filings for the years 1998–2000. These can be accessed at *www.irs.gov/ pub/irs-soi/98co05nr.xls, www.irs.gov/pub/ irs-soi/99co05nr.xls, and www.irs.gov/pub/irs-soi/00co05nr.xls.*

Since critical components of financial statements are included in corporate tax returns, you can compare the fiscal fundamentals of your organization with those of the broader industry. To simulate the recommended process, we downloaded data for Pacific Gas & Electric (PG&E) from our online broker looking at the years 1998 through 2002.

This comparison lacks the appropriate subtleties necessary to fully appreciate your corporate fiscal well-being. Nevertheless, these averages demonstrate the overall health of the industry and relative strengths of your company. Anyone wishing to promote changes within an organization must be conversant within this realm. Even a cursory familiarity with industry averages can be helpful to program managers and consumer advocates who must build business cases to support recommended initiatives.

Within the financial statements lies the knowledge base of corporate officers, with the embedded financial ratios serving as their language. Because of this, we will cover some key financial ratios used in business valuations. First, you should download the composite balance sheets and income statements from the links provided earlier. Next, you should obtain a copy of recent financial statements or recreate them from recent annual reports. Lastly, you will need to have a spreadsheet application within reach or at least a calculator. And yes, a cup of your favorite stimulant would not be wasted. While the resulting financial ratios are insightful, the calculation of these ratios can be laborious when starting from scratch.

THE FUNDAMENTAL FOUR

The most basic financial ratios compare income to expense. Differences between the two when expressed as a percent are referred to as *common size ratios.* Since we are trying to get a feel for the overall corporate picture, we will look at several common size ratios that we can refer to as the fundamental four. These are: *gross margin, operating margin, profit margin,* and the *flow ratio.*

Plotting the fundamental four across multiple years will reveal a great deal about the industry, your company, and the overall health of your service territory. In the following pages, we will do exactly that. Individual components of the gross margin will identify fundamental changes in the marketplace. Operating margins highlight the efficiency of service provisioning, while profit margins reveal management efficiency. These profitability ratios are taken from the income statement and relate to the operation of the company. The flow ratio uses information from the balance sheet to gauge the ability of the industry and the organization to generate cash, an important consideration for any investor.

Together the fundamental four reveal the overall health of the organization from the ratepayer and shareholder perspective. If these ratios are better than the overall industry and show improvements over time, you can be fairly certain your organization is in good fiscal health. Even more importantly, the fundamental four provide guidance to operational and low-income program managers.

Once you appreciate the fundamental four, you may wish to create ratios relevant to your particular department. For example, contractor expense as a percent of your total annual budget may be useful when considering staffing requirements. In fact, there are an infinite number of ratios that could be used. Utility executives and industry analysts routinely track 30 or more such ratios. For most employees, tracking the fundamental four plus a handful of ratios relevant to your operational area is sufficient to engage the interest of senior management, regulatory staff, and interveners.

The gross margin

Returning to the fundamental four, let us first consider the gross margin. The gross margin compares top-line revenue to the direct costs required to realize the revenue stream. A meaningful analogy to the gross margin is your take-home pay. This is effectively your salary minus any payroll deductions. Ideally, you would prefer to take home 100% of your salary. However, that is not the case. You have tax withholding and other voluntary/statutory contributions that reduce your effective take home pay by 20%–40%.

While this analogy is not perfect, as any accountant will be quick to point out, it will serve those without any financial management training. As such, we build upon this analogy to exemplify our other ratios.

The gross margin ratio is calculated as follows for each of our sources:

$$\text{IRS: Gross Margin} = \frac{\text{Busines Receipts} - \text{Cost of Goods Sold}}{\text{Business Receipts}}$$

$$\text{PG\&E: Gross Margin} = \frac{\text{Operating Revenues} - \text{Cost of Electricity \& Gas}}{\text{Operating Revenues}}$$

For the gas and electric industries, a key factor in this ratio is the cost of fuel. To meet consumer demand for energy, the utility must transport or consume resources in direct proportion to the demand. The gross margin captures this relationship (see Fig. 8–1).

From 1998 through 2002, PG&E realized a steady growth in revenue. Revenues grew gradually, approximately 4% annually, over the five-year period. This level of revenue growth meets our

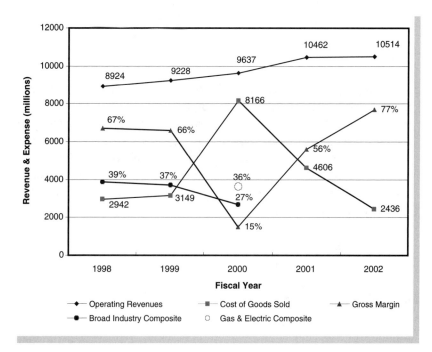

Fig. 8–1 Gross Margin Components for PG&E

expectations, mimicking stable economic growth from increases in the general population. If you do not accept this as normal, you could plot population statistics, gross domestic product (GDP), or broad industry averages over the same period. By doing so, you get a good idea of acceptable growth.

At your company, you may find growth either exceeds or trails our example. Consider why this might be so. If your organization has twice the annualized revenue growth of the industry, you need to ask why. There are three primary areas to consider: market share, market growth, and acquired revenue streams.

Most public utilities operate within a mature market. As such, market share growth does not vary much. However, should you work for a utility marketer entering a new service territory, revenue growth may double or even triple within the first few years as new customers are added. Yet for an established utility, a sustained annual growth in revenue of 8% would be significant. This would be suggestive of an economic boom across the service territory or the addition of a new revenue source. Barring these explanations, rate increases may have taken effect or a speculative surge in consumer optimism has occurred. However, increases in consumer spending rarely support broad advances over extended periods.

If revenues are stagnant or declining, you have reason to become concerned. Declining revenues suggest competitive pressures, consumer pessimism, or a deterioration of the utility service territory. For example, when a large employer relocates, the employer takes not only its contribution to revenues but also a large number of residents. Such deterioration has a ripple effect that touches other ratepayers. With fewer customers across the system, the cost of providing utility service will rise.

For low-income providers, the cost of utility service must be monitored. As consumer costs rise, low-income customers endure greater energy burdens. Utility service affordability is diminished, payments are slowed, arrearage levels escalate, and bad debts expand beyond regulatory recovery mechanisms.

The end consumer is not the only stakeholder impacted by revenue growth. Revenue growth is a desirable event for shareholders. If revenue growth outpaces the broader market, public corporations benefit from improved valuations, because investors seek high-growth companies. Conversely, corporations with declining revenues are aggressively dumped by the same investors. As such, executive management will take actions to promote sustainable long-term revenue growth.

You should also expect a proportional growth in the direct costs related to those revenues. Expected relationships are observed in 1998 and 1999, but a significant change occurred in 2000. The cost of goods sold rose to $8 billion, representing a 250% year-over-year growth.

The gross margin reflects this rise in costs, dropping from 66% to just 15%. Even a small change in gross margin can have a dramatic effect on profitability. Because of this, public utility commissions often provide mechanisms for fuel cost recovery. However, dramatic changes like those observed in 2000 will overburden the consumer, causing all recovery mechanisms to fail. As such, increased costs of goods sold must be absorbed by the utility, at least in the near-term.

With assistance from the state of California, PG&E has demonstrated gross margin improvements following the year 2000 event, albeit without the desired stability. For PG&E shareholders, gross margin improvements are necessary to reestablish profitability and regain losses from short-term changes in the marketplace.

We have a pretty good idea that something extraordinary occurred at PG&E in 2000. However, we have yet to determine if that event was localized or whether it affected the whole industry. Identifying systemic problems may be used to leverage governmental support and protect against litigation.

To determine this, we must examine the broad utility composite. First, we notice that PG&E has a much better gross margin than does the overall industry. However, upon first glance, the proportions seem inverted. The broad utility composite has a gross margin of 38%, while

PG&E recently enjoyed a margin of 66%. As such, we should check our calculations to ensure the numerator and the denominator were not mistakenly interchanged. As it turns out, the chart data is correct.

The source of this difference may be explained by the fact that PG&E is a combination gas and electric utility. We must consider the possibility that combination utilities may be fundamentally different than other public utilities. Downloading data from the IRS, we found 44 combination gas and electric utilities filed returns in 2000. The composite gross margin for combination utilities was just 36%, similar to the broad utility average. The resulting implication is that combination utilities are similar to the other 8,000 public utilities.

With the little information provided by the gross margin, we are able to conclude that PG&E operates in a substantially different market. As such, regional data may be needed to evaluate PG&E. However, comparing PG&E to other combination utilities in California would raise another set of issues. Therefore, for our purposes, we will continue to use the composite filings of all utilities as our representation of the industry.

Our second observation reveals a lower gross margin for the utility composite during the 2000 fiscal year, down 10% from the previous year. The coincidental dip suggests a broad market event took place in 2000. While no answers are given by the gross margin, a number of pertinent questions arise:

- What portion of the broad decline was a direct result of the events at PG&E?
- What events triggered the increased cost of goods sold?
- Were the events isolated, or do they represent a fundamental market change?
- What impacts will these events have on the industry?
- What impacts will these events have on utility operations?
- What impact will these events have across the service territory?

It is not our objective to answer these questions. Rather, we simply wish to illustrate that even a single ratio can provide valuable insight to the fiscal health of your organization and of the industry as a whole.

As such, the gross margin provides a foundation upon which to build. Improvements in the gross margin suggest that beneficial changes in economic conditions have occurred across the utility service territory. Depending on your functional area within the utility, you may or may not be able to contribute to these improvements. There are some prescriptive measures to boost gross margins. These include hedging against increased power/fuel costs, effective marketing campaigns, increased product awareness, and socio-economic development activities.

The net operating margin

Another fundamental ratio commonly used to evaluate operational efficiency is the net operating margin. This number is equivalent to the amount of cash your family is able to save after paying all household expenses. Consider two families that have identical household incomes. If one family is able to build a comfortable nest egg while the other runs up additional debt, we can say the family of savers manages expenses better than the family of spenders.

Similarly, corporations with larger operating margins manage their expenses better than corporations with smaller margins. Investors and city politicians like to see a surplus in income over expense. Thus a public utility that generates a net positive operating margin is more desirable than another utility that continues to operate at a loss. This is true for most utilities. However, a new utility being set up in an undeveloped area or underdeveloped country may operate at a loss for many years and still remain an attractive investment.

To calculate the net operating margin, subtract cash expenditures from the operational revenues. The resulting number is commonly referred to as Earnings before Interest, Taxes, Depreciation and Amortization (EBITDA). Dividing EBITDA by sales over the same period of time yields the net operating margin. You should note that companies may run deficits, thereby resulting in operating losses. The following equation is used to calculate the net operating margin:

$$\text{IRS: Operating Margin} = \frac{\text{Net Income} + \text{Depreciation} + \text{Interest Paid} + \text{Taxes Paid}}{\text{Business Receipts}}$$

$$\text{PG\&E: Operating Margin} = \frac{\text{Operating Income} + \text{Depreciation}}{\text{Operating Revenues}}$$

Returning to the financial statements used earlier, let us calculate and plot the components of net operating margin for both PG&E and the composite utility average.

From Figure 8–2, a few observations can be made. First, the net operating margin follows the same trend as the gross margin. Second, the gross margin impacts of 2000 were magnified in the operating margin. Third, the difference between the industry composite and PG&E's performance has narrowed.

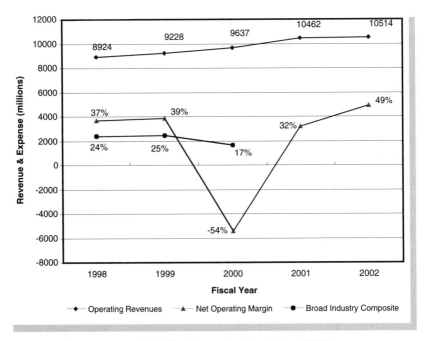

Fig. 8–2 Components of the Net Operating Margin for PG&E

Naturally, since both the gross margin and the operating margin are profitability ratios, we expect both to move in similar directions. The net operating margin is simply operating cash expenditures represented as a percent of revenue. Therefore, the cost of goods sold is a major component of this ratio. Consequently, the operating margin does indeed move with the gross margin.

However, one must be careful when interpreting this number. Often events that are not reccurring are cleverly hidden within accounting adjustments. Because of this, the financial notes attached to the income statement and the balance sheets are invaluable when interpreting these margins. If you walked through the calculations presented in the charts above, you would have seen an unusual item on the income statement of PG&E: "deferred electric procurement costs." Without this deferral, PG&E's net operating margin would look much worse. With the deferred costs, PG&E had an operating margin of –54%, compared to a margin of –121% without the deferral.

Consider what this really indicates. For every $1 million in revenues, PG&E has cash expenditures of $1.54 million and $2.21 million, with and without deferred costs, respectively. Given PG&E had annual revenues approaching $10 billion, the cash expenditures are quite significant. Respectively, the expenditures would be $15.4 billion and $22.1 billion. Our ratios suggest the deferral would be approximately $6.7 billion. In fact, the "deferred electric procurement costs" totaled $6.5 billion, just as the net operating margin suggests.

The following disclaimer was found in the year 2000 financial statements along with a declaration that PG&E filed for protection under California's Chapter 11 bankruptcy code:

> EBITDA is defined as income before provision for income taxes, interest expense, interest income, deferred electric procurement costs, depreciation and amortization, provision for loss on generation-related assets and under-collected purchased power costs. EBITDA is not intended to represent cash flows from operations and should not be considered as an alternative to net income as an indicator of the PG&E Corporation's operating performance or to cash flows as a measure of liquidity. Refer to the Statement of Cash Flows for the U.S. GAAP basis cash flows. PG&E

Corporation believes that EBITDA is a standard measure commonly reported and widely used by analysts, investors, and other interested parties. However, EBITDA as presented herein may not be comparable to similarly titled measures reported by other companies.

Given that our analysis is to identify abnormalities in the normal operations of the utility, we prefer to see this type of representation, where unusual expenses and adjustments are appropriately handled. Simply reading numbers from a chart may not provide the insight necessary to assess operational efficiencies. Yet, the financial statements remain the best place to start.

The third observation deals with the operating margins of PG&E versus the industry. The difference between the two has narrowed from the gross margins observed prior to the year 2000. A narrowing at this level suggests the normal operating costs may be higher in PG&E's service territory than across the nation. PG&E serves Northern California, where the cost of living is considerably above national averages. Thus one should expect that salaries, property values, and rights-of-way would raise operating costs above national averages. So again, we find the reported numbers reasonable.

More important than the actual net operating margin is the trend. Operating margins that show steady improvement suggest management interest in operational efficiencies. The program manager should realize that any strong proposal will be considered by senior management. When the operating margins are worsening, senior management will look for operational improvements. However, program managers may find reluctance to even the best ideas. This is because senior management must get a hold on the situation first. Board members, investors, analysts, and regulators will begin to insist on change.

Because of this, cost reductions will be the first order of business. While this is unfortunate, the short-term improvements are almost universally sought. As such, long-term improvements must wait. Appropriate actions for the program manager would be to seek both short-term and long-term alternatives. Prepare your proposals in advance of any request and wait. When requested, present your short-term ideas first then lay the groundwork to present your long-term scenarios at a later date.

Scheduling time to present your long-term initiatives in the following quarter should be sufficient. After one or two quarters of improved margins, senior management will begin to invest in long-term operational improvements. If your previous recommendations addressed near-term financial pressures, your long-term proposal will be given added weight. This is true especially where you are able to gain broad stakeholder support during the interim period.

The profit margin

The third of our fundamental four is the profit margin. Unlike the net operating margin, this ratio includes cash and noncash items. Financing options, investment strategies, and leveraging decisions accumulate into this ratio. As such, the profit margin is a key measure of management performance.

While an analogy with personal finance is not obvious, one does exist. Earlier we made an analogy for the net operating margin. We said the operating margin was the amount of cash a family is able to save over a given year. However, that is not the whole story. The IRS requires that employers withhold and deposit an estimate of personal tax liabilities. Rarely is this estimate correct. Most individuals deposit a surplus that is returned the following year as a tax refund. Instead, individuals may choose to use the money in the interim. These individuals would deposit less money than their actual tax liability. On April 15 of the following year, these individuals would submit the outstanding balance to the IRS.

To ensure enough cash is available to meet this liability, an individual may deposit a portion of his or her salary into a pretty pink piggy bank. However, if the tax liability is substantial, the individual may opt to replace the piggy bank with an investment of the appropriate maturity. The interest earned on this note would provide an additional income stream, thereby raising personal earnings. Income generated without the material participation of a taxpayer is classified as *passive income.* The profit margin recognizes beneficial tax decisions and interest income, while our other ratios do not. In short, the profit margin would be different when the piggy bank is used in place of an appropriately maturing investment vehicle.

The profit margin is the total revenues minus all expenses, as represented in the following equations.

$$\text{IRS: Profit Margin} = \frac{\text{Net Income}}{\text{Total Receipts}}$$

$$\text{PG\&E: Profit Margin} = \frac{\text{Net Income}}{\text{Operating Revenues}}$$

Like the other margins, we plot the profit margin across the five-year period beginning in 1998 and ending in 2002. The results are presented in Figure 8–3.

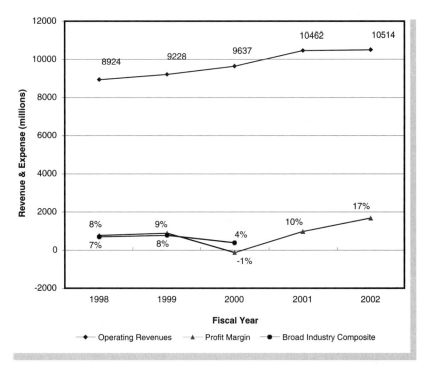

Fig. 8–3 Components of the Profit Margin for PG&E

Here we can see the significance of non-cash items on the bottom-line. In the previous charts, we observed significant differences between the results achieved by PG&E versus the overall industry. The implication was that PG&E operates in an environment significantly different than the rest of the industry. This chart confirms this assumption.

The profits realized by PG&E are proportional to those realized by the broader market despite significant differences between the net operating margins. Thus we must look for sources beyond the operational structure.

Interest, taxes, depreciation, and amortization recognized by PG&E in relation to annual revenues were greater than that recognized by the industry. When considering variances in the profit margin, the treatment of capital assets must be reviewed. Capital assets are taxed, frequently financed, and necessarily amortized/depreciated in accordance with standard accounting practices. As such, the magnitude and management of capital assets have measurable effects on profitability. While only senior management has direct responsibility for the profit margin, employees monitoring the bottom-line may be able to anticipate emerging corporate concerns.

Decreasing profit margins can trigger a sell-off of company stock and a tightening of credit lines. Senior management will be tasked with an abrupt turnaround or face mandatory retirement. Yes, even the presidents and CEOs of organizations can be removed from office. Because of this, management will initiate efforts to improve the bottom-line. A number of activities may result. These include bond offerings to restructure debt, sale of capital assets to lower tax liability, slowing of vendor payments, and a number of other management controls.

Although these controls go largely unnoticed by the average employee, nevertheless, management controls have very real financial impacts and operational considerations. Slowing of vendor payments may improve the short-term profits at the cost of operational efficiencies.

For example, a vendor that has been paid 30 days after invoicing will be concerned when payments are slowed to 60 days. Because of this, the vendor will contact the project manager for clarification. The project manager contacts the accounting staff. They will pull relevant files only to find the check has been written. The vendor will sift through the mail only to find the check missing. Miffed by this, vendor concern will eventually reach the CFO, who over time will acknowledge the vendor and clear the payment. The accounting staff notifies the project manager who, in turn, notifies the vendor. By now, the vendor has issued another invoice and the cycle resumes.

With a number of vendors taking similar action, project managers must expend resources and time handling these calls. Since payment terms are often contractually written, the CFO rarely acknowledges that payments have been intentionally slowed to improve the bottom-line. Because of this, the cycle continues to burn valuable corporate resources until some equilibrium is eventually established. Other management controls can have similar operational impacts. Delays in paying employee reimbursable expenses and travel restrictions result in growing frustrations that diminish operational efficiencies.

Effective operational managers monitoring the profit margin can anticipate these actions and manage vendor/employee expectations such that departmental inefficiencies are avoided. In addition, the program manager can appreciate the fiscal focus and develop long-term initiatives that could be introduced under more favorable circumstances.

After a period of improved profitability, management will welcome proposals resulting in long-term revenue growth and operational efficiencies. Understanding recent concern over profit margin, the program manager should avoid projects requiring capitalized investments. Even when long-term value can be demonstrated, short-term considerations will drive management approval. As such, you will need to address the near-term consequences of any and all recommendations.

The flow ratio

The last of our fundamental four is the flow ratio. The flow ratio encapsulates the credit relationships within the product lifecycle. Companies having advantageous credit relationships will have ratios approaching 0, while disadvantageous credit relationships will drive the flow ratio above 2. In general, a flow ratio below 1 is very good, while a ratio between 1 and 1.5 is solid. Before considering this ratio in more detail, let us first take a look at its calculation.

$$\text{IRS: Flow Ratio} = \frac{\text{Notes/Accounts Receivable} + \text{Inventories}}{\text{Accounts Payable} + \text{Other Current Liabilities}}$$

$$\text{PG\&E: Flow Ratio} = \frac{\text{Accounts Receivable} + \text{Inventories}}{\text{Current Portions of Bonds and LT Debt} + \text{Accounts Payable} + \text{Other}}$$

You will note that inventories and accounts receivables are on top, while accounts payables and other short-term obligations are on the bottom of the equation. Consequently, one might assume that sales are bad and paying vendors late is OK. However, this is not what this ratio suggests.

Notice that cash sales are not addressed in this equation. As such, the flow ratio only addresses credit sales. Credit sales are a valid means to increase revenues, but only if the credit sales are paid on a timely basis. Unlike a fine wine that appreciates with age, accounts receivable become worth less and less over time. As such, accounts receivable are simply another depreciating asset like the family car.

Once all avenues to collect the outstanding receivables have failed, a utility will simply write off the bad debt as an expense. Receivables with a very high probability for nonpayment can be moved from the balance sheet to the income statement. Under the operating expenses, a line item titled *bad debt* will often appear. Receivables that have been written off appear as an operating expense. This practice is common-place, occurring within all industries.

An allocation for bad debt is often included in the utility revenue requirement. This allocation is known as the *bad debt reserve*. Where uncollectibles do not exhaust this allotment, shareholders can simply pocket the remaining dollars. Where the bad debt reserve is exhausted, shareholders must pay for each dollar uncollected. For this reason, management of accounts receivable is closely monitored.

The flow ratio recognizes the accumulation and aging of accounts receivable as a detriment to profitability. On the other side of the equation, accounts payable are noted as a benefit to profitability. Consider this: the public utility is a stable entity that generates a large amount of cash from sales each and every month. As such, a vendor may be willing to wait longer for payment from the public utility than it would for a new furniture store that recently opened one block away. The utility probably has existed for several decades and has a demonstrated track record for vendor payment. Thus it can negotiate more favorable payment terms than can the furniture store lacking the same credit history.

The flow ratio captures this intangible. Credit worthiness allows the public utility to negotiate longer payment cycles. Instead of payment in 30 days, a utility may be allowed to pay bills over 60 days. As such, the utility has effectively been loaned goods or services for an additional 30 days, interest-free. Because of this, accounts payable reduce interest expense and raise profitability.

> *"The flow ratio recognizes the accumulation and aging of accounts receivable as a detriment to profitability. On the other side of the equation, accounts payable are noted as a benefit to profitability."*

The ratio of accounts receivable to accounts payable is at the heart of the flow ratio. So long as you are meeting your legal obligations, the accumulation of accounts payable is beneficial to the public utility. For example, a utility must purchase raw materials (natural gas, electricity, treated water, etc.) before the utility can distribute that material to the end consumer. If the utility can acquire the raw material under the most favorable terms and sell the same material to the end consumer for cash, the utility could earn profits on the raw material before making even the first payment.

Let us walk through the cycle to illustrate the flow captured by this ratio. A utility must first build a "warehouse" to store the raw materials it intends to sell. Through some long-term debt instrument, a loan or bond issue, the utility will finance the construction. Once the facility is in place, the utility negotiates with companies to buy raw material under a 60-day, penalty-free payment period. The material is brought to the warehouse and stored as inventory.

To earn money, the public utility will market and sell its inventory to households and businesses. The consumer is free to use the product for 30 days and has an additional 15 days to make payment. In short, the utility resells its inventory on a 45-day cycle. If all goes well, the utility has bought, stored, sold, distributed, and collected cash for the raw materials within 60 days of its original purchase. On day 46, the utility could make payment on the raw materials, having earned profits without having paid a dime to the supplier of the raw material. As such, accounts receivable would be zero and the inventory would be small, even approaching zero.

Ideally, the utility would like for this to happen. However, this is not always the case. The utility must store excess raw materials to meet unexpected demand. As such, the utility will always have some inventory on hand. Since energy and treated water are consumables, vendors are not likely to sell on such favorable credit terms. In fact, the utility may be required to pay cash for its raw materials. Consumers often purchase goods from the utility in a timely and regular basis, but occasionally make payment outside the customary 45-day cycle. As such, no free ride exists for the public utility.

The flow ratio captures the less-than-ideal financing of utility operations. As such, this ratio can be a powerful indication of corporate credit-worthiness, operational efficiency, and even long-term profitability. Because of this, the flow ratio represents a good measure of fiscal health and as such is included in our fundamental four. Plotting PG&E's flow ratio over the same period of time as the other ratios, we can make a number of observations (see Fig. 8–4). Remember, increasing flow ratios mean worsening fiscal health.

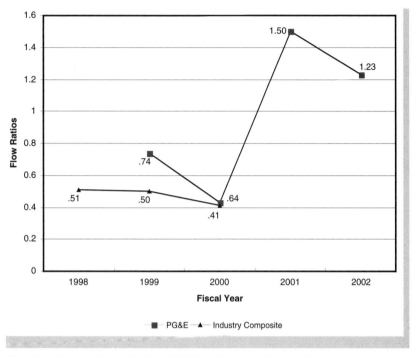

Fig. 8–4 Annual Flow Ratios—PG&E v. Industry Composite

We first observe that the utility industry as a whole has very favorable flow ratios. The utility industry composite moves from 0.51 in 1998 to 0.41 in 2000. Understanding that a flow ratio below one is highly favored, we understand the utility industry to be highly stable with strong demand for its products. Most of us would stipulate this fact without any analysis. That is precisely the value of the flow ratio. The ratio captures the underlying intangibles of a sound business case.

Since PG&E filed for bankruptcy in 2000, we expect any good fiscal measure to catch the destabilization of PG&E's overall operating efficiency. You may find it surprising that the chart above shows improvements in the flow ratio. It improved from 0.74 in 1999 to 0.64 in 2000. However, all numbers presented in financial statements trail the facts and represent events that have already passed. The flow ratio does indeed show growth in liabilities beyond that of credit sales and inventories. In fact, insolvent organizations will have short periods where the flow ratio may indeed be favorable.

However, these organizations will not be able to maintain a favorable indication for extended periods of time.

You would expect the creditworthiness and stability of an organization to decline substantially following a declaration of bankruptcy. In the case of PG&E, the flow ratio does indeed show a marked increase, rising to 1.5 in 2001 and 1.23 in 2002. While these ratios are not bad when taken individually, these values are three times the industry average and two times recent levels. As such, when assessing the current fiscal health of your organization, you must give consideration to industry and individual norms.

UTILIZING THE FUNDAMENTAL FOUR

A doctor cannot diagnose your physical fitness with a single measure. Even in a routine physical, the doctor will look at your body temperature, blood pressure, weight, and blood oxygen levels, as well as your overall medical history. To diagnose the fiscal health of an organization, the same approach is required.

The fundamental four must be monitored over a period of several years; the more history, the better. You must also track industry and regional averages over the same period of time. By doing so, you can identify norms for your organization, your region, and the broader utility industry. All of this must be done to properly diagnose potential health risks.

Again, we see the diagnostic models used within the medical industries are directly analogous to our work. Human physiology is observed, studied, and cataloged, providing us with acceptable ranges for a given measure. We know, for example, that humans have an average body temperature of 98.6°F. So when your newborn has a temperature of 100°F, you begin to worry, especially if other abnormalities begin to appear. Most parents would contact their family physician for advice without much hesitation.

Since a proper diagnosis cannot be made with just one or two measures, the doctor will ask you to bring the child into his or her office. Additional measures are taken to ensure a proper diagnosis. When all the information is returned, the doctor will evaluate these quantitative measurements using acquired knowledge and training. The doctor will consider age, sex, medical history, as well as a number of regional socioeconomic observations. By doing so, the doctor is classifying the child within a known segment of population. Comparing risk factors with potential causes, the doctor is able to make a plausible diagnosis.

Recognizing that the body temperature of an infant can vary greatly, the temperature of the newborn is not necessarily an indication of illness. However, an elevated body temperature could be associated with regional observations of a mild illness among the very young and elderly. As such, the doctor concludes your newborn has a mild virus that will pass in a few days without treatment. With the eventual passing of your child's elevated temperature, the diagnosis has been confirmed.

Similarly, the same process must accompany your efforts to diagnose the fiscal health of the public utility. Typically, the child is analogous to the corporation, the reader is analogous to the parent, and the industry consultant is analogous to the physician. In other cases, multiple roles may be defined for a given individual or organization.

Take for example a program manager. A program manager has direct responsibility for program participants, the department, and the overall organization. As such, the program manager has three children to nurture. Because of this, the program manager must routinely track 12 or more ratios to be adequately informed. Since the program manager is also expected to be a specialist in this area, he or she may also take on the role of a physician. As such, it may require a decade of direct experience for an individual to be successful in this expanded role.

Under some circumstances, the program manager may be monitored by corporate officers, thereby assuming the analogous role of the child.

To properly diagnose the fiscal fitness of your organization or department, you must understand your many roles and act accordingly. You will utilize the fundamental four highlighted in the text. You will track additional ratios relevant to your roles and routinely seek the assistance of others in an effort to ensure corporate fiscal health.

ORGANIZING A TASK FORCE

Even the best parent does not act alone. Family, friends, acquaintances, and specialists are routinely called upon to ensure your child gets the best care possible. Similarly, when assessing the fiscal health of your organization, department, program, or customer segment, valuable assistance will come from coworkers, colleagues, trade allies, and functional specialists.

Situational analysis requires a broad range of experience and expertise. As such, a fundamental tactic includes the identification of available partners and the creation of a working group. In fact, an established well-organized task force is a key success factor in the resolve of any difficult broad-ranging issue.

Task forces are commonplace in a number of arenas: politics, health, military, and economics, etc. Almost any social concern will have a number of nonprofit organizations, community groups, trade allies, and experienced professionals actively organized around the resolve of key issues. Many individuals will be actively involved or looking for opportunities to serve task forces organized around their own specialty.

Such is the case with poverty and its impact on the public utility. Many resources are available to assist utilities tasked with low-income service affordability. The resources illustrated in section II, along with a number of demonstrative programs, are just a few of the many exemplary services available. A review of these programs and discussions with experienced program managers can uncover proven strategies and innovative approaches to mitigate the fiscal impacts of utility service affordability.

So just how does one go about organizing such a task force? Well, the answer is often more easily stated than implemented. The following annotated outline provides the basic steps necessary to get started. However, the success of your task force will largely depend on the commitment of those involved. So utilize the talents of those involved, recognize their efforts, and reward successes.

Clarify your intent

A task force is useless without a cause. A task force must be charged with a specific task, preferably one with a concrete outcome. For example, a task force charged with understanding poverty will be less effective than one charged with the task of providing affordable home energy to all low-income consumers. While both tasks appear insurmountable, the latter task can be objectively measured and has a definitive resolution. As such, the latter resonates with clarity and will attract the requisite participation.

Selecting members for your task force

Individuals will join your task force for varied reasons. Some will join to extend their professional network. Others will join to pursue individual interests. Still others will join to participate in the resolution of a troubling systemic issue. Your goal is to select from these individuals members who will serve the interests of the task force.

Initially, members must be solicited from your existing network. You will have to negotiate the participation and support of key members who will guide the task force through its infancy. Later, you will need to expand the group and solicit participation from organizations and the general public. You will be looking to build a pool of talent to address the many operational considerations before your task force.

Assigning roles to task force members

Simply having the requisite talent on board does little. Each member of the task force must fill a niche within your group. The chairperson must assign each member an active role within the task force. Where an active role cannot be found, it is often best to let that person go rather than risk alienating him from the cause.

Members who lack an active role in the task force may hinder the effectiveness of your task force by involving themselves in areas covered by other members. This redundancy can be distracting and frustrating for those charged with the effort. The last thing a long-standing contributor to the task force needs to hear is the dissenting opinion of a member who is largely uninformed.

Tracking your progress

Once the task force is in place, you must decide several basics. These include how frequently the task force will meet, what methods of communication will be used, and how to report the progress of your task force. Since most groups will have difficulty meeting more frequently than quarterly, members will need a scoreboard to check task force progress. You could use something like those United Way fund-raising thermometers.

While tracking low-income utility service affordability can be elusive, the measure of success should not be. A pie representing the percent of households with active utility accounts could be one such measure. The graphic used to display the score or the units tracked is inconsequential. Members simply need to know whether or not their efforts are having an impact.

AREAS TO CONSIDER

Going back a decade or two, utilities began to see service affordability issues among the very poor. Programs were developed to address these issues, but it then became apparent that more customers than simply the very poor struggle to pay their utility bills. Government programs began to address those living within poverty. More recently, utility and government programs routinely acknowledge persons with incomes at 150% of poverty as being in need. Relevant demographics, consumption practices, and payment practices are monitored, analyzed, and published. Today, we see new issues emerging. We have found utility affordability issues in the general service population.

The working poor who have recently left welfare in favor of work now struggle against dramatically increased financial responsibility. In many cases, those leaving welfare find they are no longer eligible for government programs. These programs once provided health insurance, child care, housing allotments, and utility subsidies. As such, their limited income cannot cover the increases in financial responsibility. These people can be unaccustomed to the daily struggle of a low-wage worker. Thus many eligible individuals do not request tax credits and other assistance designed specifically for them. As such, the working poor struggle needlessly or simply fall out of the labor force back into poverty.

Another area of emerging concern involves those who are highly leveraged with personal debt. Today, the average American has several years' worth of consumer debt from purchases of perishable or depreciating assets. These include such purchases as cars, entertainment, dining, or groceries, etc. As such, they lack cash reserves to meet unexpected fiscal obligations. So when an unexpected car or housing repair is needed, the consumer will often run up additional debt. Living from one paycheck to next, the middle-income wage earner remains at risk. Unexpected job loss, credit tightening, or unavoidable expense can result in hardships that reduce impact utility payment. This consumer can be classified as the *leveraged earner.*

The leveraged earner often holds an overly optimistic view of national, regional, and personal economics. Because of this, debt levels grow ever higher. Without the expected income growth, the leveraged earner will find ordinary increases in household expense troubling. As such, increases in fuel costs or utility rates can force the leveraged earner to seek payment assistance from the public utility.

With the leveraged earner representing a significant group within the residential sector, accounts receivable can grow in both magnitude and age. As noted earlier, a slowing in the payment cycle impacts utility shareholders and ratepayers. Even worse, the overall health of the utility's service territory can be challenged, causing even greater problems for the utility.

Since the leveraged earner is often insolvent, most are *judgment-proof*. Because of this, traditional management controls cannot be used to improve debt collection. Therefore, programs must be developed for the leveraged earner. Yet, beyond the basic budget plan, no programs have emerged to address service affordability for this significant demographic.

The socioeconomic condition of the utility service territory can have impacts on the fiscal health of your organization. With economic downturns, business revenues may decline, slowing or even reversing regional growth. The result can be dramatic. The financial struggle of a single business entity can have significant impacts on the local utility.

Over the past two years, IBM has laid off more than 1,800 employees within northern Vermont. With additional regional layoffs, Vermont has seen more than 4,500 individuals lose their jobs between February 2001 and February 2002. Many of the displaced workers were faced with unemployment and an uncertain economic future. Consumer optimism decreased, regional lending tightened, household incomes declined, and consumer optimism faded. As a result, workers sought employment outside the service territory or faced the challenge of realizing regional opportunities.

An extension of the local economic condition was its impact on local businesses. For small entities, a change in consumer optimism can be damaging or even fatal. According to statistics compiled by the Corporation for Enterprise Development, 10% of Vermont's working parents earned less than 150% of the federal poverty guideline. In addition, 3.7% of the labor force is unemployed and 16.5% of the state's businesses ceased operations in 2002.[1] For the utility, these numbers represent either customers lost in the economic downturn or those who remain to struggle with service affordability. Where unemployment lingers and service affordability remains an issue, the potential for revenue erosion is present for all public utilities and private corporations.

Imagine the financial impact of a yearly decline in revenues of 5%–7%. Simply extrapolate the ratios calculated earlier with top-line revenues decreased and increased accounts receivable. Doing so, you will notice significant worsening of the fundamental four. Since industry analysts calculate and project financial performance using the fundamental four, corporate valuations decline sharply as these ratios worsen. Conversely, actions that return customers to the service territories will boost revenue estimates and operational efficiencies. This will result in more favorable valuations for the utility. In the end, the overall socioeconomic health of the utility service territory has significant impacts on the fiscal well-being of any public utility.

SEGMENTING THE POPULATION

The bottom-line for utility industry participants is that a lot more work is required before any prescriptive measures can be employed. Utilities confronted with a growing number of problems will need to invest resources to properly assess their current situation.

While many roads can lead to the same destination, one common theme to emerge is the segmentation of the payment troubled. Socio-economic factors must be used to define relevant clusters. Relevant clusters will require some descriptive names to facilitate discussions between diverse stakeholders. Research has defined clusters by looking at household income and family size. However, this model is not effective because the classification does not include work history, economic condition, and other relevant socioeconomic factors.

We recommend an approach that incorporates household demographics, regional socioeconomic conditions, and job classifi-cation. Some descriptive clusters were identified previously: notably, the *low-income, near poverty, working poor,* and the *leveraged earner.*

While these are starting points, they are not based on a scientific sampling across the entire industry. As such, these clusters will require modification. For example, the low-income segment could contain clusters of more relevance. These could be TANF recipients, SSI reliance, the newly impoverished, chronically poor, homeless, and housing abandonment, among others.

The development of appropriate clusters will rely on a statistical analysis of your customer base. In addition, the analysis must be corroborated across the nation. Only then will we know for certain what significance a given cluster has on the utility industry.

Further segmentation by payment behavior is also warranted. For example, a leveraged earner may prioritize the utility bill differently than would the chronic poor. A leveraged earner may choose to pay credit cards first because of late fees, interest charges, and credit dependency. The chronic poor may pay the utility first to ensure safety and stability.

If this is the case, then differing strategies will be required for the two population segments. The leveraged earner may respond to economic incentives, while the chronic poor could not improve payment behavior even with the stiffest penalties. As such, utilities may wish to employ a segmentation matrix to identify effective affordability measures.

As can be seen in Table 8–1, the number of possible measures can escalate as a multiple of the number of defined clusters. Consequently, the number of clusters should be based on statistically significant differences between payment behavior and socio-economic conditions. When done properly, each cell represents a unique behavioral cluster.

While the process is easily illustrated, the practice often requires specialized skills. For many organizations, market segmentation will be contracted to specialized consultants. However, program managers should understand the basic process in order to facilitate and manage those engaged in the effort.

Table 8–1 Example of a segmentation matrix

Clusters	Perfect Payer	Near Perfect		Jackpot Payer
Chronic Poor	$\text{Measure}_{(1,1)}$	$\text{Measure}_{(1,2)}$	...	$\text{Measure}_{(1,m)}$
SSI Dependent	$\text{Measure}_{(2,1)}$	$\text{Measure}_{(2,2)}$	...	$\text{Measure}_{(2,n)}$
TANF Recipient	$\text{Measure}_{(3,1)}$	$\text{Measure}_{(3,2)}$	...	$\text{Measure}_{(3,n)}$
LIHEAP/HWAP	$\text{Measure}_{(4,1)}$	$\text{Measure}_{(4,2)}$	...	$\text{Measure}_{(4,n)}$
Near Poverty	$\text{Measure}_{(5,1)}$	$\text{Measure}_{(5,2)}$	...	$\text{Measure}_{(5,n)}$
Working Poor	$\text{Measure}_{(6,1)}$	$\text{Measure}_{(6,2)}$	...	$\text{Measure}_{(6,n)}$
Leveraged Earner	$\text{Measure}_{(n-1,1)}$	$\text{Measure}_{(n-1,2)}$	...	$\text{Measure}_{(n-1,n)}$
Recently Unemployed	$\text{Measure}_{(n,1)}$	$\text{Measure}_{(n,2)}$	...	$\text{Measure}_{(n,n)}$

To realize value from the segmentation matrix, the assigned task force must brainstorm potential measures for each behavioral cluster. Strategies must be developed along with a series of tactical measures using the broad range of skills, experience, and expertise within the task force. While each behavioral cluster could require differing tactical measures, in many cases the tactics employed in one cluster will be advisable for members of other clusters as well. As such, the number of measures required can be reduced to manageable levels.

For each unique measure, the task force will explore methods to implement and market the defined measures to appropriate customers. This is the heart of situational analysis. First, define your needs through comprehensive market research. Second, identify gaps between observed need and current offerings. Third, develop strategies and tactical measures to fill the observed gaps. Lastly, effectively implement the defined measures with integrated monitoring and evaluation.

ASSESSING THE NEED FOR LOW-INCOME PROGRAMS

While the approach outlined previously addresses general issues, no specific guidance has been provided to signal the need for low-income programs. We will attempt to address this topic using the fundamental four in conjunction with behavioral clusters.

Since cluster analysis requires a specialist, it is wise to address overall need before expending resources on a detailed analysis of your customer base. To address the fiscal health of your organization, we must return to the analysis of gross margin, net operating margin, profit margin, and the flow ratio. An observed weakness among these fundamental four warrants an extended analysis of the fiscal health of your organization.

First, you must look at revenue growth. A decline in revenues or even a slowing in yearly growth signals a deterioration of the utility service territory. Any economic downturn will exacerbate the plight of the low-income population. There are usually insufficient resources available to serve the current low-income population. Consequently, an economic downturn will tend to increase the number of customers eligible for government and utility affordability services. With the current resource pool being spread across a greater number of recipients, eligible applicants will be refused services. As such, the requests for payment negotiation will rise, with outstanding receivables resulting. This will result in long-term consequences for the utility ratepayer and shareholder.

The second indication of low-income need is a narrowing of the gross margin. The gross margin captures the variable cost of utility service, a large component of which is fuel and procurement costs. With these costs being transferred to the end consumer, the increasing energy burdens can exacerbate affordability issues. Customers having trouble paying the current energy bills will have even greater trouble with the increased monthly bill. Excessive energy burdens place undo stress on, and pose politically unacceptable risks to, the low-income population.

A third indication of low-income need is an unfavorable or dramatic change in the flow ratio. Since increases in accounts receivable cause the flow ratio to rise, service affordability is well represented by this ratio. Any movement of this ratio

Perhaps the most common and influential indicator of growing need is simply a statutory requirement for low-income programs. Often industry advocates working for the public utility commission are the first to raise relevant concerns regarding the low-income.

requires careful consideration. You must identify why this ratio rose. Did your company sell off assets, thereby removing short-term obligations? Have receivables grown substantially? Has the amount of bad debt risen above the allotted reserve? The flow ratio captures a negative influence on the overall business delivery infrastructure. Even so, a thorough investigation of individual components within the flow ratio will be required to fully appreciate the growing concern over the low-income population.

Perhaps the most common and influential indicator of growing need is simply a statutory requirement for low-income programs. Often industry advocates working for the public utility commission are the first to raise relevant concerns regarding the low-income. Only then are utilities eager to get involved. However, at this stage the utility is totally defensive. Utilities often view low-income mandates as regulatory inefficiencies to their business.

Despite the overwhelming need for more affordable utility service, many utilities simply do not see the economically disadvantaged as a valuable customer base. As such, low-income programs are seen as unnecessary expenditures that serve to raise the cost of utility service. With many utilities coveting the least-cost provider status, even the most reasonable affordability and conservation programs clash with executive mandates for lower operational costs. This is true even when these programs earn a guaranteed return.

When any one of the four scenarios is realized within your organization, a low-income need is a near certainty. However, low-income need does not in itself justify the development of special programs or even tactical measures. The only way to identify the need for low-income programs is to segment your population on payment behavior and socioeconomic factors. Identifying these behavioral clusters is a key component in the development of low-income programs and a necessity for any relevant gap analysis.

Generally, there will exist as few as three or as many as 12 unique behavioral clusters. These clusters will span income classification. At times this will require fundamental changes in operational policy and procedures. Other clusters, such as the chronic poor, may consist only of low-income customers. Where low-income clusters show poor payment behavior, targeted low-income programs warrant investigation.

A number of business cases should be considered qualitatively. Where long-term benefits to both shareholders and ratepayers are anticipated, the development of relevant business cases should follow. Armed with relevant statistics, strategies, and tactical measures, you are ready to assess the viability of low-income programs within your organization.

NOTES

[1] Woo, L., and W. Schweke. 2003. 2003 Development Scorecard for the States, *http://drc.cfed.org/grades/vermont.html.*

9

FROM CONCEPT
TO REALITY

OVERVIEW

Humanity is continually frustrated by common misconceptions that clash with reality. In our culture, the belief that a single idea can change the world or bring us fortune is not lost on the young. Many creative minds are wasted in the indeterminable rationalization that their ideas are simply too grand to be accepted. They squander opportunity for action and instead invest in their own victimization.

How many of us ponder aimlessly because we lack the persuasiveness to sell our concepts to those important people with whom we entrust our future? In fact, many persons are defined by these ponderings. Take the struggling artist who is ahead of her time, the undiscovered actor serving drinks in the neon light, or the maverick employee frustrated by lack of recognition. Consider the enraged advocate who lacks financial support. So fall the innovators of affordability programs.

Any good idea or business concept requires fertile soil before it can sprout. In the business world, the soil is depleted of its nutrients by the aggressive growth demanded by each and every harvest. As such, those wishing their concept to germinate must prepare the soil before introducing the seed. Only with laborious patience will you be able to raise valuable business concepts into viable business ventures.

Defining a need for low-income programs is just the first step. Many hours of effort are needed before even the most advantageous program is funded. Like the overnight pop star who struggles for 10 or more years before striking a record deal, each business concept must age until the soil is made rich.

This chapter highlights the critical process of preparing your business concept. We demonstrate the importance of self-assurance and the relentless motivation needed to build broad support for your initiative. We identify critical stakeholders whose values and objectives must be considered. We reiterate the language barrier that exists between corporate executives, regulators, program managers, implementers, and advocates. By the end of this chapter, you will recognize the tedium in store for the aspiring individual innovating within a mature industry.

We call this process *program development*. Unlike program design, which deals with implementation issues, program development seeks the initial funding necessary to raise a good idea from concept into reality.

PEOPLE ARE FUNDED, NOT IDEAS

If broad support is to be realized for your ideas, strong leadership will be required. People, not ideas or concepts, are funded. Start-ups succeed because of the drive, stamina, and positive attitude of individuals who are able to convince others that their business concept is invaluable to the targeted community.

That same level of passion will be needed to rally support for a low-income initiative within your organization. Whether you work for the government, a neighborhood service provider, or a public utility, your personal motivations will be evaluated alongside any business idea that you choose to represent.

To realize funding for your programs, you will first need a broad base of support. As such, you must talk with a number of individuals and organizations to demonstrate that your business concept is viable. Notice that we choose the word demonstrate! It is essential that you are able to document the strength of your ideas, the need for your services, and the support of the community. All of these factors are fundamental to your success.

Prepare yourself for a long journey paved with hardship. Demonstrating the need for a service offering is much easier than demonstrating support for the offering. As a result, many barriers will be raised along the way. Some individuals and organizations will acknowledge the need, while others will not. Those who do acknowledge the need may or may not offer their support. At times, even a testimonial that a real need exists will elude you. As such, you must be both patient and persistent. Relevant stakeholders must be identified, persuaded, and signed before you move forward. This is the basis for any business case.

THE LOW-INCOME PERSON AS A PRIMARY STAKEHOLDER

We first begin by understanding what is meant by *primary stakeholder.* A primary stakeholder is any individual or organization benefiting directly from a proposed service offering. For example, the low-income population must be considered a stakeholder for any service related to energy assistance, service affordability, usage reduction, and community development.

While the low-income customer has little individual clout, the overall number of low-income persons across the nation can leverage a wealth of support. With 25% of the nation identifiable as low-income, the political clout of this population can be leveraged to build support for your initiatives. A low-income provider network already exists in the form of government agencies, private foundations, and advocacy groups. As such, any low-income initiative has a base of likely supporters. Your goal is to leverage their presence and to document the enthusiasm around your business concept.

For the low-income population, much of the need is assumed or easily demonstrated from previous research. Government census statistics can be used to illustrate the number of individuals and families living in poverty. Their average household income can be compared to monthly and annual expenses, such as housing, groceries, daycare, and utilities. It does not take much effort to demonstrate that a need really exists. In many cases, household income will be far less than even the most conservative estimates of household expense.

Furthermore, the government census also tracks appliance penetration and household statistics, making comparisons to our standard of living very easy. What percent of low-income families own a car, have more than one television, or own a gas range? How many square feet are available to each resident? Answering similar questions about the low-income population in your service territory can help you develop the proper perspective.

While we all struggle with monthly living expenses, the nature of our struggle versus the struggle of the low-income must be better understood. Although the average middle-class family has financial worries, they enjoy a standard of living far beyond that of those living in poverty. As such, the risks associated with the financial pressures are very different.

When we fail to meet our financial obligations in a timely manner, we face mounting late fees and short-term setbacks that could result in some level of embarrassment. For example, we may not be able to support school functions at the same level as other parents. This is a much different consequence than the family who cannot provide medicine for an ailing adult or sick child. Nor is our embarrassment equivalent to losing utility service at a time when summer heat or winter cold is fast approaching.

Understanding and communicating differences between our standard of living and that of those living near poverty is essential to leverage support from other influential entities. Demonstrating a personal understanding of those you plan to serve is an elementary step. It is necessary in the process of demonstrating that the services offered through your program can and will rectify a specific need within that population.

Care must always be taken to ensure you can successfully resolve the chosen issue. While you may be unable to resolve poverty in total, your program must resolve at least one consequence of poverty. Many of the same principles relevant to organizing a task force are also present in developing a business concept.

One area that needs additional attention is utility service affordability. A low-income program that improves long-term payment behavior would be desirable for a number of secondary stakeholders. However, before moving forward, let us consider other primary stakeholders of low-income programs.

Service Providers as Primary Stakeholders

The program you are considering may involve a number of service providers. Utilities may outsource a majority of low-income program functions. As such, you may find community-based organizations conducting outreach and intake and a nonprofit organization providing program services. You may find a private company evaluating program impacts and consulting groups assisting with program design and infrastructure development.

Recognizing this fact, a number of providers will be needed to implement your initiative. A successful business case will identify a handful of organizations that routinely provide the necessary services. You will want key contacts within those organizations to acknowledge their interest in the resulting work. They must demonstrate a resource pool that could be made available within the desired timeframe. In short, you are qualifying potential service providers for any future contract offerings. Where possible, these relationships should be documented in nonbinding letters of intent.

By doing so, you will be able to demonstrate the viability of your business case and implementation plan. This is particularly important when involving nonprofit and community-based organizations. A for-profit entity actively seeks growth. Consequently, resources are often in place to exploit unexpected growth opportunities. This is not the case for most nonprofit agencies.

Nonprofit organizations often rely on annual grants and donations to maintain even modest staffing levels. Private sector contracts are a welcome source of revenue but require planning. Nonprofit groups may require board approval before adding staff, expanding services, purchasing necessary assets, or extending facilities. When using nonprofit agencies, even members of the existing low-income network, implementation may take several months or even a year to get started.

Where program services are innovative, established providers may be scarce. In these cases, both for-profit and nonprofits will struggle to fill the niche. As a result, moving from concept to reality will require planning horizons spanning several years. In addition, program services will require some level of trial and error. Often practices and policies established on paper will require significant modification before even the most critical services are effectively implemented.

"For energy efficiency programs, you may actually lower revenue streams. However, you do so by lowering the risks associated with those revenues. As such, you can demonstrate shareholder value by showing the reduced revenues are more secure than higher revenues without your initiative."

To succeed, you must demonstrate a great deal of pride, patience, and tolerance. In addition, your company will need to show similar restraint. The key will be to set optimistic, yet realistic, goals and to achieve small successes very early in the process. To do so, you must understand stakeholder interests.

One of the best methods of identifying stakeholder interests is simply to ask each participant to set the measurements by which they will be judged. For an outreach agency, you may ask for the number of campaigns that will be attempted in the first year, the second year, and so forth, along with anticipated response levels. For intake agencies, you may ask for the average cost per enrollment. For service providers, you may want to identify the number of jobs that can be completed monthly. Simply let them choose the numbers that best reflect operational efficiency.

By allowing service providers to choose the measurement, you will get a good indication of what interests these organizations have in your proposed business. The actual numbers chosen by the stakeholder do not matter at this point. Rather, you simply want to document their willingness to support your venture. Understanding the desired role of each service provider is essential to the development of your business delivery infrastructure.

YOUR ORGANIZATION
AS A PRIMARY STAKEHOLDER

The most obvious stakeholder is perhaps the most often forgotten. You will be asking your organization to allocate financial resources and personnel to your interests. As such, you must consider the interests of your organization. You must demonstrate more than just a need. You must tap into an unspoken desire for the organization to support your efforts. While this is a critical success factor, most individuals will find support for their efforts only after enduring a great deal of frustration and repeated setbacks. To avoid this, we outline a few steps that may ease the process.

First, you must recognize that all private organizations are owned by a group of individuals who demand annual and even quarterly returns on their initial investment. For government agencies, such as a municipal utility, the owners are politicians who are often elected by individuals who also demand returns to supplement the tax-base. As such, your organization is controlled by individuals looking for a return on the assets acquired by years of investment. Consequently, you must ask yourself, how does my initiative add to these returns?

Second, you must understand that individuals operate under a risk-reward model, whereby additional risk increases desired returns and reduced risk lowers expected returns. The justifications for your initiatives must address this model. If it produces financial returns directly, then you may adopt a purely financial model. Where your program offers no significant improvement in either revenue growth or cost reductions, you must demonstrate that corporate risks are somehow reduced.

For energy efficiency programs, you may actually lower revenue streams. However, you do so by lowering the risks associated with those revenues. As such, you can demonstrate shareholder value by showing the reduced revenues are more secure than higher revenues without your initiative. In either case, you demonstrate an ability to manage the anticipated returns.

Third, you must recognize that your organization consists of a number of individuals who may or may not be aware of the anticipated returns. As such, you must effectively communicate the importance of these returns and the method through which your initiative will improve these expectations. In fact, the management of expectations is the single most important aspect of business case development, leading us to the next point.

You must establish expectations with each individual in your organization and repeatedly meet those expectations. While developing your business case, you are soliciting an acknowledgement of expected program impacts. If they accept those consequences, then you can rely on their support. If you request that a department manager supply a range of services, then you must ensure support for those resources within your plan. Because of this, you will be making commitments to a number of individuals at all levels of management throughout your organization. As such, your career will be influenced by your ability to manage and meet the expectations established by your advocacy.

YOU AS THE PRIMARY STAKEHOLDER

Because you are asking others to support an initiative, you have a significant stake in the outcome. If the program is successful, you will have the satisfaction of helping those in need. At the same time, you will have enhanced shareholder value. As such, your efforts will be appreciated and rewarded in time. If, on the other hand, your initiative raises shareholder and ratepayer concern, your career may be hindered. Individuals acknowledging this impact must confront emotions that will rise throughout the development, design, implementation, and monitoring of the program.

Personal rewards must be considered carefully at the early stages of program development. A desire for immediate and direct financial rewards will establish incorrect driving forces that will become clear as you seek support from other stakeholders. If these desired objectives do not line up with the objectives of the other stakeholders, your initiative will not generate the broad support needed to raise concepts to viable ventures. Consequently, you must have a genuine interest in the service offerings, the expected outcomes, and resulting stakeholder impacts.

Early in my career, I was actively brokering a deal between a software company and an energy service company where I was employed. Having recognized an opportunity to improve operational efficiencies, I presented the software company to corporate executives. This was my pet initiative for several months. During a chance interaction, the founder of the software company asked what I wanted from the deal. The honest truth was that I wanted nothing; however, without recognizing my stake in the venture, my initiative was suspect.

How could anyone promote a venture without having any vested interest? I realized much later in my career that there was a significant interest in the venture for myself. Executives from both companies were investing time and effort to broker a deal that would not happen. As such, the time and effort I spent was more than wasted; it was a hindrance to my advancement within the energy service company. Without my vested interest, the deal lost momentum as the two companies struggled to clarify synergies. As such, each initiative that I suggested from that point forward was carefully scrutinized.

The lesson learned was significant. You have a vested interest in any initiative you choose to undertake. While you may not control the end result, you do have a role in the process and perhaps the outcome. Those from whom you are requesting support must understand your role in each. Your ability to garner support for your initiative will depend on your passion, enthusiasm, and commitment in the ideas you espouse. Identifying relevant stakeholders and understanding their interests will guide your presentations and enhance your ability to generate interest. Ultimately it will help you secure funding for your initiative.

THE UTILITY
AS A SECONDARY STAKEHOLDER

The public utility generally has two interests in all low-income offerings. The utility must ensure program funds are used to generate long-term financial returns or to mitigate unacceptable risk. These impacts must be clarified by the utility. Quantifying only the direct impacts of program offerings can miss substantial benefit streams that flow from the program itself. The follow-on effects, realized from the program results rather than directly from program services, are considered *secondary impacts*.

Take as an example a conservation program. If the conservation program is successful, program participants will reduce energy consumption significantly. As a result, utility revenues will be reduced. If so, then how does the conservation program improve shareholder return? When that question is asked, you must be able to justify spending shareholder money to lower corporate revenue. Could you handle that question?

If not, you have overlooked other impacts resulting from the program. By reducing customer billings, program participants have reduced energy burdens and improved service affordability. This was observed within Columbia Gas of Pennsylvania's 1993 Low-Income Usage Reduction Program. Customer billings were reduced, allowing customers to pay a higher percent of their heating bills. On average, customers participating in the program made the same payments following the installation of conservation measures as they made prior to program enrollment. As a consequence, program participants who once accrued arrears annually were able to reverse the trend, paying down past debt despite coincidentally lower government assistance.

The impact to the shareholder was reduced revenue risk. While the program lowered revenues for program participants, accounts receivable showed annual improvements. As such, the usage reduction program was valuable to shareholders. Why? In addition to the direct impact to accounts receivable, many financing options are tied to this number. As such, when receivables show improvement, the utility will realize lower interest expense, improved access to capital, and higher investor returns.

Anticipating these secondary and tertiary impacts will be necessary if you are to dispel common misconceptions regarding program impacts. The same will apply to initiatives you wish to sponsor within your organization. Given that the public utility is an influential stakeholder, your low-income initiative must address shareholder and ratepayer concerns if utility funding is being sought.

THE GOVERNMENT AS A SECONDARY STAKEHOLDER

The government is also an influential stakeholder of low-income initiatives. In fact, almost any action taken within the public utility involves regulatory oversight by responsible government agencies. Rate increases impact economic development. Marketing raises issues of consumer protection. Deteriorating utility infrastructures threaten national and regional security. And service affordability and reliability issues threaten public safety. As such, governments closely monitor a utility's actions.

Regulatory agencies, advocates, and politicians make up the government within our context. Driving factors of each must be considered. Most program initiatives will require approval by the governing boards and regulatory agencies before program expenditures can be recovered by the utilities. Because of this, government support must be sought and obtained.

Generally, the government will be interested in three critical areas: public welfare, ratepayer impacts, and tax implications. Most program managers will realize the need to address public welfare. Utilities must provide reliable and affordable energy to all who desire service. Home energy, telephone, and water are considered essential and must be provided to everyone willing to pay a reasonable fee for those services.

The public utility, end consumers, and government entities struggle with the reasonableness of utility costs. For example, an ongoing debate asks whether or not a funding threshold should exist for annual home energy expenses relative to household income. This ratio is known as the energy burden of the household. Many believe an energy burden in excess of 15% of household income is onerous. Yet, we find very low-income homes can easily have energy burdens in excess of 30%. This is 10 times the energy burden of a typical middle-class home.

As energy burdens rise, the affordability of utility service raises concern for public welfare. Increases in the utility average rate per unit of consumption can substantially increase the cost of utility service. For these reasons, regulators and advocates scrutinize rate requests before adopting any position on proposed programmatic changes. Utility program initiatives must pass the gauntlet of regulatory and administrative scrutiny. Therefore, care must be taken when outlining the program scope to ensure adequate services can be provided at acceptable costs

The third government hurdle is tax consequence. Understanding the tax implications of your proposed initiative will surely assist in government approval. Will your program add to the general tax base? Do you plan to utilize government funds? Does the program reduce customer dependence on government programs? Will your initiative fill gaps in government assistance?

One important consideration is job creation. Each employment opportunity generates tax revenue and adds to the general tax base. As such, initiatives resulting in regional employment are highly desired by government officials. Reducing government expenditures also has positive implications. Reducing dependence on state-run programs can extend resources to individuals who would have otherwise been denied assistance due to lack of funds.

Your initiative will have a range of influences that extend beyond the program participant. In developing your program, you must consider the overlap that exists between your initiative and existing government programs. Doing so will maximize your chance of garnering support of influential government entities. Clearing governmental barriers during the conceptual phase of program development is an essential aspect of program development.

THE COMMUNITY
AS A SECONDARY STAKEHOLDER

In many ways the government is simply a surrogate for the community. Politicians and regulators are tasked with protecting the populous and spurring community development. As such, many of the same governmental stakeholder concerns are applicable to the general community. However, some key distinctions can be made.

First, the residents of a community will be concerned with the impacts your initiatives may have. A number of community development programs discussed in chapter 7 may significantly alter communities. For example, the National Brownfield Revitalization Bill signed into law by President George W. Bush in 2002 supports the reclamation of vacant industrial sites. This is important for low-income advocates, because areas of concentrated poverty often remain in the wake of these abandoned properties.

Chester, Pennsylvania is one city taking advantage of this program. The Keystone Opportunity Expansion Zone provided tax incentives that revitalized one of PECO's old power plants into an office building. Other developments include The Shops at Wellington Ridge. This development has provided more than 200 new jobs for low-income residents. These jobs were created due to the center's development and the state's provision for added highway access to stimulate the local economy. This resulted in long-term employment opportunities for surrounding communities.

The development of once-vacant land provides needed economic stimulus for areas of concentrated poverty and serves as a model for urban development. Jump Street USA seeks to locate other retail outlets in Philadelphia's other economically disadvantaged communities.

In fact, Philadelphia has supported a number of notable revitalization projects, such as Penn's Landing, Convention Center, and the Arts District.

These projects were economic successes, providing needed economic stimulus in areas of concentrated poverty. However, care must be taken to ensure unintended consequences are manageable. While employment opportunities were created, not all jobs were accessible by the low-income population. As such, job training, transportation planning, and job placement assistance were required. With the economic development, the surrounding areas gained popularity. The resulting housing development drove up area rentals, increased automobile traffic, and raised infrastructure requirements. Some low-income families were displaced from their homes.

Because the unanticipated impacts of economic expansion remain unstudied, little data is available. Yet, the benefits of economic development on the low-income population are largely assumed. As such, you will need to anticipate community concern and identify available resources to secure community support. Testimonials from community agencies, local politicians, entrepreneurs, and residents will add significantly if you are proposing community development initiatives.

Despite your efforts, the displacement of existing tenants and the shrinking availability of affordable housing will necessarily result. Your task is to include as much support as possible for those displaced. At the same time, you must recognize that low-income home owners can benefit as property values increase, and that many individuals will move from subsistence in pursuit of prosperity.

TERTIARY STAKEHOLDERS

A number of tertiary stakeholders will exist for each secondary impact spawned from your initiative. For example, area businesses positively impacted by a community development program will benefit the vendors and customers of those businesses. Similarly, affordable housing advocacies may be interested in the displacement of families resulting from the economic boom. The dichotomy created by programs will spark interest from media outlets, calling additional attention to your program.

The advocacies, vendors, customers, and media represent just a handful of tertiary stakeholders in any strategic initiative. While these impacts can trickle indefinitely throughout the utility service territory and beyond, the question arises, where do you draw the line?

BOUNDARIES FOR YOUR BUSINESS CASE DEVELOPMENT

The breadth and depth of your research will contribute to the critical assessment of your strategic initiative. The more information you have on each stakeholder, the better able you are to justify program services. However, there are limits that must be respected, including time, financial resources, and value.

Quantifying tertiary and quaternary impacts will add little value to your business case and may even detract from your ability to sell your concept to relevant stakeholders. Demonstrating astronomical financial returns will not be believable, especially in the era following the dot-com boom. Considering too many stakeholders will also create logical barriers. For example, drawing a two-dimensional object, like a square, is easier than drawing a three-dimensional object, like a cube. Both of these are exponentially less difficult than drawing a four-dimensional object, such as the tesseract.

So where are the boundaries? We suggest a simple approach of quantifying all primary and most secondary impacts with supportive research. Elusive secondary impacts should be qualified along with influential tertiary impacts. To accomplish this, you must identify and talk with as many primary, secondary, and tertiary stakeholders as possible. Ask each of these contacts to document their support and/or concerns in writing. Then carefully consider what documents, stakeholders, and impacts are notable to adequately communicate program benefits and risks to utility shareholders and ratepayers. It should be noted that participant benefits are often assumed to be both substantial and obvious. Otherwise, voluntary participation would be nonexistent.

PASSING THE ELEVATOR TEST

We have discussed actions that must be taken to successfully develop your strategic initiative, but we have done little to demonstrate when this task is complete. Here we will identify the basic documents and knowledge base that signal your preparedness.

Clearly, your strategic initiative must be concise, lucid, and valuable. The *elevator test* is a technique used to demonstrate your ability to adequately communicate your concept. Assuming you have a strategic initiative that has been under consideration for some time, you should be able to communicate the value of your initiative to each relevant stakeholder. If this is so, you are ready for the elevator test.

Consider any stakeholder (for example, the corporate executive) and meet that person in the lobby of a 10-story building for a short elevator ride. After your initial greetings, enter the elevator and take a short ride to the 10th floor. During the two-minute ride, you are to describe, or even better, convince the corporate executive to support your strategic initiative. If your concept is indeed concise, lucid, and valuable, you will have no problem with this task.

However, for most of us, the first attempt will demonstrate a miserable ability to communicate even the simplest concept. As such, practice will be required. After mastering the elevator test for one stakeholder, you must repeat it for all primary and secondary stakeholders. What you will find is the elevator test is passed only after careful consideration has been given to the specific interests of each stakeholder.

Returning to the corporate executive, let us give it a try. If we are to be successful, no introduction is necessitated. The elevator arrives...

> *"I'm glad we had a chance to meet today. I have been considering a strategic initiative that could improve profitability ratios that have been declining over recent quarters. When you have some time, I would like to present how negotiated payment programs targeted at the 'working poor' and the 'leveraged earner' can lower accounts receivable by as much as 20% in just three months. If I could demonstrate long-term shareholder value by leveraging existing programs, would you support such an initiative?"*
>
> *"I guess...sure!"*
>
> *"Great, when would be a good time for you?"*

Did the text capture your attention? I hope so, because it is true! So, what characterizes a successful elevator test? The answer lies in the results you have realized. Were you able to gain the shareholder's interest? Were you convincing? Were the results targeted at the party with whom you were speaking? Did the individual agree to support your efforts?

If so, then you need only to negotiate the necessary resources to launch your initiative. If not, then you must consider why the attempt was unsuccessful. In general, failure to gain support may extend outside the elevator test. Outside influences, such as a budget crisis or other pressing matters, may have ultimately led to your inability to gain support. However, this is just a reason and should not be taken as an excuse to cease your pursuit.

This is where passion, patience, and tolerance are needed. In the end, you must identify the critical issues facing each stakeholder and target that person's interests in your elevator tests. However, identifying these driving influences may require some ingenuity that is outside the scope of our discussion.

THE CONCEPT PROSPECTUS

After a successful pitch, supporters of your initiative will want to better understand your proposed offering. A *concept prospectus* is a short document, 1–4 pages in length, that outlines the business case.

The concept prospectus is divided into four areas. These are understanding of stakeholder concerns, recommendations for resolution, demonstrating stakeholder support, and requesting stakeholder action. We will discuss the contents of each section.

Understanding of stakeholder concerns

The understanding of stakeholder concerns will highlight the needs and desires of the stakeholders identified for your initiative. Who are the primary and secondary stakeholders? What concerns do they share? How have they addressed these concerns? What remains to be done? Where do stakeholder concerns lie? All are important questions to demonstrate your understanding of their need. Having passed the elevator test for each stakeholder, you should have no trouble with this task. So let's move forward.

Recommendations for resolution

The second area of consideration is your recommendations for resolution. Building on the elevator test, you must specify in added detail what services will be needed and how these services will be delivered. The challenge here is to properly scope your recommendations. Your recommendations must convince the reader that the problem will be resolved, while not getting bogged down with the details to be addressed when designing specific offerings. We are left with a high-level review of critical implementation strategies.

Demonstrating stakeholder support

By demonstrating stakeholder support, you are highlighting the achieved value for each enabling stakeholder. In this area, you should identify specific individuals and organizations that have demonstrated support for your initiative. For example, you may point out that the utility revenue recovery group is eager to see your program developed. You might explain that it will curb the growth in accounts receivable and payment negotiations among the working poor, which has burdened staff and stressed departmental budgets. As such, the reader understands who is supporting the initiative and why.

Requesting stakeholder action

The final section recognizes your need for additional support. Requesting stakeholder action demonstrates that the program is not yet fully developed. Additional actions are needed from the recipients of your prospectus if the program is to move forward. A call to action is needed if you are to motivate those who support your ideas, lifting concepts to reality.

STAKEHOLDER PRESENTATIONS

The purpose of the concept prospectus was simply to pique the interest of influential stakeholders. Naturally, questions will arise from the prospectus that you must address in person. Each stakeholder invitation represents a significant opportunity for you and your concept. As such, each presentation must be given careful consideration.

You should understand who will be in attendance and what their interests are in the presentation. This will take a little effort and may delay the meeting, but it is important to understand the roles of each individual. With this knowledge, you can tailor your presentation in much the same way your elevator test was customized for each stakeholder.

Sometimes this information will not be available, or individual roles will not be identified. At that point, you must make assumptions as to why and to whom you will be presenting your concept.

The presentation should be an extended version of your elevator test. As such, the statement drafted for the elevator test is a good opening for most presentations. Going back to the elevator test illustrated earlier, we find the same important points embedded in the statement. These include

- Declining profitability ratios
- Possibility of lowering accounts receivable 20%
- Negotiated payment programs as a recommendation
- Targeting the working poor and leveraged earner
- Demonstration of long-term shareholder value
- Need for additional support from stakeholder

Simply walking through each of these points could easily take 20 minutes to one hour. As such, you can simply build your presentation from your previous work. The only remaining caveat is to understand and address the individual personalities of those in attendance.

SECURING SUPPORT TO MOVE FORWARD

At the end of each presentation, you will be asking for a commitment. Most individuals will want to keep these commitments abstract. Your goal is to have them solidify exactly what the individual or organization is committing. The most demonstrative way for this to happen is to get a written document, or even better, a check. In essence, that is your goal. You want to sell your concept.

To turn concepts into viable business ventures requires passion, patience, and tolerance. The path before the program developer leads to a gatekeeper whose riddle, in effect, must be answered if you are to pass.

Most of us have bought a car. During the final stages of the sale, the salesman will ask you to write a small check to demonstrate your commitment to the sale. While the check is by no means a firm commitment on your part, the salesman has taken your abstract desire for the automobile to a concrete written action. The salesman understands this step is very difficult for most individuals. As such, he can demonstrate to himself and management that you are ready to purchase the car. All that remains is to establish proper terms and conditions. For the car dealer, the remaining tasks are simply delivering the specific car and offering appropriate financing.

You have a similar role in the development of a program. You must address the market demand for your products or services and demonstrate value in your ability to meet market demand. You also must highlight why you can be trusted to deliver on those demands. In essence, to successfully develop a strategic initiative requires salesmanship.

If you do not possess this quality, you must either find another who does or simply accept the task as beyond your current capabilities. To turn concepts into viable business ventures requires passion, patience, and tolerance. The path before the program developer leads to a gatekeeper whose riddle, in effect, must be answered if you are to pass. Only after you endure and reflect upon the journey, do you realize the satisfaction of having raised the necessary funding for your proposed initiative.

10

DESIGNING YOUR PROGRAM

OVERVIEW

Once you have raised the necessary support for your initiative, you now must focus your attention on the implementation issues before you. Program design is the first and most critical aspect of a successful program launch. You must carefully consider what services are to be offered, to whom these services are targeted, and how those services will be delivered. You also must consider what objective measures will be tracked to evaluate program performance.

Unlike the activities recommended in the previous chapter, during program design you will be required to conceptualize and negotiate specific stakeholder involvement. This effort will involve resources from various departments within your organization, as well as some external expertise. In this chapter, we will highlight the core activities necessary to complete program design.

Since many approaches lead to a successful program launch, we do not espouse a specific recipe or process. The following text is not meant to be a manual for your efforts. Rather, we underscore the basic components of program design in an effort to guide your efforts. Our goal is simply to promote the value of, and need for, comprehensive design activities. If you are looking for a text on program design, there are many available to the public. This chapter is not such a text.

While many initiatives exist outside the utility industry, we will focus our attention on the design of utility affordability programs. The reason for this is simple. This book is designed to encourage and inform utilities on the value of low-income initiatives and how they may be developed. As such, the utility affordability program is a good place to start.

Utility-sponsored energy assistance programs involve a range of stakeholders and represent a complex initiative appropriate for illustrative purposes. We will draw upon our experience to highlight specific activities that have yielded positive results over the long-term.

KEY SUCCESS FACTORS

To begin our discussions, let us highlight a few key success factors. The items included here are correlated with program success. As such, you should seek to ensure these items are present in your program design plan. In the following text, we will highlight the importance of executive-level involvement, support from low-income providers, a sound business delivery infrastructure, and appreciative participants.

Executive involvement

One of the primary success factors noted by our research is executive level support. Unlike large construction projects that may cost billions, most low-income initiatives involve only modest financial investments, typically several million dollars annually. Because of this, affordability programs are often well within the budget authority of middle management.

Most affordability initiatives do not require executive support. However, the involvement of executive management can speed project start-up, avoid costly operational barriers, and lengthen the lifespan of a typical program. As such, executive level involvement should be sought immediately. For program pilots, understanding executive motives and expected outcomes is essential for establishing your program within the utility. For on-going programs, executive involvement is often the only means to grow your initiative from an established base level.

One poignant statement made by a utility executive clarifies this point. Speaking to a program manager after an executive briefing, the president said, "You have been running this program for 20+ years and this is the first time I understood its contribution to the bottom-line." While the program manager was pleased by this recognition, the statement shows that executives may be largely uninformed about the value of low-income initiatives.

Many affordability programs result from regulatory mandates and judicial settlements. As such, utility affordability programs often represent a compromise to mitigate risk associated with other executive endeavors. Utilities must do better. By involving senior level management in the creation of your low-income initiative, the issues and opportunities you see can be better incorporated in the company's strategic planning. Ultimately, this will clear the path for more advantageous initiatives in the future.

Gaining executive involvement may seem self-explanatory. However, it is neither common nor well understood. Executive involvement is important for obvious reasons as highlighted above but also for other reasons that may not be so evident. For example, reporting project activity to senior management can avoid costly delays in implementation. This was readily apparent while working on two projects within a single utility. The first was an on-going home weatherization initiative and the other an emerging afford-ability program mandated by the state.

Administrators of the home weatherization program could not gain priority for information requests without escalating concern through several layers of management. The latter program had senior management attention and maintained a diverse workgroup of more than 20 individuals supporting information technology requirements. Because of senior management involvement, the stark contrast between the two programs soon surfaced. The utility infrastructure group realized the value of a low-income data warehouse and gained senior level support for its development. In the end, operational efficiencies were realized in both programs, thereby improving long-term shareholder value.

Other departments will also have their own priorities. As such, you must compete for resources from relevant stakeholders. Members of the revenue recovery group are often busy with monthly collection targets and on-going regulatory activity, leaving little time to participate in other internal affairs. Similarly, the legal department will have its own concerns, as will the marketing group. In fact, obtaining appropriate and consistent resource participation may be the most significant hurdle to effective program design.

During program development, you garnered support for your initiatives by demonstrating value to the stakeholder group. Despite their support, you will have trouble securing a reliable talent pool. Since everyone has day-to-day tasks requiring attention, even those with the best intentions may not be able to allocate the time needed to fully support your initiative.

Executive level involvement may be the only means of overcoming this task. Senior management can encourage employee participation and authorize new hires to ensure departmental operations are covered. With company executives removing staffing constraints, departmental concerns over resource allocations are unjustified, provided you allow enough time for each department to hire and train new employees.

Individuals who still resist participation in the face of executive level support should be involved only after careful consideration. With operational issues covered, you must decide what other reasons may be driving resistance. In many cases, your initiative was not anticipated and does not fit well in a desired career path. Your initiative may have delayed a project of his or hers. Or there may be extenuating circumstances that inhibit the person's involvement.

In any case, program design requires a significant commitment in the form of time and resources. As such, those involved must be able to focus on the task before them. For some, program design is a painstaking process of little significance. Naturally, identifying those with this attitude is important. Without executive level involvement, these individuals can hide behind operational responsibilities, masking their own personal reservations.

Utility executives can easily overcome internal barriers. Yet, they may prove even more valuable in tapping external resources. Utility executives have established relationships within the local community and with industry professionals, vendors, and politicians. As such, an executive willing to beat the drum on your behalf can raise awareness and support for your initiatives both quickly and reliably. For example, executives may have trusted relationships with sympathetic politicians who can clear regulatory hurdles and ease bureaucratic restraints. They may even provide matching grants to support your efforts.

Senior management will be active in a number of community development initiatives. They may be members of the local area chamber of commerce. As such, business alliances can result when specific vendor participation is desired. With executive level support, securing industry participants is often much easier and more timely than attempting to develop those relationships yourself.

Initial support from the low-income provider network

Also important are the community action agencies that make up the low-income provider network. Like many nonprofit groups, program services are offered by a limited number of employees and supported by a handful of volunteers. During program development, you likely sought and obtained the support of executive directors at several key agencies. During program design, you will need a firm commitment from each agency.

> *"Moving agency attitudes regarding your program from tempered enthusiasm to firm commitment is essential for your program to move forward. You and your organization must realize this and prepare accordingly."*

This will require board approval from most nonprofit organizations and community-based organizations. Naturally, the executive director is the most influential person involved. Because of this, you should be certain each executive director understands your initiative and the available funding. Many times the executive director will pitch your initiative to the board. In other cases, you may be called into attendance. If so, then you must be ready to present to the board. Like stakeholders identified during the development of your program, the board must understand quickly your intended services, the target population, and the expected outcomes.

Well-rehearsed scripts that have successfully passed the elevator test are invaluable during program design. Moving agency attitudes regarding your program from tempered enthusiasm to firm commitment is essential for your program to move forward. You and your organization must realize this and prepare accordingly.

Once support for your initiative has been approved, additional work will be necessary to bring the agencies on board. Key agency staffers must get involved in the early stages of program design. Several brainstorming meetings will be necessary to identify essential program offerings, critical delivery constraints, and significant driving influences for the local populous. With the initial considerations given proper consideration, community-based organizations will require training, access to key data, and clear deliverables before moving forward.

Business delivery infrastructure

Many of you will not have heard the term *business delivery infrastructure* outside this text. Yet, you often subconsciously select organizations with well-defined and efficient business delivery infrastructures as strategic partners.

Organizations with significant business delivery infrastructures are often well established, experienced, and efficiently operated. In short, these organizations are known for delivering quality services in significant quantity, and they will own recognizable brands.

The reason for this is simple. Organizations delivering services will develop business processes and information systems to ease the provisioning of services. Over time, the investment in these business processes and the underlying technology lead to recognizable and reliable operational efficiencies. This infrastructure allows for the delivery of program services in an efficient and proven timeframe. This reliability creates a brand of sorts that attracts even more clients. As such, these organizations will grow, attracting and retaining the best talent. In the end, these organizations will have the best technology, proven business processes, and loyal expertise.

The totality of these factors is the business delivery infrastructure. It is comprised of the people, the processes, and the technology. Identifying organizations possessing the best of all three will help to support rapid growth during economic booms and to survive economic downturns. As such, these organizations are valuable trade allies.

However, it is rare that any one organization will possess all three. Even more rare is a network of organizations operating together, sharing the same pool of talent, and providing synchronized product or service delivery through an integrated information system. Because of this, there exists no ideal business delivery infrastructure.

In the design of your initiative, you must seek an acceptable level of performance that can grow in conjunction with expanding program services and increasing levels of participation. To better understand this, let us consider each component individually.

People. Within our context of program design, the term *people* refers to both the organization and the individuals within that entity. For an organization to operate efficiently, employees must be well informed, conscientious, and committed to the delivery of product or services. To ensure this, a number of steps must be taken.

Those involved in your project must have both the responsibility and authority to fulfill their roles. It does little good to assign responsibilities to individuals lacking the capacity to undertake the necessary actions. Asking your 10-year-old daughter to manage your household budget would be foolish. She likely would do her very best to assist the family. However, she probably would not fully appreciate the consequences of missing a few mortgage payments, delaying bill payment, or simply allocating too many resources to a sibling.

Even with the specialized education and training, you would likely feel uncomfortable assigning this role to her. The reason for this is simple. She was not responsible for the purchase of the house, the escalation of credit card debt, and certainly not the upbringing of her older sibling. You were responsible for those actions. As such, your 10-year-old daughter cannot take a personal interest in the eventual outcome, even if it does impact her future. Even more to the point is the fact she has no legal authority to refinance your home or write checks on your behalf. Nor does she have guardianship of her older sibling.

Recognizing your 10-year-old daughter cannot be assigned the role as head-of-household is a no-brainer. Yet in the business world, we see examples of misappropriated responsibility just as preposterous, especially in areas of rapid growth. During the IT boom of the 1990s, technically savvy professionals were in very high demand. Computer hardware and software companies expanded rapidly. Individuals were needed to manage emerging clients, lead implementation teams, and design software solutions.

The result was a notorious realization of the Peterson Principal. Individuals were rapidly promoted to increasing levels of incompetence. When the economic upswing ended, many emerging managers were stranded as companies trimmed their workforce. During the following period of rebuilding, a number of managers were left to contemplate new career paths. In a stark realization, these individuals had to acquiesce the fact that their previous assigned roles simply fit neither their desires nor their capabilities.

Programmers trained in the linear construction of efficient algorithms found themselves designing event-driven components for a vaguely understood industry. As such, many programmers sought to make the business process more efficient by introducing technological innovations. Unfortunately, this is a costly mistake of inexperience that is repeated often.

A better approach is to identify what business decisions are being made within the industry and to design components to make those decisions easier. A business consultant easily understands this. Asking a schooled programmer to analyze a business segment is not much different than asking your 10-year-old daughter to manage your household budget. Yet, it happens repeatedly.

We should consider people within the framework of your business delivery infrastructure. In doing so, we are asking you to identify appropriate roles for individuals and organizations within the development, design, and implementation of your initiative. In fact, few individuals can be effective in these various phases.

While asking an implementer to assist with program design is perfectly understandable, asking an implementer to lead design activities may be a serious misappropriation of resources. We are not suggesting that implementers be excluded from the design process. Rather, we simply suggest careful consideration must be given to their role. In fact, a frustrated implementer looking for career opportunities may be the ideal candidate for leading the design of program services. This could be the case if the frustration stemmed from a sense of underutilization within the day-to-day responsibilities.

Even with the appropriate persons involved, people will need on-going support. Their roles must be clearly defined and adequately communicated. The number one priority in program design is to set and manage the expectations of all involved. To do this, you must be open, available, and supportive. If training is needed, you must provide it. If additional resources are called for, you must identify support for those resources. When interpersonal issues arise, you must monitor and facilitate an acceptable resolution. In short, leading program design takes an enormous effort and great attention to the needs of those involved.

Processes. In addition to the people, there are also *processes.* To successfully deliver quality services, a logical flow from one business process to the next must be developed to fulfill client expectations. Those involved must be able to develop workflows that achieve the desired objectives.

A good place to begin the design of business processes is the segmentation of your residential population. A great deal of information is available about household incomes and appliance saturation. Most utilities access these resources but often fail to take additional steps, such as querying their own information systems for relevant payment behavior.

The segmentation of payment behavior can produce meaningful classifications. Sampling low-income households will reveal a number of payment patterns. Some households will pay the entire amount due in a timely manner. Other customers will have an even better payment pattern, paying a levelized payment in advance of peak seasonal usage. Then, of course, a number of customers will negotiate payments that lag behind home energy use. Still other households will allocate financial resources to other priorities, leaving the utility in arrears. Clearly, the payment patterns of these households have varying impacts on utility cash flow.

One of the first attempts to evaluate the impact of payment behavior occurred in the early 1990s. The Pennsylvania Utility Commission (PUC) mandated the collection of monthly payment history for the Low-Income Usage Reduction Program. To simplify data collection, the PUC asked utilities to report whether the customer made a full, partial, or missed payment. While this sounds simple enough, those involved struggled to come to a consensus. For those wishing to pursue a similar path, we suggest you either hire a professional or adopt the following payment classification (see Table 10–1).

Table 10–1 Payment Classification Matrix

Payment Made?	Variance Trend	Payment Classification
Yes	Decreasing/Static	Full
Yes	Increasing	Partial
No	Irrelevant	Missed

With the payment classifications defined, you may wonder why a specialist is recommended for customer segmentation. With just this single variable being collected during an 18-month period, exactly 387,420,489 possible patterns exist! And generally even more variables will be added to the segmentation matrix, such as customer segment, size of arrears, and risk assessment.

One way to simplify the segmentation is to create a chart similar to that used by Stephen Covey in his best seller, *The Seven Habits of Highly Effective People.* Doing so produces a graph similar to Figure 10–1.

Having filled this chart with random numbers, the 250 customers are more or less evenly distributed. Even so, some clustering emerges. For example, a group of customers have severe, but not terribly urgent, need. However, since the data points are random, no statistically significant clusters are observed. In the real world, the distribution is not random, allowing natural clusters to emerge.

In Figure 10–2, three distinct customer segments are observed as indicated by the light ovals. The first cluster contains customers with less severe needs, but some degree of urgency. This cluster is representative of utility customers who have recently missed a payment. The second cluster is composed of customers with greater need but more time to deal with the issues. These customers may be characterized by growing arrearage levels from regular partial payments.

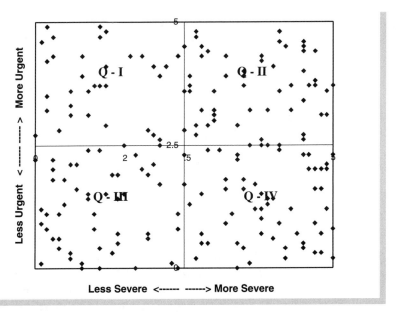

Fig. 10–1 Randomized Customer Set

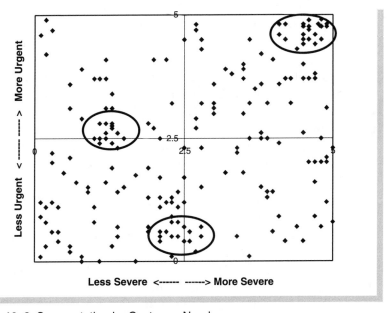

Fig. 10–2 Segmentation by Customer Need

The third cluster is composed of customers who have severe needs and little time to react. With regard to payment behavior, the third cluster represent customers with large arrears resulting from several missed payments. Because these customers are facing service termination, these customers receive much attention within the industry, while the other customer segments are ignored, if acknowledged at all. Without proper attention, one cluster can migrate upwards in both urgency and severity, making any satisfactory resolve elusive. Dynamic segmentation of customers identifies the migratory pattern of evolving needs.

By understanding these patterns, program managers can customize business processes to suit behavioral patterns of individual segments. The value of customized processes is increased customer satisfaction, improved participation rates, and enhanced program effectiveness. In recognition of these facts, online retailers are now investing hundreds of millions of dollars on personalization engines to identify and serve consumers based on behavior.

Amazon.com is the most notable example. Customers browsing titles can see what other books were purchased by individuals with similar interests. By doing so, Amazon.com is able to up-sell and cross-sell relevant merchandise. In addition, returning customers receive recommendations on music, videos, and books based on past purchasing decisions. The reward for their investment in dynamic segmentation has been persistent top-line revenue growth!

Underlying technology. This leads us to our third component, the *underlying technology*. Information technology is often needed to support customer segments and delivery services. However, each solution has its strengths and limitations. The most common limitation is that embedded business processes are assumed.

In these standard offerings, you will find the primary functionality necessary. Yet, some customization will be inevitable. Hence cost inefficiencies arise as you begin to adjust available technology to suit your specific needs. By choosing organizations that specialize in the delivery of particular services, you insulate yourselves against such cost. As mentioned earlier, organizations that have historically provided services will already have invested in these customizations.

As such, we come full circle. Business processes are carried out by people with the aid of technology developed by people responsible for the delivery of service. This cycle defines the business delivery infrastructure. Without it, your program will struggle to meet growing demand for services and will not realize optimum cost-effectiveness.

Appreciative participants

No program can be successful without first cultivating the appreciation of program participants. Programs that do not serve participant needs will not warrant participation, and the intended objectives will linger unmet. On the other hand, programs providing real value earn the gratitude of their participants.

"The greatest benefit to your program will be the authentic appreciation of past participants.
By managing customer expectations, participants will tolerate the necessary inconveniences required to deliver program services."

The greatest benefit to your program will be the authentic appreciation of past participants. By managing customer expectations, participants will tolerate the necessary inconveniences required to deliver program services. In fact, all aspects of your program will improve with the demonstrated appreciation of program participants. Testimonials can be leveraged to increase public awareness, encourage program participation, and access continued funding.

OTHER DESIGN CONSIDERATIONS

Program design activities must address each of the five distinct aspects of program delivery: *outreach, intake, service provision, evaluation,* and *reporting.* When designing your program, it often helps to discuss each component independently, despite obvious overlaps. In the subsequent pages, we will define each aspect of program delivery, suggest likely participants for program planning, and highlight key design considerations.

Program outreach

Outreach is defined by the *American Heritage Dictionary* as the "systematic attempt to provide services beyond conventional limits, as to particular segments of a community."[1] This is an ideal definition for low-income initiatives. While radio, print, and television can be effective at reaching a broad demographic, grassroots marketing techniques often work better for the low-income population. Flyers, word of mouth, agency referrals, church announcements, and other methods can build on the success of other regional programs.

While a grassroots effort is the most effective at delivering specific messages, mass media builds on public awareness to generate program referrals. For example, radio and print ads may draw the attention of many consumers. Only a small percentage of consumers will meet the eligibility guidelines, and an even smaller percentage will take the desired actions. Thus mass media may not appear effective. Yet, the effectiveness of mass media is often under-rated within low-income initiatives.

Looking at response rates to various solicitation efforts, we find referrals are near the top of the every list. Some of those referrals come from previous participants, others from neighbors, and still more from the respondent's extended family. *Trusted referrals* are a significant factor in a respondent's decision process. To enroll or even inquire about program services, respondents will independently verify the information heard. As such, several touch-points are often necessary before even a single action is taken.

For this reason, mass media ads and bulk mailings can be extremely effective. An individual whose interest has been piqued by an assistance program will seek independent confirmation from friends, relatives, and trusted organizations. This sort of unsolicited confirmation is typical prior to making a program inquiry. Similarly, a trusted organization may unknowingly confirm the validity of an emerging initiative. An announcement in a church bulletin or news-letter may confirm an ad seen in a local paper several weeks earlier.

The broad level of awareness generated by media coverage not only assists in the confirmation of program legitimacy but also generates funding support. Government agencies, charitable foundations, and even private businesses can support only those programs that are known and understood.

Broad public awareness has the additional benefit of removing consumers from isolation. An understanding that others are struggling with similar issues explains in part the rationale for energy assistance and affordability programs to the general consumer. As such, the stigma associated with program enrollment is lifted.

Because both grassroots and mass-marketing techniques are needed to encourage low-income participation, a dilemma often arises. Just how does one successfully reach the low-income consumer? In the end, all methods must be considered, with the most promising approaches being tested. Only by tracking outreach effectiveness across your service territory will you find the correct mix for your target population.

Program intake

Responding to program inquiries, facilitating program enrollment, qualifying program applicants, enrolling successful applicants, and confirming program participation are all part of the intake effort. Community-based organizations and selected service providers typically run these activities. Sponsoring organizations administer quality standards, monitor participation levels, and support program participation. Exceptions to this structure do exist. General program inquiries may be directed to customer service centers first, allowing the utility to certify and refer respondents to all applicable offerings.

Another exception is seen in those states with consolidated energy programs funded through universal service riders. For example, the state of Vermont has a number of very small utilities. So consolidating energy programs through a single entity makes a great deal of sense. Beyond the administrative savings generated through program consolidation, smaller utilities are now able to offer a diverse range of programs that would otherwise be impractical. In these cases, a single entity typically manages both program outreach and intake. Thus they take on the roles more typically seen split between the sponsoring organizations and selected implementers.

Whatever arrangement you select for your program, the need to track referrals must be integrated with your intake activities. These so-called touch-points should document both the reason for the contact and the various outreach efforts contributing to the call. Tracking the activities requested during customer contacts can generate a number of operating efficiencies.

Where general inquiries dominate customer interactions, efficiencies can be realized in several ways. This can be accomplished by implementing fax-on-demand, posting responses to frequently asked questions, or customizing voicemail options. Alternately, if callers are requesting enrollment, unnecessary overhead can be eliminated by routing calls to local intake agencies or providing an online enrollment process.

Another area of focus should be on the various contributing factors leading to the call. Is the contact a result of a direct mailer, regional ad campaign, or news coverage? Who provided the referral? When did the respondent first decide to make the call? Did he or she have any trouble reaching us? These questions along with others help us understand the decision process leading to the desired action. Unfortunately, sometimes it is difficult to ascertain this information in a convenient, unobtrusive manner. However, surveys can follow each customer contact to gather the desired information.

Getting respondent information prior to an actual contact would be highly desirable, because unintended biases can be avoided. An interesting alternative may be to use the time while the customer is on hold to conduct a short survey. If this is impossible, a carefully crafted voicemail structure could serve the same function. While complex voicemail navigation can obstruct the intake process, the benefits resulting from this approach seem to outweigh the potential inefficiencies.

Another area to consider is the infrastructure available to support intake activities. Intake requires fielding program inquiries, facilitating program enrollment, and qualifying program applicants. It also involves enrolling successful applicants and confirming program participation. To successfully implement this, the intake agency must be aware of program offerings, eligibility criteria, and recent promotional activity. In addition, the agency must be able to track pending applications.

Agency employees will require ongoing training, regular program updates, and a database of some sort. Questions of quantity will typically arise. How much training is needed? At what frequency should updates be provided? How much should be spent on the tracking system? Anyone involved in program design will understand this immediately.

Consultants without a firm grasp of program scope may simply not understand the budget constraints and will attempt to sell unnecessary functionality, customization, and scope. While it is good practice to invest in the delivery infrastructure, too much investment at the early stages can tie a program to inefficient business practices. A preferred approach is to apply moderate levels of investments that are flexible and can evolve with your program offerings.

The WarmChoice Program offered by Columbia Gas of Ohio did just that. During the early years of the program, WarmChoice utilized several small CAP agencies that had no information systems at all. The initial thought was to put in place a small database to serve the first few years of program development. To meet this need, I wrote some simple database programs more than 14 years ago. They are still in use today. Because of the data model, agencies have been able to add functionality to their systems in small increments. Over the entire period, I would be surprised if these five agencies spent a total of $200,000 on software development. This would be the base implementation fee for many tracking systems sold today.

Similarly, training was ramped up gradually over time. Thus, long-term employees benefited from training targeted to their specific needs. Through this graduated investment paradigm, the program was able to mature along with its infrastructure. Today, the program still operates and continues to outperform nationally.

Service provisioning

Needless to say, no program achieves national recognition without attention being given to the technical aspects of service delivery. While the agencies selected under the Ohio WarmChoice program were not known for outreach or intake, each agency was already participating in the state weatherization program. As such, the chosen service providers were technically skilled in home weatherization. Despite this, Columbia Gas of Ohio insisted on and supported ongoing training.

Paying close attention to technical innovations and proven techniques, WarmChoice increased energy savings five-fold in the five years overlapping my involvement. Although I would like to think my involvement was causative of this achievement, it clearly was not! Nearly five years after my involvement ended, WarmChoice was still focused on the technical aspects of service delivery, raising savings levels even higher.

Even more impressive is the number of individuals who have remained with the program for the last 10 years. The administrative staff, quality assurance inspectors, community action agencies, agency program directors, and many staffers have remained involved with the program throughout. This consistency in staffing is certainly one of the many outstanding features of the program. Without significant turn-over, operational efficiencies were realized on many levels.

First, the expense of finding experienced replacements for departing talent was to a large extent avoided altogether. Second, the low turnover ensured the training provided remained within the program, thereby maximizing training cost-effectiveness. Third, the lessons learned from long-term service delivery were effectively folded into operations. Last, customer service was improved from a deep understanding of the concerns facing program participants.

The loyalty cultivated within the WarmChoice Program and within the community agencies did not occur by accident. Choosing agencies and employees with a demonstrated interest in the program offerings provided synergies that would otherwise take years of careful oversight to grow. As such, those designing program delivery options should involve those within the established low-income network.

Those with demonstrated success with certain aspects of program offerings should be leveraged. For example, you may wish to expand an agency's service territory rather than look for other agencies to fill geographical gaps. Likewise, agencies with specialized offerings, such as technical training, may serve as preferred providers or even be offered exclusivity in key areas.

On the other hand, emerging agencies with proper leadership may be ripe for cultivation. An emerging service provider will typically rely heavily on one or two key business relationships. As such, you may be able to negotiate favorable terms and impose operational restrictions that favor program success. Also, these agencies do not have an established infrastructure. While this can be a substantial hindrance, appropriate investments can realize efficiencies unavailable elsewhere.

However, one caution exists before an emerging entity is selected as a provider. The entity must be stable. To ensure this stability, due diligence may be required before offering a contract. You want to ensure competent leadership will remain on board throughout, appropriate levels of funding are secure, agency documents are accessible, and the willingness exists to adopt lessons learned. If all these conditions are met, an emerging entity, like a newborn, will reflect the values you instill upon them. By nurturing an agency's early growth, significant operational efficiencies can be realized.

Monitoring and evaluation

This will require ongoing monitoring and evaluation efforts. By integrating monitoring activities with day-to-day activities, service providers benefit from incremental adjustments to service delivery. This prevents onerous reengineering following a special operational review. Similarly, periodic evaluations provide incremental feedback on issues that are not affordable or technically feasible on a daily, monthly, or even annual basis. As such, monitoring and evaluation should be part of program design activities.

While both are important to ensure program cost-effectiveness, monitoring activity is needed for management control. I became involved in a direct-load control project after monitoring activities revealed production levels for a few contractors were significantly higher than those of long-term staff. For the first few months, it was thought the contractors simply outperformed staff because of production incentives. As such, the project manager was often praised for boosting production levels. However, our employees voiced their suspicions about these production levels.

With ongoing monitoring efforts, we identified those installers with the highest productivity levels. Coincidentally, all were contractors reporting to a single supervisor. A closer examination revealed two installers we had never met. While not unusual, it raised additional concerns. Focusing our monitoring efforts on those jobs approved by this single supervisor, we pulled the invoices of these installers and began checking the physical installations. Our goal was to ensure quality work was maintained despite their production levels. What we found confirmed everyone's suspicions.

The installers had billed for jobs that physically were not completed. In short, these installers were padding their daily workload by creating fake invoices. In addition, several installers could not be confirmed. As part of our monitoring efforts, a meeting of installers was called. Not surprisingly, the missing installers failed to show. A number of reasons were given. However, we soon found these installers simply did not exist. In the end, the monitoring efforts found the project manager, field supervisor, and a single field technician had colluded to defraud the company and our client utility. However, their scheme did not last long, and the parties faced both civil and criminal charges.

Without the monitoring efforts, this scheme could have gone unchecked for a very long time. As such, all programs must monitor the work of their service providers. In general, 10%–15% of jobs are reviewed along with associated paperwork. Additionally, inspectors should conduct *ride-alongs* to ensure a personal interaction exists between the field and administrative staff. By doing so, both the quality and legitimacy of work can be verified.

In addition, these relationships help bridge the gap that often exists between labor and management. Closing this gap is a critical component of successful program design. In areas where union shops are present, this relationship is often strained from a history of conflict. However, this history can be overcome through relationships and boundaries formed via ongoing monitoring efforts. With a full awareness of expectations and a formal evaluation process, job performance can be critiqued without individuals taking personal offense to management scrutiny. This is often a surprising and welcome revelation for those involved in the management and administration of strategic initiatives.

While monitoring is often associated with short-term feedback, program impact assessments add value to ongoing and emerging initiatives. Initially, impact assessments are used to monitor program achievements and to establish a baseline for expected results. Early assessments are compared with other initiatives across the continent to assess relative performance. Where a program is underachieving, an impact assessment may justify policy changes, technical innovations, or a process review to boost program results. These types of assessments are often associated with pilot programs. However, even mature programs require periodic review.

In general, we recommend impact assessments every three years and process reviews every five years. The exception would be where significant policy changes have been implemented or programmatic concerns have been raised. In those cases, we suggest appropriate assessments be conducted to measure the impact and efficiency of policy revision or to address specific program issues. Program evaluators are often consulted to determine which assessments may be required. Hence our recommendation is to have a program evaluator on retainer who is familiar with program services, key providers, and geography. By doing so, necessary assessments can be implemented quickly and at much lower cost.

Establishing a baseline of savings is necessary for pilot programs. However, mature programs often require assessments that extend beyond primary and secondary impacts of program offerings. Taking time to extrapolate tertiary impacts can demonstrate program impacts well beyond your initial consideration. This information is particularly important if program funding becomes unstable or you simply wish to expand the program.

The study of tertiary impacts often reveals long-term shareholder and ratepayer value. Hence, regular process and impact assessments are indispensable. They are vital to communicate program impacts to executive management, utility shareholders, public service commissions, and/or interveners.

To understand what is meant by primary, secondary, and tertiary impacts, let us look at a home weatherization program. The primary impact of home weatherization is an improvement in home-heating and cooling efficiency. A standard impact assessment will quantify energy savings as the difference in normalized annual consumption before and after weatherization. Simply stated, energy savings represent the average change in energy use following program services given the same weather conditions and behavioral characteristics.

Today, many utilities recognize that arrearage levels also decline following home weatherization. This secondary impact is a direct consequence of lower participant bills, especially for those struggling with excessive energy burdens. Utility service that was once unaffordable becomes more affordable as the home becomes increasingly energy efficient. As such, accounts receivable are reduced.

While this is a recognizable benefit to the utility and ratepayers, the consequent tertiary impacts are rarely quantified. If we are to consider tertiary level impacts, we must ask the question, what impact does lowering accounts receivable have on the utility and its ratepayers?

As explained earlier in the book, a number of tertiary impacts arise from lower accounts receivable. First, the cost of carrying debt is reduced. This will mean a great deal to your revenue recovery group, but it is still accounting jargon for the average program manager. In short, the cost of carrying debt can be thought of as finance charges. Second, collection expenses are often reduced or even eliminated. If a customer is able to keep current on his utility bill, a whole sequence of collection activity can be avoided. Third, when service becomes affordable, requests for payment arrangements are unnecessary. As such, additional expenses are avoided.

The fourth advantage is that consumers realize disposable income that is likely to be spent in the community, thereby stimulating the local economy and improving the service territory. Finally, lower accounts receivable impact the corporate credit rating and therefore impact access to capital. This factor alone can have huge impacts on shareholder return, reliability of service, and ratepayer expense.

As we can see, a number of tertiary impacts exist that are not often quantified. The value of the previously stated tertiary impacts could easily add up to several hundred dollars per participant annually. In fact, this is just the tip of the iceberg. We have not touched on health or safety considerations that could reduce corporate liability, nor have we considered the quaternary impacts. Needless to say, the financial benefit of the home weatherization program can be quite substantial over a 10-year planning horizon. Depending on the size of your program, these impacts can have substantial long-term benefits that are not often related back to the home weatherization program.

Because of this, impact assessments that look at a broad range of economic factors can uncover value in low-income initiatives that often remain hidden. Similarly, process assessments can reveal opportunities to expand your offerings, improve service offerings, and discover cost-effective service delivery options. Combining impact and process assessments on a regular basis could generate considerable interest in your program offering.

Program reporting

While evaluation and monitoring are largely an information technology fueled by human effort, program reporting is information accumulated and generated from technology. Because short-term feedback is required to successfully manage operations, tracking systems have been developed to gather and analyze relevant program data.

Despite the fact that many low-income initiatives have existed since the early 1970s, current information technology still lacks critical functionality. For example, many utilities offer several initiatives to the same target population. In the low-income sector, the state of Pennsylvania has mandated several universal service programs. These include customer assistance and referral evaluation services, customer assistance programs, low-income usage reduction plans, and utility hardship funds. All of these assist customers struggling with service affordability. However, each utility may employ a number of systems to implement the suite of low-income initiatives, thereby raising program costs unnecessarily.

A better solution is to find a system with a flexible data model supporting a range of low-income initiatives. However, these systems are not easy to find. Having run a software company for several years, I have concluded that universities instruct computer science students how to automate business processes rather than how to facilitate business decisions. This is a grave mistake for most service industries.

If we look at the previous four universal service programs, each offering is different. Consequently, the business processes and practices supporting each vary significantly. If the software simply automates these processes, then it is impossible to find common ground. The resulting effect is the use of four independent tracking systems, one for each program.

A better solution would be to facilitate the business decisions. With this focus, a common denominator can be found within the universal service initiatives. All seek to help the consumer with service affordability. As such, customers may flow through the customer assistance and referral evaluation services to one or more of the remaining three programs. Using a single tracking system to track this flow would improve operations as well as yield program reporting that is unavailable today.

However, to date, only fully integrated customer relationship management (CRM) systems have sought to achieve this functionality. Unfortunately, most of these systems are cost-prohibitive and often fall short of the desired objective. Today, this is unacceptable.

As such, companies are developing software to support multiple low-income initiatives via an information system that is decision-based. To accomplish this, a flexible and comprehensive data model is required. By working with program developers, systems are being developed to facilitate business decision-making and enhance service provisioning. The end result is lower implementation costs, improved service delivery, and improved program reporting.

"Program managers extending new services should consider the use of available systems from companies specialized in the development of information technology for energy service programs."

While many systems could be designed in this manner, most companies simply lack the necessary expertise or industry experience to offer a comprehensive decision-based program tracking system. Such work requires an analyst with experience in both program delivery and full life-cycle software development.

Finding a person with expertise in both areas is essential for success. Otherwise, large teams of program managers, services providers, and technologists must have regular meetings to transfer knowledge between the various participants. While appropriate in concept, rarely do these large investments in both time and personnel result in the desired implementation.

As such, modifying internal information systems in support of low-income initiatives can be a costly and time-consuming endeavor. Program managers extending new services should consider the use of available systems from companies specialized in the development of information technology for energy service programs. Program managers should insist on the support of multiple initiatives. With recent technological advances, a single management and program tracking system can be used to support direct load control, appliance rebates, payment plans, and other consumer services.

INTEGRATED SERVICE DELIVERY

This brings us to our last point: integrated service delivery. It has been a goal for many years across industries, departments, and agencies to integrate offerings where similar target markets exist. In fact, this concept was leveraged by dot-com executives to spark interest in a new economy.

Portals began to appear that addressed the needs of specific populations. Napster and Apple targeted those looking for a diverse library of music. Both successfully established a peer-to-peer network to access and download music in a digital format. Other successful portals emerged, at times appearing as single-interest retailers. Amazon.com is one such example. Initially, Amazon.com sold only books. However, with a swelling base of consumers, Amazon.com was able to expand into videos, CDs, and electronics. Today, Amazon.com looks more and more like a giant department store where almost any product can be purchased from a single point of entry.

This in many ways should be the goal of the low-income provider network. The low-income individual should be able to enter a single point and access all forms of available assistance. However, we are nowhere near this reality. Simply stated, no portal exists for low-income service delivery. Government programs are found in one area while programs sponsored by regulated industries are found in another. Even today, most utilities offer a range of programs to serve the low-income population. Yet, the utility still requires several points of entry to take advantage of the available assistance.

A consumer may first call the customer service line to request a payment negotiation. Through an initial assessment, the customer service representative may refer the customer to a CAP designed to help the low-income. The consumer is then transferred. The CAP agency establishes an affordable payment arrangement but stipulates that the customer must also apply for federal energy assistance and home weatherization. Two applications are forwarded to the customer. If both are filed, the consumer will then receive a cash grant as well as home weatherization, assuming the program is currently available.

However, these programs may have additional stipulations. For example, the customer may be required to request regional energy assistance and/or agree to installation of an automated meter-reading device. The consumer must follow through with these initiatives, signing proper releases and making additional applications. The scenario often continues indefinitely.

While providers often refer consumers to available assistance, little consideration is given to the process the low-income consumer must tolerate to access these funds. Already strapped and burdened by financial need, the typical low-income consumer has little time for repeated application to the many service providers. We often overlook that TANF requires additional efforts, such as employment search or job training. Other regulated businesses such as banks, hospitals, and insurance companies offer similar assistance, having unique eligibility requirements and enrollment processes.

The demands faced by the low-income applicant quickly become untenable. The growing requirements placed on the consumer seeking public assistance can be discouraging. The result is that many consumers will simply delay application or avoid public assistance altogether. In both cases, the low-income consumer loses the opportunity to participate in programs that would alleviate many financial constraints.

While this affects low-income consumers directly, those consumers opting out of available assistance also impact the ratepayers and long-term shareholders who are often left to shoulder the consequences of nonpayment. Consequently, we must do better at designing our initiatives.

Instead of designing one program at a time, utilities should redesign low-income initiatives so that enrollment in one program qualifies the participant for all available assistance within the utility. Creating a single point of entry for all available assistance would generate cost efficiencies and improve the levels of assistance received by participants. This is important for all stakeholders.

The more that can be accomplished per customer interaction the greater our return from low-income investments. Ideally, enrollment in utility programs would qualify consumers for government programs, refundable tax credits, banking assistance, and medical insurance. While the logistics of these interactions raise significant barriers, ensuring comprehensive assistance within a single entity's low-income offerings is viable. Program administrators should set this as a goal and make it a continual focus.

As new program offerings are added, design activities should include all available forms of assistance. If we are to reap the benefits of our low-income initiatives, a conscious effort must ensure the integration of service delivery and ease intake requirements between program offerings. Where direct enrollment is impossible between assistance programs, utilities should make clear all regional offerings for their consumers. Each dollar of assistance that enters the household frees financial resources for the program participant. The long-term goal should be to help needy families rise above the financial constraints that have shackled them to an unfulfilling existence of dependence. Only through informed decisions and responsible actions leveraging available assistance will these families rise to self-sufficiency.

Through the provision of comprehensive assistance and targeted knowledge transfer, the utility can revitalize low-income communities. This will improve socioeconomic conditions within its service territory that serves the ratepayer and will reward the long-term shareholder.

Notes

[1] Houghton Mifflin Company. 2002. *The American Heritage Dictionary of the English Language* (4th ed.).

11

PUTTING IT
ALL TOGETHER

OVERVIEW

The question that most often gets put to us is whether or not a single approach can be recommended as best. The common answer is a resounding *no*. However, I believe the more appropriate answer is a definitive *yes*. While each low-income initiative has it own unique characteristics and distinct operational considerations, a standardized approach can integrate program offerings with other low-income initiatives. Operational efficiencies transcend simple cost containments and generate exponential returns on utility investments in low-income initiatives.

For the utility, we recommend an approach that is both fiscally responsible and responsive to the socioeconomic needs of the utility franchise. Through the following process, utilities can expand low-income initiatives in a manner yielding long-term shareholder value.

1. Assess corporate fiscal concerns.

2. Segment the population on payment behavior and socio-economic condition.

3. Develop a business case around fiscal concerns, segmentation data, political climate, and socioeconomic needs within the service territory.

4. Integrate program offerings to fulfill business objectives and minimize barriers to participation.

5. Build a reliable and efficient business delivery infrastructure through gradual recurring investment.

6. Monitor service delivery and assess program impacts.

7. Communicate findings to participants, providers, and the public.

8. Redesign service delivery when program offerings are added.

9. Actively manage the five program components: outreach, intake, service provisioning, evaluation, and reporting.

10. Target economic development activities in areas of concentrated poverty.

11. Leverage federal, state, and regional initiatives of public, private, and charitable organizations.

12. Never lose sight of technical innovations that serve evolving consumer demand.

While these steps outline the general approach, they do not highlight the basic characteristics of successful low-income initiatives. In an effort to summarize industry best practices, this final chapter will make specific recommendations based on our survey of notable low-income initiatives. We will cover the integration of energy assistance, utility affordability services, usage reduction programs, and targeted community development. Used together they can generate long-term shareholder value, meet ratepayer scrutiny, and provide participants with the opportunity to progress towards financial self-sufficiency.

MONEY IN THEIR POCKETS

Regardless of our own prejudice, the truth remains that all across North America, individuals and families struggle to meet financial obligations.

Steve Rhode, president of a nonprofit financial health center, says that more than one-half of American adults struggle to control spending and debt.[1] When coupled with the economic downturn that followed September 11, 2001, the American middle class suffered financial distress. This financial distress followed decades of broad economic expansion.

With 25% of households living near poverty and home energy costs rising to near-record levels, more than 50 million households are struggling with the cost of food, water, and shelter. For the public utility, the financial distress translates into rising uncollectibles. Regulatory recovery mechanisms do little more than treat the latest symptom of utility service affordability. To address the underlying interaction between poverty and the public utility, industry participants must take action to preserve the health of the local economy.

Individuals unable to find employment because of health-related issues, factory slowdowns, or job loss may begin slip undetected into financial distress. We must acknowledge that affordability issues extend beyond the low-income population. Middle-income Americans and even some high-earners can falter in the face of mounting debt. Despite the varied circumstances of those in financial distress, at the core, all payment-troubled consumers struggle with cash flow. Some households lack the necessary income, others simply lack disciplined spending, and still more exhibit some hybrid of the two.

Families must learn to successfully manage cash if payment troubles are to be overcome. Unfortunately, managing cash flow requires financial skills, personal responsibility, a long-term outlook, and discipline. For most, these activities require lasting behavioral change. Not unlike giving up smoking or losing excess weight, fiscal responsibility can be elusive for many.

The only reliable way to resolve financial distress is to raise cash inflows and lower outlays. Earnings and loans improve cash inflows. Pretty simple stuff, but managing cash outlays can be tricky. Reducing cash outlays requires one to trim expenditures, renegotiate debt, and access subsidies.

"Low-income energy affordability will not change overnight. However, there is hope. If households were to access available low-income assistance and lower home energy consumption by just 20%, preliminary findings suggest home energy burdens would return to manageable levels."

Each requires a level of sophistication in and of itself. For this reason, a well-developed provider network exists to assist low-income families in this effort. Federal programs, such as the LIHEAP and HWAP, lower excessive energy burdens placed on households. Other federal programs like TANF, refundable tax credits, housing allotments, and some federal subsidies offer cash grants to provide for basic necessities and resolve crisis situations.

One key strategy in serving the low-income population is to identify and integrate nonenergy subsidies to effectively raise household income. In recent years, the average LIHEAP grant was just under $300, while a qualified low-income wage earner may accrue an earned income tax credit (EITC) in excess of $4000. This is an order of magnitude greater than the largest LIHEAP cash grant. Not only are the tax credits refundable, they can be advanced. By advancing the tax credit, low-income families benefit from reduced tax withholdings, raising net take-home pay.

The EITC is just one example. In fact, utility subsidies can be found in a number of affordable housing programs. To ensure families are not displaced from their homes, homelessness prevention programs may provide grants to forestall utility service termination. To improve tenant conditions and lower shelter costs, affordable housing programs may embed utility subsidies for the low-income. The USDA offers food stamps and school meals, lowering living expenses and thereby freeing cash so that families can afford adequate shelter. And private foundations award cash grants and offer gifts to families in financial distress. Our research estimates assistance for low-income families is in excess of $90 billion annually. Focusing solely on the $1.8 billion available through LIHEAP is clearly shortsighted.

To access available dollars, affordability programs must be expanded in scope and integrated with other low-income programs. Low-income energy affordability will not change overnight. However, there is hope. If households were to access available low-income assistance and lower home energy consumption by just 20%, preliminary findings suggest home energy burdens would return to manageable levels.

If this is true, then the chronic poor can be served profitably, and accounts moving out of poverty can be served at even greater margins. A special-purpose entity may be required before profits can be realized from serving those near poverty. Nevertheless, utilities can improve returns by investing in low-income initiatives.

Individuals moving from poverty towards self-sufficiency represent the greatest challenge for the public utility as well as the greatest potential for low-income initiatives. If an individual can successfully achieve financial self-sufficiency, the benefits to the utility, its shareholders, and the surrounding community are maximized. Yet little has been done by utilities to move individuals from welfare to work. Most would argue that such objectives are outside their charter. While I once agreed with this sentiment, my opinion has changed.

Low-income consumers are looking for a hand up, not a handout. Afforded opportunities to earn a decent living, most would accept the day-to-day responsibility of employment with enthusiasm over the tough, well-trodden path of poverty.

Rarely are such opportunities afforded those in poverty. Limited income often means these families do not have reliable trans-portation. As such, employment opportunities must exist within their neighborhood. For urban dwellers, aging infrastructures often discourage new business development. In rural areas, limited popula-tion densities discourage the location of large employers. Even so, some notable exceptions do exist. Such exceptions include the opening of Honda's Maryville plant or the development of Penn's Landing in Philadelphia. On the whole, business development has moved to suburban areas.

While suburban development improves the utility service territory, many low-income laborers are unable to access these new jobs. As such, the low-income problem is exacerbated, while new lines are stretched to keep pace with the urban sprawl. A better solution for utilities is to promote economic development within areas of concentrated poverty with the same fervor provided suburban communities.

Take for example Columbus Circle within the city of Philadelphia. A once-abandoned warehouse district known as Penn's Landing has grown into a thriving retail district with notable employers. Such businesses as Wal-Mart, Target, and Home Depot are anchoring retail outlets along the seaport. By establishing outlets on once-dilapidated property near lower income communities, families were able to access the new jobs. Today, the area thrives. The economic stimulus of just one brave retailer revitalized a once-deteriorating community. With this success, the city of Philadelphia has funded similar revitalization projects, spurring an economic boom for the city.

Private utilities should actively participate in these revitalization projects. Beyond charitable giving, the public utility can offer rate incentives to large employers. These can be offered to employers who take up residence in abandoned properties or within areas of concentrated poverty. Additionally, utilities should consider occupying or relocating operations to areas needing economic stimulus. By providing employment opportunities within low-income communities, the utility can access affordable labor while improving the economic conditions of those with historically poor payment behavior. As such, utilities are able to lower operational costs, improve accounts payable, and fuel growth through a single initiative.

The utilities are in a position to help put money into the pockets of those in financial distress. This has several benefits to the utility. The utility can expand shareholder returns through lowered operating costs, improved fiscal efficiencies, and enhanced business valuation.

CHARITABLE GIVING TO ACCESS CAPITAL

Access to capital on preferred terms is a basic tenet of sound fiscal management. For capital-intensive businesses, such as utility distribution companies, the cost of capital can dramatically impact shareholder return. As you might expect, the utilities monitor known factors, such as corporate credit ratings, business valuations, and financial ratios. Initiatives improving these factors are given considerable weight by senior management.

Unfortunately, low-income initiatives are not often considered investments. Instead, low-income initiatives are thought to benefit only program participants at the expense of utility shareholders and ratepayers. Generalizations such as this cause utilities to miss opportunities within a significant segment of the residential sector, the low-income population.

Charitable giving is one such opportunity. But how can giving away money help utilities improve shareholder returns? Reading this question, you are likely to have one of two typical responses. Either you will agree that no benefit can be derived from charitable giving, or you will take the opposite position. This view relies on networking, community development, or corporate branding to generate eventual returns. However, both answers dismiss the immediate return generated by targeted charitable giving.

To exemplify this point, let us focus on one key factor: accounts receivable. Rising accounts receivable raise cash requirements, lower credit ratings, and diminish business value. They negatively impact the share price of publicly traded companies. Programs that lower outstanding receivables can quickly improve shareholder value and need to be considered by the utility executive.

Home weatherization demonstrates this ability, as do affordability programs. However, neither produces the immediate results accomplished through charitable giving. In the United States, corporations are able to expense 10% of taxable income as charitable contributions. Yet, in 2002, utilities contributed just $235 million on $32 billion of net income. This is less than 1% of taxable income. The critical question remains, could the utilities have benefited from increasing charitable giving?

Established fuel funds, and even federally funded LIHEAP providers, routinely lack the financial resources to address growing demand. Consumers are forced to choose between basic necessities: food, housing, water, heat, electricity, or medicine. Such a choice is incomprehensible for most of us, and the politicians agree!

Virtually all energy assistance funds are classified as charitable organizations. Contributions made to energy assistance qualify as charitable giving. Because of this, utilities can effectively transfer aged receivables to an expense item without exceeding established bad debt reserves.

In the past, utilities were forced to fund energy assistance programs from overcharges and/or civil penalties. Such was the case in a recent ruling by the Georgia Public Service Commission (GA PUC). To settle accusations of slamming, the GA PUC required a contribution of $400,000 from Energy America to the state's Low Income Home Energy Assistance Program. In other cases, new funds were established through these settlements. In 2003, St. Louis-based AmerenUE and the Missouri Public Service Commission used a $9 million settlement. This was used to launch a one-month program directing $3 million to eliminate past due balances of those economically disadvantaged.

As can be seen from these recent rulings, settlements are still used to fund energy assistance. However, utilities and even their shareholders are beginning to realize the value of regional fuel funds and energy assistance grants. Voluntary contributions by the utility and its shareholders are more common today than ever. Evidence of this trend can be found in the monthly bulletins published by the National Fuel Funds Network. Despite growing support for regional fuel funds, utilities should consider raising contribution levels.

Energy assistance grants provided to the low-income population flow back into the utility as cash payments. As a result, receivables are reduced along with collection expenses. Because of this, utility shareholders benefit along with ratepayers and program participants. To demonstrate these benefits, let us follow the flow of utility fuel fund contributions.

Returning to IRS utility consolidated statements for 2000, we notice that charitable giving accounts for 1% of taxable income on revenues of $757 billion. Outstanding receivables totaled $211 billion. Making an assumption that 20% of the outstanding receivables are from low-income customers, we estimate that $42 billion of the receivables are at risk across the utility industry.

If we consider the industry as a single entity, we can appreciate the magnitude of the problem. A CFO may sell low-income receivables to private collection agencies for 20¢ on the dollar. Having read earlier chapters, you suggest to the CFO a mechanism through which 95% of receivables can be collected. Coincidentally, the collections target many utilities. Although you capture his interest, the CFO remains skeptical. You explain that giving $45 billion to energy assistance funds targeting past due accounts could eliminate 100% of accounts receivable. Now even more skeptical, the CFO chooses a few expletives to get you to explain how this would work.

You explain contributions return to the utility during the following peak heating/cooling season. While this has no impact on revenues, the $45 billion in customer payments effectively move outstanding low-income receivables from the balance sheet to the income statement as a pretax expense. Because of the timing of cash inflows and outlays, year-end cash balances are lower by $2.25 billion. However, this amount is returned via the resulting decrease in tax liability. The $45 billion charitable contribution would lower income taxes by $16 billion. Similarly, the reduction in assets would also serve to lower the annual net worth tax in applicable states and counties.

On the other side of the coin, utilities have taxable incomes of just $29.2 billion. This is far less than the $45 billion contribution discussed. Obviously, the entire balance of low-income arrears could not be resolved in a single year. Still, more manageable contributions of $2 billion annually could substantially reduce receivables. Although net income would be approximately 10% lower, profits would be reduced by just 6.4%. While the reduced earnings could temporarily lower share price, long-term share-holders will benefit in several ways. These benefits result from accumulated tax benefits, improved access to capital, and unspecified reductions in operating costs.

For utilities with accumulated debt resulting from recent mergers and acquisitions (M&A) activity, the reduction in earnings may be justified to lower debt service. In addition, the resulting operational efficiencies and balance sheet improvements will lower the cost of capital and improve credit scores. Under the right corporate circumstances, charitable giving may be a valid approach to access capital on more favorable terms.

WORKING WITHIN CONSTRAINTS

No matter how much capital is available, a chronic segment of the low-income population will remain in poverty and will continue to struggle with service affordability. Even the most comprehensive low-income initiative will fail to encapsulate the entirety of those in need. As such, we must work within constraints. This may discourage the altruistic. However, an opportunity exists to substantially alter the realities of those served through low-income programs. This can be done without regard to regulatory restrictions, budgetary constraints, or operational realities. We simply must be practical in our design and selective in our implementation.

Consumer need differs in both severity and urgency. Serving only those with the most urgent requirements (i.e., facing termination of service) fails to recognize the severity of the problem. Committing limited resources to indifferent debtors with untapped financial reserves and relatively low outstanding balances will never be cost-effective. This is especially true if you compare this to serving customers with substantial arrears who have requested resolution through an affordable amortized payment schedule.

By segmenting the population on utility payment behavior and socio-economic condition, market oppor-tunities will be discovered. For example, a concentrated area of poverty may exist within your service territory. If so, an economic stimulus targeted at this area may do more for service affordability than any annual cash grant. Other segments may include a geographically dispersed population of low-wage earners who are best served by refundable federal and state tax credits. Still other segments require only time to resolve service affordability issues, such as recently displaced workers.

> *"An acknowledgment of the practical constraints confronting low-income initiatives is required. Strategic targeting of notable market segments yields a practical solution characterized by offerings that are comprehensive in depth but narrow in the breadth of those served."*

Initiatives under development must consider individual consumer need to realize expected operational efficiencies. An acknowledg-ment of the practical constraints confronting low-income initiatives is required. Strategic targeting of notable market segments yields a practical solution characterized by offerings that are comprehensive in depth but narrow in the breadth of those served.

EXTENDING
THE BOUNDARY

The inelasticity of home energy consumption has long been assumed within the utility industry. As such, assistance has been focused on those with limited incomes. Yet, many payment-troubled segments exist outside those with income levels near the federal poverty guidelines. Even dual-income households can experience payment troubles. With mounting consumer debt, even upper middle-class households can struggle with monthly financial obligations. To successfully address the effects of the recent economic downturn, boundaries of existing initiatives must be extended, both in breadth and in depth.

With recent welfare reform, TANF recipients could lose federal assistance if work is not found within the allotted timeframe. Those able to work are encouraged to leave government programs and find employment. This has led to an expanded class of the working poor.

The working poor experience a number of problems that challenge even the best coping skills. Child care, transportation expenses, health care, and other household expenses represent a burdensome reality for those recently employed. Emerging financial obligations and reduced assistance levels expose the working poor to many risks, including a return to the welfare subsidies.

Any initiative promoting economic self-sufficiency must be sensitive to these issues. As such, nontraditional offerings must be considered as an integral part of the overall assistance. Referrals to related assistance help ease the transition back to work. However, more integration is needed.

Each assistance program requires individuals to be means-tested repeatedly. Individuals entering the labor force simply cannot afford the time needed to navigate program requirements. Few employers are sympathetic to new employees repeatedly asking for time off. Even when time is available to meet with service providers, transportation often becomes an issue, because providers are often located in various parts of the county or metropolitan areas. Short of a universal enrollment center conveniently located, the working poor and others will be left to scavenge for available assistance.

A great need exists for a universal enrollment center, whereby persons seeking assistance can be means-tested and screened for eligible programs across a number of industries. These centers could verify residence, income, asset accumulation, outstanding liabilities, credit risk, and family demographics, and screen individuals for program eligibility. Individuals meeting program requirements could automatically receive program benefits without repeated intervention and time commitments.

For the low-income population, the ability to access initiatives across industries is basic to their efforts to become self-sufficient. A number of utilities are currently experimenting with a joint-enrollment program. In it, TANF and SSI recipients are enrolled into the states LIHEAP, HWAP, and private energy assistance programs. This increased breadth in offerings seeks to maximize individual participation in energy assistance programs.

While this is a good first step, these programs often ignore offerings outside the narrow scope of the energy industry. Why not leverage programs offered by other regulated businesses like banks, mass transit, telephone and cable companies, Internet service providers, and hospitals? Why not include private initiatives from local retailers that provide senior citizen and low-income discounts? Why not administer individual deposit accounts or promote refundable tax credits? The answer given by utilities is often quite simple: these services are outside our mandate! While this may be true, as mentioned earlier, only a comprehensive and sustainable offering will lead to self-sufficiency.

Offerings for the chronic poor must address the basic needs. As needs moderate, cash grants may alleviate temporary financial difficulty. When employment is sought and found, transportation subsidies and refundable tax credits become paramount. When stable employment is realized, individuals must establish deposit accounts, access credit, and maintain regular checking accounts to break the cycle of high-cost payday loans. As incomes rise from continued employment, household expenses must be managed, often requiring a crash course in personal finance. And in all cases, local economic development must be sought to promote the general well-being of the utility service territory.

If we are to provide meaningful help to those in need, we must look beyond our mandate at the emergent needs of the population we are serving. Only after the depth and breadth of public assistance is expanded will operating efficiencies reward utility ratepayers and shareholders.

TRUST
BUT VERIFY

Low-income providers must be trusted to implement program services. However, they must also be monitored. The cautionary slogan made famous by President Ronald Reagan while negotiating a nuclear arms treaty with the former Soviet Union is applicable here: Trust but Verify.

For a number of reasons, all administrative entities must monitor and evaluate the performance of their service providers. If for no other reason, management controls require contract terms to be monitored for compliance. Without monitoring, fraud is inevitable given the passage of enough time. However, if we trust our providers, monitoring and evaluation efforts require additional justification.

The actions of your best employees are monitored and their performance is evaluated, and the performance of your selected service providers should be evaluated, also. Monitoring and evaluation provide the data necessary for an objective assessment of contractor performance and program efficiency. With objective measurements in place, administrators are able to make informed policy decisions and mentor service providers toward higher performance standards.

Successful programs have integrated compliance monitoring, technical training, and in-field critique as part of their daily operations. They regularly review 10%–15% of all jobs. When problems are noted, the percent of jobs inspected for a given person, organization, or program can be raised to provide the necessary oversight. Coupled with periodic process assessments, program managers are able to manage program cost-effectiveness.

Similarly, assessments are repeated frequently to evaluate intended and unintended impacts from program offerings. Baseline impacts are established through annual studies during the developmental years and tapered when intended impacts plateau. One area for improvement is the inclusion of cumulative, secondary, and tertiary impacts of low-income initiatives. Typically, only primary impacts are evaluated, especially early in the program life.

Focusing impact assessments on known outcomes is a common mistake. For example, home weatherization programs often look only at yearly changes in normalized annual consumption. By doing so, program impacts are grossly understated. During a recent study for Columbia Gas of Ohio, we found no degradation in achieved savings during the years subsequent to program participation. As such, cumulative effects of home weatherization accrue, providing compounded returns that are rarely recognized. In addition, decreasing arrearage levels also accrue as secondary impacts.

In this example, cost-effectiveness was demonstrated only by the accumulated impacts of both arrearage and energy savings. However, we know that many program impacts have yet to be counted. With the eventual inclusion of those added impacts, program expansion will be easily justified.

Selling Your Successes

One important reason to verify program impacts is to leverage program results. Building upon recent accomplishments is a proven approach to raising support. Most readers understand that programs must demonstrate the ability to achieve desirable outcomes in order to receive continued funding. However, selling your successes can extend far beyond subsistence.

Notable programs rely on third-party assessments to demonstrate results and actively sell their successes to a wide range of industry participants and program stakeholders. Model programs find funding support, establish brand equity, and generate consulting revenue. Sometimes a choice must be made between funding an established offering with demonstrated success and funding an emerging interest addressing similar needs. Barring any significant differences, the established program will receive far greater support. Like private brands, public service brands retain value.

A number of organizations are recognized by the general population and convey some meaning, despite people having only a superficial understanding of specific service offerings. Organizations like the Red Cross and United Way are often trusted as providers of international goodwill. However, many individuals would have trouble listing even a handful of services and programs supported by these organizations. That inherent trust is a result of brand equity bolstered by media support.

Similarly, governmental programs also hold brand equity. Head Start is just one of those programs. Within our industry, brand awareness is far less reaching and may account for the modest levels of support. Two of the government's largest low-income initiatives, HWAP and LIHEAP, have far less recognition within the general population than does a more recent initiative, EnergyStar.

I will not pretend to understand the development of brand equity and all its ramifications. However, I cannot deny its value. Raj Sethuraman of Southern Methodist University found "the low income group was very influenced by brand image and tended to favor national brands."[2] In relation to commodity-like grocery products, a price premium of 20% over store brands was not unusual. Recognizing this is much different than energy services, we searched for brand studies related to the low-income initiatives highlighted throughout this book. Unfortunately, brand value has not been widely tracked, and the results are not generally made public.

Yet, we know from experience that trusted referrals are heavily relied upon by program participants. This fact alone suggests a predisposition to brand susceptibility. However, this trust is often associated with the referring agency or individual rather than with a specific initiative. For example, a utility weatherization program may be less trusted than the local church or TANF agency that provided the referral. Still, the general population holds utilities in very high regard. As such, utility-sponsored initiatives have some built-in brand equity and transferable goodwill.

The challenge facing program managers is to leverage existing brand equity to differentiate program offerings from the number of unlawful and ill-reputed offerings targeted at the low-income, elderly, and disabled. A well-branded name can ease intake efforts by avoiding the need for continued reassurance by service providers.

Branding within program offerings using branded uniforms, handouts, door hangers, and advertising helps in this differentiation. Also, branding program services help with word-of-mouth referrals. Participants in a well-branded home-weatherization initiative are unlikely to forget the program name. Similarly, providers of cash assistance are unlikely to be forgotten, especially if arrearage forgiveness and budget counseling were among the offerings.

On the other hand, community development initiatives and payment negotiations are often associated with the utility and not the individual program. To avoid this, program managers must actively promote the program brand. Successful managers will establish brand equity by selling successes via public service announcements, regular marketing techniques, and event sponsorship. A combination of these efforts leads to increased community awareness and brand recognition that translate into public support.

For any significant initiative, a plan must be in place to communicate program success to a range of stakeholders. Company executives, regulators, service providers, program participants, and the general ratepayer will want to understand the program impacts, each with a different viewpoint. Participants will want to know what to expect from the program. Regulators will monitor participant interactions and ratepayer charges. Company executives must remain informed to address shareholder interests. And perhaps most importantly, general ratepayers must remain informed if they are to continue funding low-income initiatives. As such, program administrators must sell their successes and build on past accomplishments.

FEASTING ON
THE FOREFATHERS

No matter how successful a program becomes, the offerings must be regularly scrutinized to address relevant issues facing share-holders, ratepayers, and the target demographic. As such, programs grandfathered in from previous rate cases must be critiqued and altered to meet current demands. I refer to this process as *feasting on the forefathers.*

We cannot afford to linger on past successes as justification for continued support of existing initiatives. In chapter 8, we looked at the fundamental four as an indication of corporate need. Building on this analysis, we created strategic initiatives and developed supporting business cases to obtain the necessary funding. This analysis must be repeated periodically to determine if similar conditions exist today. If not, then different initiatives will be required. On the other hand, if the same conditions persist beyond a reasonable period, then one must consider the inability of the chosen initiatives to achieve the desired outcome.

In either case, change is required. Within a regulated market, change can be a costly endeavor. Building support within a diverse group of stakeholders can be difficult. A great deal of inertia serves to retain current offerings without alteration. However, such consistency under changing conditions is simply unreasonable.

Program managers, service providers, and even participants must be willing to accept changes in the composition of service offerings. Utility executives, regulators, and shareholders must first demand periodic justifications of existing programs and demand changes to align with long-term ratepayer and shareholder interests. Only by replacing legacy programs with up-to-date strategic initiatives will shareholder and ratepayer concerns remain a critical focal point.

SEGREGATION, STILL AN ISSUE

Perhaps the greatest challenge is the integration of low-income programs. Cash assistance programs, service affordability options, usage reduction programs, and community development initiatives are commonplace within the utility industry. Most utilities will offer a suite of programs directed at the disadvantaged, low-income, aged, and disabled. The challenge is to integrate these offerings and stream-line service offerings under a single, well-branded effort.

Our survey of offerings demonstrates that many utilities are now referring and often requiring participants to apply for cash assistance as a condition of participation in other strategic initiatives. Some utilities have gone a step farther with automatic enrollment. Through this process, participants enrolled in one form of assistance are automatically enrolled in other available programs.

These are certainly steps in the right direction. Asking customers to prove their income eligibility only once per annum is not only more cost-effective, it also helps boost participation rates. This ensures that customers get all the available assistance due to them. However, enrollment into separate initiatives retains inefficiencies that could be eliminated through the integration of program services into a single branded offering.

Even better would be a universal enrollment center that qualifies individuals for assistance across industries and encapsulates all government programs. While this objective may be unrealistic in the near-term, certainly a single branded program encompassing the offerings of a single utility is a reasonable endeavor.

Branding assistance programs within a single entity of the utility ensures the goodwill created is retained by the sponsoring entity. Of course, where multiple utilities share service providers, greater efficiencies can be realized. This is true even when each utility retains a single branded assistance program. In fact, the service provider is in the position of generating brand equity for its organization by leveraging the offerings they administer.

In short, the integration of program offerings yields increasing efficiencies benefiting ratepayers while building long-term shareholder value through brand-equity. As such, two important points are to be made. Sponsoring utilities are better served if the brand is retained versus the funding of universal programs offered via a separate entity. Second, obvious efficiencies are gained by integrating services within a single offering.

> *"Branding assistance programs within a single entity of the utility ensures the goodwill created is retained by the sponsoring entity. Of course, where multiple utilities share service providers, greater efficiencies can be realized."*

Taking these two points together, an opportunity for a utility specialized in the service of economically disadvantaged accounts may prove not only viable, but also profitable. For the brave investor, an opportunity exists to consolidate low-income accounts under a statewide combination utility offering gas, electric, water, telecom, and cable services.

THE TORTOISE
V. THE HARE

We are at a point where strong leadership is required to focus investors on long-term shareholder value. Growth in the investment market over the last 20 years has raised expectations, forcing many utilities to take on significant risk to meet short-term investment targets. The recent collapse of Enron and Montana Power coupled with the equity concerns facing PG&E remind passive investors that protections are needed within the industry.

Focusing on the condition of service territory is perhaps the best place to start. As the socioeconomic conditions of the service territory improve, so will utility revenues and shareholder return. For the CEO, the ultimate win-win-win strategy is to fuel economic stability across the breath of the utility service territory.

This type of leadership is rare. Economic development takes time to mature. The relocation or attraction of large employers may take years rather than months. As such, it may be easier to promote suburban sprawl rather than prioritize the use of abandoned facilities that often require greater planning horizons and rezoning. Yet, the value of utilizing existing infrastructure versus building new lines across vacant land is analogous to the race between the hare and the tortoise.

Developers often look for vacant land to build residential and commercial property. Utilities will extend services to these areas to spur growth and realize an expanded customer base. Yet, these suburban expansions often exclude those economically disadvantaged. Without reliable transportation to these suburban developments, low-income persons have trouble accessing new jobs or improvements in living conditions. Unlike the average consumer who can rely on credit to move in pursuit of economic opportunities, many disadvantaged populations simply lack this option. Instead they must risk all capital reserves to simply relocate across town. Without guaranteed employment, this migration is too much to ask.

The result is that the economically disadvantaged are stuck in areas of concentrated poverty that grow worse with each passing year. The impact on the utility is predictable. Service affordability issues continue to escalate. With the escalation of unpaid arrears, utility credit ratings and business valuations decline, along with operating efficiencies.

Long-term investors should not tolerate this scenario. Instead, economic development initiatives should prioritize development that creates jobs for those with the greatest need. As such, areas of concentrated poverty should be given considerable weight. Regional incentives are often available for development within empowerment zones. Utilities stand to reap long-term benefits by supporting or even promoting expansions within these areas.

For example, utilities could offer large employers at-cost utility service for a number of years to spur economic development in target areas. The lost margins are compensated by increases in regional employment, increased service affordability, and small business development. Focusing on the long-term benefits to rate-payers and shareholders is a critical component of valuable low-income initiatives.

Where the most difficult customers are served profitably, the remaining customers yield even greater margins. Hence, low-income initiatives that effectively serve those in need ultimately generate long-term shareholder value and eventually increase operating margins. Utility companies can profit from the development of low-income initiatives that improve the overall condition of the utility service territory. But before we can realize a return, we must first be willing to invest in low-income initiatives rather than acquiesce to mandated universal service provisions.

NOTES

[1] Rhode, S. 2002. Half of Americans Repeatedly Struggle with Debt. Myvesta (Mar. 21). *http://myvesta.org/news/releases/032102PRMoneyBehaviors.htm.*

[2] Young, M. B. 2000. Why Consumers Pay More for National Brands. MSI Report No. 00-110. (Fall) *http://www.msi.org/msi/insights/ins00f-d.cfm.*

Index

INDEX ❧ *367*

M

R

V

W–X

Y–Z